The Word is
Near You
on Your Lips
and in Your
Heart

Reflections on the Weekday Readings for
the Liturgical Year 2023–24

Fr Martin Hogan

Published by Messenger Publications, 2023

ISBN: 9781788126472

Designed by Brendan McCarthy
Typeset in Times New Roman & DIN Condensed
Printed by Hussar Books

Messenger Publications,
37 Leeson Place, Dublin D02 E5V0
www.messenger.ie

INTRODUCTION

This book is the eighth publication of reflections on the weekday readings for the liturgical year. I have tried to ensure that none of the reflections repeat those in the earlier publications. The reflections in this book are based predominantly on the gospel readings for the weekdays of the liturgical year 2023/24, with occasional references to the first reading. They follow the sequence of the weekdays of the liturgical year, beginning with the Monday of the first week of Advent on 4 December 2023, and concluding with the feast of Saint Andrew on Saturday, 30 November 2024. On the weekdays of any liturgical year, we read from a large proportion of all four gospels, with the Gospels of Matthew, Mark and Luke featuring especially in Ordinary Time, and the Gospel of John featuring more prominently in the seasons of Lent and, especially, Easter. In and through these gospel readings we encounter the living word of the risen Lord to his Church. These short reflections attempt to listen to the gospel readings on their own terms while showing how they can continue to speak to our lives today.

Many people feel drawn to basing their prayer on the scriptures, in particular the gospels. It is hoped that these reflections will serve as a help to prayer. They may also be of service to priests who seek to offer a short reflection on the readings of the day at the daily Eucharist. Where there is a weekday Liturgy of the Word, with or without Holy Communion, they can be read as a reflection on the readings. On most weekdays, the same readings are proclaimed in the Church throughout the world. To read and reflect upon the readings for the weekdays of the liturgical year is to go on a spiritual journey with the universal Church.

The title of this book of reflections is taken from Paul's letter to the Romans: 'The word is near you, on your lips and in your heart' (Romans 10:8). Paul is quoting here from Deuteronomy 30:14. For the author of this book, the 'word' corresponds to 'this commandment that I am commanding you today' (Deuteronomy 30:11), which he identifies with 'loving the Lord your God, walking in his ways' (Deuteronomy 30:16). The author had earlier stated that 'the Lord your God will circumcise your heart and the heart of your descendants, so that you will love the Lord your God with all your heart and all your soul, in order that you may live' (Deuteronomy 30:6). Keeping the commandment of the Lord is not about striving after something that is far away, 'in heaven ... beyond the sea' (Deuteronomy 30:12–13). Rather, it entails a surrender to what God has already placed in the heart of his people. Inspired by this text in Deuteronomy, Paul interprets the 'word' in Deuteronomy 30:14 as 'the word of faith that we proclaim' (Romans 10:8), the gospel of Christ crucified and risen. For Paul, it is the gospel that resides within the human heart and finds expression in the open confession with our lips. Romans may be the latest letter of Paul to have come down to us. In his earliest letter preserved in the New Testament, his first letter to the Thessalonians, Paul identifies 'the word of God that you heard from us' as 'God's word, which is also at work in you believers' (1 Thessalonians 2:13). Paul had a strong conviction that the word of God, the word of the Gospel of Christ, resides deep within the hearts of those open to receive it and is powerfully at work there. When we listen to this word, we are listening to our deepest selves, to the Lord speaking to us from deep within our hearts.

It is my hope that these reflections will help the reader to listen to the word of the Lord, the word that 'is near you, on your lips and in your heart'. These reflections come from my own efforts to listen to the Lord's word in the circumstances of my own life. Every reader could write a different set of reflections based on their own personal listening. The word of God that dwells in us richly (Colossians 3:16) can speak in myriad ways to each one of us. As Saint Ephrem, a fourth-century Syriac-speaking deacon of the church of Edessa, expresses it so well, 'God has hidden in his word all kinds of treasures so that each one of us, whenever we meditate, may be enriched by it. His utterance is a tree of life, which offers you blessed fruit from every side.'

4 December, Monday, First Week of Advent

Matthew 8:5–11

Today's responsorial psalm is from a small collection of pilgrim psalms in the Book of Psalms, psalms prayed by pilgrims on their journey to Jerusalem and its Temple, the House of God. 'I rejoiced when I heard them say, "Let us go to God's house".' There is a great sense of expectant longing in these pilgrim psalms for the meeting with the Lord that awaits the pilgrim in the Temple, where it was believed that God had chosen to dwell. That sense of expectant longing is very much the mood of Advent. Advent is the season that calls out to us to be pilgrims once more. For us Christians, it is Jesus who is now the House of God, the one in and through whom God has chosen to dwell. Jesus is Emmanuel, God with us. In Advent we are journeying with expectant longing towards the celebration of the birth of Jesus, Emmanuel. At a deeper level, we are journeying towards what Jesus in the gospel reading calls the feast in the kingdom of God, that banquet of eternal life at which many will be present from north, south, east and west, alongside the great patriarchs of Israel. We are called to make this journey with the same attitude of expectant longing shown by the Roman centurion in today's gospel reading, when he said to Jesus, 'Just give the word and my servant will be healed'. As we continue on our pilgrim way, we are invited to keep on entrusting ourselves to the Lord's word, in that same spirit of hopeful faith shown by the centurion.

5 December, Tuesday, First Week of Advent
Luke 10:21–24

Today's gospel is one of the places in the gospels where we hear Jesus praying. He praises God in the joy of the Spirit for revealing the mysteries of God's kingdom to mere children, as distinct from the learned and the clever. The learning of those who claimed to already know God and God's will blocked them from hearing what God was trying to show them through his Son Jesus. In contrast, those who did not claim to know, who were genuinely searching, were open to receive what God was revealing through Jesus. These were the 'children' Jesus speaks about in the gospel reading, those who acknowledged their own need and were open to receive. The religious experts missed the opportunity of God's visitation through Jesus, whereas those who would have been written off as knowing nothing of God or of God's law welcomed God's visitation and rejoiced at the year of God's favour that Jesus was inaugurating. Jesus' prayer reminds us that when it comes to God, being too sure of our knowledge can be a dangerous thing. We have to keep acknowledging our need for light. Advent is a season to enter into that poverty of spirit that keeps us open to what God wishes to show us. Such openness of spirit finds expression in the humble prayer, 'Come Lord Jesus'.

6 December, Wednesday, First Week of Advent
Matthew 15:29–37

There is a very striking portrayal of the compassion of Jesus for the broken and needy in today's gospel reading. He initially healed the lame, the crippled, the blind and those unable to speak, all of whom had been brought to him by a large crowd. He then noticed how hungry this large crowd was; he was concerned for their physical well-being. He didn't say, as we might be tempted to say, 'I have done enough compassionate work for today. It is time for me to move on.' When faced with human need, he could not but respond with a compassionate heart. The disciples were of a different frame of mind, perhaps more like ourselves. When Jesus mentioned the hunger of the crowd to them, they answered, 'Where could we get enough food in this deserted place to feed such a crowd!' As we might say today, they were telling Jesus, 'Don't even think about it!' However, Jesus could not but think about it and he prodded his disciples to think about it: 'How many loaves have you?' The discovery that seven loaves and a few small fish were available wouldn't have inspired anyone with hope or confidence. Yet, this was all Jesus needed to feed the hunger of the crowd. His compassionate heart could work powerfully through the smallest of human resources. The gospel reading suggests that we need to give the Lord's compassionate heart space to work through us. The Lord never turns aside from human need but sometimes he can only address it with our help, even though we may feel we have very little to offer him. The task can seem so much greater than the resources at our disposal. We wonder if it is worth our while to begin at all, yet we will often be surprised and amazed at how powerfully the Lord can work through our seemingly limited resources and efforts, if we trust that he can and will do so.

7 December, Thursday, First Week of Advent
Matthew 7:21, 24–27
We know that a house is as good as its foundations. If the foundations are flimsy, the consequences for those who live in the house can be catastrophic, especially if unusual stress is placed on the

building because of weather or some other disturbance of nature. The most important part of the house is that which is not immediately visible. In the gospel reading, Jesus draws on that image of the house to speak about the foundation of our lives as human beings. He declares that entrusting ourselves to him, listening to his word and trying to live by his word, will provide a foundation for our lives that will enable us to withstand the great storms of life. We need some solid ground under us as we go through life. Jesus presents himself as that solid ground. If we build our lives on all he says and does, he will prove to be a rock, enabling us to stand firm even when the disappointments and sufferings of life leave us feeling very vulnerable. As human beings we long for security at many levels. Jesus tells us that we will find our ultimate security in him if, in the phrase of Saint Paul, we allow his word to dwell in us richly and then to bear fruit in our lives.

8 December, Friday, The Immaculate Conception of the Blessed Virgin Mary

Luke 1:26–38

Gerard Manley Hopkins, in his poem, 'The Blessed Virgin compared to the air we breathe', concludes with a prayer to Mary: 'Be thou then, O thou dear / Mother, my atmosphere; / My happier world, wherein / To wend and meet no sin'. Today's feast celebrates Mary as that happier world. She was untouched by that sin of Adam referred to at the beginning of today's first reading. Because Adam rebelled against God's will for his life, he was uncomfortable in God's presence. He hid from God and God had to call out to him, 'Where are you?' Mary had no reason to hide from God because she was always open to doing God's will. She lived her life in the light of God's presence. She was, in that sense, full of God. It was because Mary was so full of God from the first moment of her conception that she could respond to God's call to her through the angel Gabriel with the words, 'Let what you have said be done to me.'

The principal church in our diocese is in Marlborough Street in Dublin city. We usually call it the Pro-Cathedral. However, its official title is Saint Mary's (the Immaculate Conception). We don't often speak of Mary as Saint Mary. Yet today's feast celebrates Mary's sainthood, her sanctity. We consider her the greatest of all the saints because we believe that she was holy from the first moment of her conception. No more than any of the other saints, Mary was not removed from the struggles and sufferings of the human condition. Something of her struggle comes through in today's gospel reading. She was initially deeply disturbed by the words of the angel Gabriel. She was full of questions in response to Gabriel's good news: 'How can this come about?' Luke goes on to tell us in his gospel that Simeon announced to her that a sword would pierce her soul. According to the Gospel of John, she stood at the foot of the cross suffering the agony of watching her only Son die a slow and painful death. It was in the midst of all the struggles and pains of life that she lived out her 'yes' to God's will for her life.

Mary's holiness from her conception does not remove her from us. She is our companion on our pilgrim journey. She is given to us as a perpetual help. That is why, in the 'Hail Mary' prayer, we ask her to pray for us 'sinners' now and at the hour of our death. Paul reminds us in the second reading that before the world was made God 'chose us in Christ to be holy and spotless and to live through love in his presence'. Paul spells out there our calling from the beginning of time. Mary has lived that calling to the full; she was holy, living through love in God's presence. We look to her to help us to live out that same calling. In the words of the Preface of today's Mass, she is an advocate of grace for God's people, for all of us. She prays for us for the grace we need to be as generous as she was in responding to God's purpose for our lives.

9 December, Saturday, First Week of Advent
Matthew 9:35–10.1, 6–8

The opening verse of the gospel reading gives us a sense of all the work Jesus did during his public ministry. He made a tour through all the towns and villages, teaching in the synagogues, proclaiming the good news of the kingdom and curing all kinds of diseases and sickness. Jesus clearly did not spare himself in doing the work God had given him to do, yet he knew that even he could not do God's work alone. When he saw crowds that were harassed and dejected, even after all the work he did, he didn't respond by saying he had to work harder. He responded by asking his disciples to ask God to send labourers into God's harvest. The harvest was so rich, the work to be done so great, that Jesus could not do it alone. Many labourers were needed, through whom Jesus would work. That is why he went on to send out his twelve closest disciples to do the same work he had been doing, proclaiming the good news of the kingdom and curing all kinds of diseases and sickness. Yet Jesus knew that even these twelve could not do all God's work that needed doing. Many more labourers would be needed. The Lord needs each one of us to be a labourer in God's harvest. Each of us has a combination of gifts and experiences that the Lord needs to continue God's work in the world today. Each of us has a unique role to play in helping the risen Lord to bring more of the kingdom of God to earth. There is a corner of God's harvest that needs our labour. The Lord wants to work through each of us to bring his healing and life-giving presence to bear more fully on the world. None of us, no matter where we are on our life's journey, is surplus to his requirements.

11 December, Monday, Second Week of Advent
Luke 5:17–26

In the gospel reading we have a very good image of faith in action. The friends of the paralysed man were so intent on getting their friend to Jesus that they went to the extreme of creating an opening in the roof of the house where Jesus was teaching and letting their friend down in front of Jesus. The gospel reading states, 'Seeing their faith Jesus said, "My friend, your sins are forgiven you".' It was not so much the faith of the paralysed man that caught Jesus' attention as the faith of his friends. The man was literally carried to Jesus by the faith of his friends. There is an image there of what all of us are called to be for each other within the Church. We are called to carry each other by our faith. Our own faith in action carries others. Sometimes we need the faith of others to carry us when our own faith seems weak. Saint Paul says in his letter to the Romans that the life and death of each one of us has its influence on others. He would also have said that the faith of each one of us has its influence for good on others.

12 December, Tuesday, Second Week of Advent
Matthew 18:12–14

In the gospel reading Jesus tells a parable about a shepherd who notices when one sheep out of a flock of one hundred goes astray, and who is sufficiently concerned about that one sheep to go searching for it, even though it means leaving the ninety-nine unattended. The one, and not just the many, matter to this shepherd. The shepherd is an image of Jesus who is always portrayed in the gospels as engaging not just with crowds but with individuals. In the language of John's Gospel, he is the good shepherd who knows his own by name. The risen Lord relates to us not just as anonymous members of a group but as individuals. He calls each of us by name. In Matthew's Gospel the parable is not just an image of how Jesus relates to us, but of how we are called to relate to each other. We are to call each other by name; we are to respect the uniqueness of each other, relating to one another as unique and irreplaceable images of God. Meeting with one person has potentially as much value as meeting with a large group. The parable suggests that one individual is as deserving of our attention as a gathering of many.

13 December, Wednesday, Second Week of Advent
Matthew 11:28–30
We can all grow tired and weary, especially as we get older. Our physical energy levels are not what they were. We may feel the need for a nap in the afternoon. According to the first reading, even 'young men may grow tired and weary, youths may stumble'. The weariness in question there is not so much a physical weariness but a weariness of spirit. We can suffer from a weariness of spirit at any age. We struggle to get up and go, to invest ourselves in the task at hand, to give of ourselves to others. Physically we may be strong, but there is a lethargy about us. It is often part of the human condition. That first reading suggests that it is not part of God's condition: 'He does not grow tired or weary'. The Lord is always actively engaged with us. He is always coming towards us. We pray the simple prayer during Advent, 'Come, Lord Jesus', a prayer that recognises that the Lord is always on the way towards us. The Lord never retreats into himself in a kind of weariness of spirit. He is always fully alive, vibrant and dynamic. In the gospel reading, he invites us to come to

him in our weariness of spirit and draw life from his presence to us: 'Come to me, all you who labour and are overburdened, and I will give you rest.' The word 'rest' suggests not so much inactivity but revival and renewal, as in one of the lines of the psalm, 'The Lord is my Shepherd': 'Near restful waters he leads me to revive my drooping spirit'. Each day, in prayer, we can turn to the Lord in our weariness of spirit and open ourselves to his reviving presence. When we turn to the Lord in hopeful trust, the promise at the end of today's first reading can come to pass for us: 'Those who hope in the Lord renew their strength; they put out wings like the eagles.'

14 December, Thursday, Second Week of Advent
Matthew 11:11–15

In the gospel reading, Jesus says something very striking about John the Baptist: 'Of all the children born of women, a greater than John the Baptist has never been seen.' The greatness of John consists in his willingness to embrace the role that the prophet Elijah was expected to play in the age of the coming of the Messiah. It was believed that Elijah would be sent ahead of the Lord to prepare a way for him. In referring to John as the promised Elijah, Jesus is implicitly referring to himself as the promised Messiah. Having made that striking statement about John the Baptist, Jesus then makes an even more striking statement, declaring that the least in the kingdom of heaven is greater than John the Baptist. John did not live to see the coming of God's kingdom through the life, death and resurrection of Jesus. He was executed by Herod Antipas shortly into the public ministry of Jesus. Jesus is reminding his disciples of how privileged they are. We are all being reminded of how greatly graced we have been, graced in a way that even John the Baptist wasn't. We have been given a great deal through the life, death and resurrection of Jesus and the coming of the Spirit, not on the basis of anything we have done, but purely as an expression of God's love for the world. In the language of the Fourth Gospel, Jesus has come among us full of grace and truth, and from his fullness we have all received. We spend our lives trying to appreciate fully all we have received and are receiving from God through the life, death and resurrection of his Son, and then learning to give generously to the Lord and others out of all that we have received.

15 December, Friday, Second Week of Advent
Matthew 11:16–19

There are several passages in the gospels where Jesus either relates directly to children or speaks of them. All of the passages note the warmth of his relationship with children. Today's gospel reading suggests that Jesus is a keen observer of how children behave. We have to imagine two groups of children in the marketplace. One group tries to engage the other group in their games. They first pretend to be the musicians at a wedding, but the other group are unmoved: 'you wouldn't dance'. They then change tack and play at being the singers of dirges at a funeral, but the other group is equally unmoved: 'you wouldn't be mourners'. Jesus reads this scene as a commentary on what is happening in the adult world. His contemporaries were unmoved by the somewhat mournful message of John the Baptist, and they were equally unmoved by Jesus' own joyful message, his proclamation of the good news of God's loving reign. They dismissed John the Baptist as possessed, and Jesus as a glutton and drunkard. 'We played the pipes for you, and you wouldn't dance'. We don't often think of Jesus as a piper, playing a tune that invites people to dance. In a sense, the music of God is played through the life and message of Jesus, as well as through his death and resurrection. We are invited to tune in to this celebratory music, to be moved by it and to allow it to shape our lives. We show we are the Lord's followers by dancing to his tune, moving to the promptings of his Spirit.

16 December, Saturday, Second Week of Advent
Matthew 17:10–13

At the time of Jesus there was an ancient Jewish tradition that just before the coming of the Messiah God would send the prophet Elijah back to earth to prepare people for the Messiah's coming. 'I will send you the prophet Elijah before the great and terrible day of the Lord comes. He will turn the hearts of parents towards their children and of children towards their parents … ' (Malachi 4:5–6). That tradition is behind the question of the disciples to Jesus in today's gospel reading, 'Why do the scribes say then that Elijah must come first?' Jesus identifies John the Baptist as the promised Elijah, and, by implication, he is identifying himself as the Messiah. Yet, as Jesus goes on to say, 'they treated him [John the Baptist] as they pleased'. John had been beheaded by Herod Antipas. Jesus then announces that he will suffer the same hostile fate as John the Baptist: 'The Son of Man will suffer similarly.' Jesus announces that his contemporaries have already rejected God's messenger sent to announce the coming of the Lord and they are soon to reject the Lord himself. We can all fail to recognise God's messengers. We can even fail to recognise the Lord himself when he comes to us. Advent is a time when we pray the prayer, 'Come, Lord Jesus'. We might also need to pray the prayer, 'Lord, help me to recognise you when you come'. The Lord can come to us in ways that we had not expected. He can come to us even in and through those circumstances of our lives that seem to suggest he is absent. He can come to us through people whom we might not associate with the Lord. The Lord is always coming in a whole variety of guises. He is often most powerfully present at those moments when we sense his absence. We pray this Advent for eyes to recognise his various comings to us.

18 December, Monday, Third Week of Advent
Matthew 1:18–24

Today's gospel reading gives us Matthew's account of the birth of Jesus. Luke's account of Jesus' birth has so caught the imagination of artists and storytellers down the centuries that Matthew's account has found itself somewhat in the shade. In Luke's account of Jesus' birth, Mary is more to the fore than Joseph. In Matthew's account it is Joseph who is to the fore. In our gospel reading the annunciation of Jesus' birth is made to Joseph, not to Mary. He needs reassuring when he discovers that Mary, his betrothed, is pregnant before they have come to live together as husband and wife. Out of consideration for Mary, he had initially decided to divorce her informally, until the angel Gabriel announced to him the true nature of Mary's pregnancy: 'She has conceived what is in her by the Holy Spirit', and the true significance of the child in her womb: 'She will give birth to a son and you must name him Jesus, because he is the one who is to save his people from their sins.' Apart from the name Jesus, the name 'Emmanuel', 'God-with-us', found in the prophet Isaiah, will also apply to him. Mary's child will be the presence of the merciful God among us. In response to that annunciation, that revelation, Joseph took Mary home as his wife. The gospel reading gives us a picture of Joseph struggling to discern what God is asking of him in a situation he doesn't fully understand. We are all like Joseph in that regard. We make a decision, thinking it is God's will for our lives, and then we have to review it as it becomes clear to us that perhaps this is not what God is asking of us. We are always trying to discern God's call, what God is asking of us in the here and now. As a man who had much to discern, Saint Joseph can be a very good companion for us in those complex moments in our own lives when there is much to be discerned.

19 December, Tuesday, Third Week of Advent
Luke 1:5–25

We are used to hearing bad news. Most of what passes for news on our news programmes is bad news. What's wrong with the world always seems more newsworthy than what is right with it. When we do hear good news, we can sometimes become a bit sceptical of it. We wonder if it is really true; we start to look for the downside. In today's gospel reading, the angel Gabriel proclaimed good news to Zechariah; his wife Elizabeth would finally have a son, and a special son who will be great in the sight of the Lord, who will be filled with the Holy Spirit, and who will bring many of the people of Israel back to the Lord their God. However, Zechariah couldn't bring himself to believe this good news. It was too good to be true. 'How can I be sure of this?' he asked. He couldn't allow himself to savour this good news and to rejoice in it, as the angel had invited him to do. His failure to hear resulted in an inability to speak. He was silenced and had no power of speech. Our failure to listen always impacts negatively on what we say and how we say it. Good speaking springs from careful listening. Like Zechariah, we can be slow to hear good news, including the good news of God's loving initiative towards us through Jesus. We might think that this may be good news for others, but not for me. Surely, God did not send his Son for me. Yet, as the angel said to the shepherds on the night of Jesus' birth, 'Today … a Saviour has been born to you', and each one of us is included in that 'you'. We spend our lives learning to listen to this good news, this gospel, absorbing it so that it shapes who we are, what we do, what we say and how we say it.

20 December, Wednesday, Third Week of Advent
Luke 1:26–38

The gospel reading portrays Mary as saying 'yes' to God's call to her to become the mother of God's Son. Yet the gospel suggests that her response to God's call did not come easily to her. Initially she was 'deeply disturbed' by the greeting of the angel. She raised a probing question in response to the further words of the angel. 'How can this come about?' she asked. She eventually arrived at the point where she could say, 'Let what you have said be done to me'. However, the reading suggests that she only came to that point after a lot of struggle. We are reminded of Jesus in the garden of Gethsemane. His prayer eventually brought him to the point where he could say, 'Not my will but yours be done'. Again, that was only after a great struggle, in the course of which he had prayed, 'Remove this cup from me'. The experience of Mary and of Jesus suggest that responding to God's call, remaining faithful to God's will for our lives, will always involve a struggle of some kind. The nature of that struggle will be different for each of us. However, we engage in that struggle knowing that we are not alone in it. The power of the Most High will overshadow us, as it overshadowed Mary; the Holy Spirit will come upon us, as it came upon Mary. In our struggle to be faithful, we are also encouraged by the words of Gabriel to Mary: 'nothing is impossible to God'. As Mary's adult son, Jesus, will go on to say, 'for God all things are possible'. Mary herself is also a resource in our struggle to be faithful to the Lord's call, which is why we ask her to intercede for us, to 'pray for us sinners, now and at the hour of our death'.

21 December, Thursday, Third Week of Advent
Luke 1:39–45

I am often struck by the way people greet each other here before Mass begins. It is very obvious that people are glad to see one another and, if some are missing, others ask about them and wonder how they are. The way we greet people, welcome them, can bring a blessing to them. In today's gospel reading, the way Mary and Elizabeth greeted one another was a source of blessing for both of them. Upon arriving at Elizabeth's home in the hill country of Judah, Mary, we are told, greeted Elizabeth and, because of Mary's greeting, Elizabeth was filled with the Holy Spirit. It would be wonderful if we could all greet others in ways that brought the Holy Spirit to life in them. Not only was Mary's greeting of Elizabeth a source of blessing for her, but Elizabeth's subsequent greeting of Mary was a source of blessing for Mary. In greeting Mary, Elizabeth declares her the most blessed of all woman, because of the special child she was carrying in her womb, and also because she had believed the word of promise that the Lord had spoken to her through the angel Gabriel. If you read on, we discover that Elizabeth's way of greeting Mary inspired Mary to pray her great prayer, the Magnificat (tomorrow's gospel reading). Here was a meeting between two women which brought each of them closer to the Lord. There is a pattern here for all of us. Our calling is to be present to others, to greet others, in a way that brings them closer to the Lord and creates a space for the Lord to come alive more fully within them.

22 December, Friday, Third Week of Advent
Luke 1:46–56

Today's gospel reading is the prayer that we have come to know as the Magnificat. It is prayed every evening by those who pray the

Evening Prayer of the Church. In the opening part of this prayer, Mary praises God for what God has done for her: 'he has looked upon his lowly handmaid'. Mary sees herself as the humble servant of the Lord. She is aware that, by the standards of the age, she had no status or standing. Yet she is also aware that God chose her for a very special role; she was to be the mother of God's Son. In the remainder of her prayer, Mary recognises that God's choice of her, someone whom the world would consider lowly and of no consequence, is in keeping with how God has related to his people in the past. It is the lowly whom God has exalted; it is the hungry whom he has filled with good things. In contrast, the proud of heart, the princes of this world, have been routed and cast down. Mary's prayer recognises that it is only those who are aware of their need of God, those who know their poverty before God, who will experience God's saving presence, God's helping hand. At this time of the year, we are invited to come before the Lord in our poverty, in our neediness, like Mary, like the shepherds at the time of Jesus' birth. If we do so, we too will know the joy of his saving help and come to discover the great things that the Lord can do for us.

23 December, Saturday, Third Week of Advent
Matthew 1:57–66
Some time ago, I did some research on my family tree. My father's name was Patrick Hogan and his father's first name was John. Not only was my grandfather called John, but so was my great-grandfather and my great-great-grandfather. It brought home to me how the naming of a newborn child was a very traditional business in past generations. The child very often took the name of the father or mother or of some other significant close relative. It wasn't usual to choose a name that had never been used in the family before. We find that tradition at play in today's gospel reading. When Elizabeth

and Zechariah's child was born, the expectation was that he would be called Zechariah after his father. When Elizabeth declared that he would be named John, following on from the message of the angel Gabriel, the neighbours and relations all piped up, 'But no one in your family has that name.' It took the written word of Zechariah to confirm what Elizabeth had said. Their son would not be called after their father, but would be called John. What's in a name you might ask? Many Hebrew names had a meaning and the name John means 'The Lord is gracious'. A new era of God's gracious, loving presence was about to open up with the birth of Jesus, and Elizabeth and Zechariah's son would prepare people for Jesus' coming. God was doing something new, and age-old conventions, such as around the naming of children, had to give way before this wonderful newness. God continues to do something new today through his Son, now risen Lord, and we all have to learn to let go of conventional ways of doing things so that the ever-new work the Lord wants to do today can find full expression among us.

26 December, Tuesday, Feast of Saint Stephen, Martyr
Matthew 10:17–22
A day after celebrating the birth of Jesus we celebrate the death of the first martyr, Stephen. We move from a birth to a death very quickly. Today's feast brings home to us the words of Simeon to Mary and Joseph as they brought the child Jesus to the Temple: 'This child is destined ... to be a sign that will be opposed.' Not only would Jesus be opposed, but so also would those who witnessed to him, like Stephen. The loss of someone so gifted as Stephen must have been a great blow to the early Church. The Acts of the Apostles refers to him as 'full of faith and the Holy Spirit' and 'full of grace and power'. After he was stoned to death, Acts says that 'devout men

buried Stephen and made loud lamentation over him'. The other disciples did not simply weep silently over his death but wailed publicly, so great was their loss. Yet some good came out of this loss. The Lord worked powerfully through the martyrdom of Stephen and the persecution of the Church that followed. The Acts of the Apostles says that those who were scattered because of the persecution went from place to place proclaiming the word where it had never been preached. Today's first reading also tells us that a young man named Saul witnessed the killing of Stephen and approved of it. He went on to become the great apostle to the Gentiles. Perhaps the martyrdom of Stephen was somehow instrumental in Paul's transformation from zealous persecutor of the Church to its most dynamic missionary. Today's feast reminds us that the Lord can bring new life out of all our losses. In the words of today's psalm, the Lord remains our rock and our stronghold in the midst of our painful losses. As Jesus declares in the gospel reading, 'the Spirit of your Father will be speaking in you'. If we entrust ourselves to the Lord at those times of loss, if we commend our spirit into his hands, we will experience his saving help.

27 December, Wednesday, Saint John, Apostle and Evangelist
John 20:2–8
Yesterday was the feast of Saint Stephen, today we celebrate the feast of Saint John, traditionally understood to be the author of the Fourth Gospel. Whereas Stephen was martyred as a young man, John, or the disciple Jesus loved, as he is referred to in today's gospel reading, seems to have lived a long life. Like Stephen, the beloved disciple was a wonderful witness to Jesus. Yet, whereas Stephen witnessed to Jesus primarily by his death, the beloved disciple witnessed to Jesus primarily by his life. He was the eyewitness who was close to Jesus in love and who witnessed to what he had seen and

heard by his preaching and teaching, and eventually by inspiring the writing down of the Fourth Gospel. In this gospel the beloved disciple is described as close to the bosom of Jesus at the Last Supper. The opening verses of John's Gospel, the Prologue, describe Jesus as close to the bosom of the Father. This disciple has the same loving relationship with Jesus that Jesus has with God the Father. The beloved disciple is the disciple we can all become. We are all invited to have the same intimate relationship with Jesus that Jesus has with the Father. In the words of the Fourth Gospel, we are called to abide in Jesus' love just as he abides in the love of the Father. If Christmas is the feast of Immanuel, God with us through Jesus, today's feast reminds us that we are called to be with Jesus as he is with the Father, to be present to him in love as he is present to the Father in love.

28 December, Thursday, The Holy Innocents
Matthew 2:13–18

The portrayal of Herod the Great in today's gospel reading is in keeping with what is known about him from the historical records. He owed his power to Rome and, having gained power, he did everything possible to retain it. In his later years he seems to have become especially paranoid, seeing threats to his power all about him, executing members of his family whom he suspected of wanting to overthrow him. The wise men from the east had told him that an infant king of the Jews had recently been born. To eliminate any possible threat to his power, he ordered the death of all children under two years of age. The gospel reading displays a figure who embodies ruthless, self-serving power to an extreme degree. We don't have to go back two millennia to find such figures. They are all too contemporary. Many children continue to suffer terribly because of the decisions such powerful people make. It can be difficult to discern any light in such dark and dangerous rulers. They seem to be the polar opposite of what is said of God in today's first reading: 'God is light; there is no darkness in him at all.' Elsewhere in this letter, the author states, 'God is love', suggesting how 'God is light' is to be understood. The reading acknowledges that there is some darkness in all of us: 'If we say we have no sin in us, we are deceiving ourselves.' We may not be like Herod, but we are all aware that the light of God's love does not yet fully shine through our lives. Even when the princes of darkness, like Herod, do their worst to others, something of the light of God's love often shines brightly through those who suffer from their cruelty. It is there in today's gospel reading in the care that Joseph shows for his wife and child as they try to escape a murderous tyrant. How often in the midst of wars unleashed by despots does God's light of love shine forth in various ways. Our calling is not just to curse the darkness but to reveal ever more fully the God of light and love who became flesh in the person of Jesus and wishes to become flesh in all of our lives.

29 December, Friday, Fifth Day in Octave of Christmas
Luke 2:22–35
In the opening chapters of his gospel, Luke portrays Jesus' parents as faithfully observing the Jewish Law. In this way he wants to stress that the movement that became known as Christianity has its roots deep in the Jewish faith. In the Jewish scriptures, especially in the prophet Isaiah, Israel's role was to be a light to the Gentiles, to reveal the light of God to the world. According to our gospel reading, the elderly Simeon, a devout Jew, recognises Mary and Joseph's child as the one who is to embody this calling of Israel. He is to be a light to enlighten the pagans, and in being faithful to this role he will bring glory to Israel. Simeon had spent his life looking forward to

'Israel's comforting'. When Mary and Joseph entered the Temple with their newborn first child on that day, Simeon's longings and hopes were brought to fulfilment. It has been said that Simeon has become the patron saint of those who, having found meaning at last in their lives, are able to let go and surrender to the Lord. His prayer of surrender has become part of the Night Prayer of the Church. We pray that prayer as people who have been graced by God's light shining through Jesus. Like Simeon, we have come to recognise Jesus as the light to enlighten the pagans and the glory of Israel. Every time we light a candle in church or at home, we are acknowledging Jesus as the light of the world and we are also recognising our own need for his gracious light as we struggle with the various forms of darkness in our lives.

30 December, Saturday, Sixth Day in the Octave of Christmas
Luke 2:36–40

There are several women in Luke's Gospel who welcome the coming of God through the person of Jesus. Mary, the mother of Jesus, and her cousin Elizabeth are especially noteworthy, and then there are the sisters, Mary and Martha, the woman who washed the feet of Jesus with her tears and dried them with her hair, Mary Magdalene and the other women who accompanied Jesus and his disciples on their travels and provided for them out of their means. Anna in today's gospel reading belongs in their company. She had been a widow for most of her adult life, her husband having died after only seven years of marriage and Anna herself now being eighty-four years old. Her devotion to God through prayer and fasting made her sensitive to the coming of God's special messenger, the child of Mary and Joseph. When she saw Simeon with the child in his arms, she immediately recognised the child for who he was, and began praising God and speaking about the child to others. Her response to recognising the true identity of this child was twofold, towards God in prayer, and towards others in proclaiming to them the good news that God had come to deliver his people through this child. The portrayal of Anna in the gospel reading reminds us that prayer makes us sensitive to the Lord's presence. Prayer attunes us to the various ways the Lord comes to us. Anna also shows us how to respond to the Lord's coming to us, his presence with us. Like her, we respond firstly by giving praise to God. We also respond by proclaiming the good news of the Lord's presence to others. We do this above all by allowing the Lord to be present to others through us.

1 January, Monday, Mary, the Holy Mother of God
Luke 2:16–21

I am very fond of that prayer of blessing at the beginning of today's first reading. It is the blessing of Aaron over the people of Israel. It is a prayer of blessing any of us could pray for others, silently or aloud. That prayer of blessing contains a hope, a wish, for those for whom it is prayed. That hope came to be realised above all with the birth of Jesus to Mary and Joseph. It was then that the Lord God made his face to shine upon us and was gracious to us. It was then that he uncovered his face to us and brought us peace. There are two references to the face of God in that blessing: 'May the Lord let his face shine upon you … May the Lord uncover his face to you.' God let his face shine upon us and uncovered his face to us with the coming of Jesus. It was a strongly held belief in the Jewish tradition that no one could see the face of God and live. Yet God showed us his face through the birth, life, death and resurrection of Jesus. Jesus was God with us, Emmanuel. As mother of Jesus, Mary was mother of God-with-us, mother of God. When we venerate Mary as mother of God, we are making a statement about her child, Jesus. He is God's face made visible to us. It is by showing our face to one another that we become recognisable. In showing his face to us through Jesus, God has become recognisable. Jesus has revealed the face of God to be a face of love, a love that seeks out the lost, brings back the stray, suffers with those who suffer, brings new life out of death, a love that does not come to an end. There is much to ponder here. According to the gospel reading, Mary treasured all the things the shepherds said to her about her newborn child and pondered them in her heart. God had given Mary much to ponder in calling her to be the mother of his Son, the mother of God. There is much to ponder here for all of us, as we contemplate the face of God in Jesus, Mary's Son.

2 January, Tuesday before Epiphany
John 1:19–28

The priests and Levites ask John the Baptist two questions in today's gospel reading, 'Who are you?' and 'Why are you baptising?' The more fundamental of the two questions is the first one, because the answer to the first question determines the answer to the second question. It is because of who we are that we do what we do. It was because John was the voice crying in the wilderness to draw people's attention to the presence of Jesus among them that he was engaged in the water ritual of baptising that prepared people to receive Jesus with open hearts. The question 'Who are you?' is one of the most fundamental questions of life because our identity is the foundation for what we do and why we do it. We all need to keep returning to that question 'Who am I?' It can be answered at different levels, 'I am Irish, I am a bus driver … .' At the deepest level of my being, who am I? What is my deepest identity? John the Baptist was very clear about his deepest identity, which is why, when asked, he could deny that he was the Messiah or Elijah or the Prophet. As the voice, he was the witness to the Word, the light of the world. John the Baptist points us in the direction of our own deepest identity, which is to be a witness to Christ. Saint Paul would even go further and say, 'It is no longer I who live, but Christ who lives in me.' Our deepest identity is our Christ identity. It is that identity that is to shape all we do and why we do it.

3 January, Wednesday before Epiphany
John 1:29–34

It seems that John the Baptist had an aversion to saying, 'Look at me'. He was very clear that his calling from God was to make a very different statement, 'Look at him', 'Look at Jesus'. He declares in today's gospel reading, 'It was to reveal him to Israel that I came baptising with water'. John was a very impressive figure. Many people went out to him in the wilderness and looked to him. He had his own followers. Yet he consistently deflected people's vision away from himself towards the one who 'ranks before me because he existed before me'. His opening words in that reading are 'Look, there is the Lamb of God who takes away the sins of the world'. 'Look at him', he is saying, 'Go to him and follow him.' Even though in our culture many people are saying in a very forceful way, 'Look at me', and, by implication, 'Be like me', the voice of John the Baptist continues to sound forth, calling upon us to look at Jesus, to go to him and become like him. Having looked upon the Lord and come to him, John the Baptist would be very clear that there is a further step we need to take and that is the step of witnessing to the one upon whom we have looked, to whom we have come and whom we have received into our lives. John the Baptist was one of the great witnesses to Jesus. He can inspire us to live lives that in some way or other point to the Lord, lives that witness to the values that he lived and died for, the values of God's kingdom.

4 January, Thursday before Epiphany
John 1:35–42

In today's gospel reading John the Baptist introduced two of his disciples to Jesus, saying to them, 'Look, there is the Lamb of God'. It was because of what John the Baptist said to his two disciples that they began to follow Jesus. Jesus could then speak to them directly: 'What do you want?' 'Come and see.' The Lord wants to speak to each one of us directly, but he often needs others to pave the way. A person of faith takes some initiative towards us, and then we discover the call of the Lord for ourselves. John the Baptist created a space for Jesus to engage directly with his disciples and for them to respond. According to the gospel reading, that pattern then repeated itself. One of John the Baptist's two disciples was Andrew. Having spent time with Jesus, having developed a personal relationship with Jesus, Andrew then introduced his brother Simon to Jesus. He created a space for Jesus to engage personally with Peter and for Peter to respond. What John the Baptist did for Andrew and what Andrew did for Peter, Peter would go on to do for many others. He created a space for the Lord to relate in a very personal way to others and for them to respond. We can each give thanks for all those who introduced us to the Lord, who played the role in our lives that Andrew played in the life of Peter, that Peter played in the life of many others, and that, later on in John's Gospel, the Samaritan woman played in the life of her townspeople, and that Mary Magdalene played in the life of the other disciples on Easter Sunday morning. Both these women played a significant role in bringing others to the Lord. Each of us is called to bring others to the Lord, perhaps just one person. We don't have to be great missionaries to introduce someone to the

Lord. Very often our own quiet and faithful witness to the Lord and his way of life will, in time, bear that rich fruit for others.

5 January, Friday before Epiphany
John 1:43–51

Dublin people often have a prejudice about Cork people. It is sometimes expressed in the saying, 'The only good thing to come out of Cork is the road to Dublin'. That is city prejudice, but there can be small town prejudice too, and we see something of that in today's gospel reading. We learn from the final chapter of John's Gospel that Nathanael was from Cana in Galilee, which is not too far from Nazareth. When Philip finds Nathanael to tell him that he had found the long-awaited Messiah, Jesus son of Joseph, from Nazareth, Nathanael replies, 'From Nazareth? Can anything good come from that place?' It has to be said that Nazareth was a small village, off the beaten track, with no claim to fame; it isn't mentioned even once in the Jewish scriptures. Yet something, someone, wonderful came out of Nazareth. This very ordinary place was the home of God's only Son, the Word who was with God in the beginning and who was flesh in Nazareth. Having met Jesus for himself, Nathanael began to see that there was much more to Jesus than he could ever have imagined, 'You are the Son of God, you are the King of Israel'. Even that insight was only the beginning of Nathanael's journey of discovery. Jesus promises him, 'You will see greater things … You will see heaven laid open and, above the Son of Man, the angels of God ascending and descending.' Nathanael will eventually come to appreciate that Jesus was the one through whom heaven was coming to earth; this man from this very ordinary village, Nazareth, was God in human form. We can all be tempted to ask a version of Nathanael's question, 'Can anything good come out of this place, this situation in my life, this person … out of me?' The gospel reading is reminding us that the ordinary is often charged with the presence of God. Something good, something of God, can come out of any of us, even when we seem to ourselves to have little to offer.

6 January, Saturday, The Epiphany of the Lord
Matthew 2:1–12

There is a tradition in certain parts of Latin America that on the feast of the Epiphany a small plastic baby Jesus is hidden in a cake baked specially for the feast day. The hiding of the plastic figure signifies the efforts to hide the child Jesus from the evil intentions of King Herod. As the cake is cut, the slicing knife represents the danger posed to the infant Jesus by the cruel king. In some places the tradition is that whoever gets the piece of cake with the small figure of Jesus is obliged to host the next family gathering on 2 February, the feast of the Presentation of the Lord. In other places, the one who finds the plastic figure receives gifts from those present. These traditions make tangible both the dangers that threatened the child Jesus as soon as he was born, and the excitement of discovering the child Jesus, the son of Mary and Joseph, to be Emmanuel, God-with-us. If the danger posed to the child Jesus is represented by King Herod, the excitement of discovering the child Jesus is expressed by the magi from the east who, on arriving in Bethlehem, fell to their knees to worship the infant king of the Jews and then offered him their gifts of gold, frankincense and myrrh.

The word 'Epiphany' means a showing forth, a setting in the light. Today we celebrate the good news that God showed forth his Son to all the nations, Jews and pagans alike. It is the pagan visitors from an unnamed city of the east who reveal to us how to respond to God's showing forth of his Son, God's gift of his Son. Jesus was born into a Jewish world and these visitors from the east were strangers in that world; they were outsiders. It often takes strangers, outsiders, to show us how to respond to God's gift of his Son, how to appreciate the great riches of our faith, the presence of Christ in the Eucharist and in the other sacraments, the life-giving message of the scriptures, in particular, the gospels. In recent years there has been a huge increase in the number of people coming to live among us from abroad. They often bring an enthusiasm and appreciation for the treasures of the faith, that we, perhaps, have lost somewhat. They have enriched the Church by their readiness to share their gifts and energies with the Church here in their adopted homeland.

Although in the emerging tradition of the Church the visitors from the east have become kings and are portrayed as kings in our traditional cribs, they are not called kings in the gospel reading. They are called 'magi', translated as 'wise men'. The term 'magi' referred to people who had special knowledge, experts in some field or other, and in the case of our magi, it would appear, experts in astronomy or astrology. The rising of a new star suggested to these 'magi' the birth of a new Jewish king, to whom they wished to do homage. They saw a new light and they chose to follow the light, wherever it led them. They represent all those, of whatever creed or persuasion, who seek to follow the light, the light of truth. The magi are the ancestors of all of us who seek the truth. It was their own natural skills of searching and interpreting the skies that launched them on their search. Those natural gifts brought them to Jerusalem, but the gospel reading suggests that they needed the guidance of the Jewish scriptures to direct them to Bethlehem, where the infant king of the Jews would be found. Reason and the revelation of Scripture worked together to bring them to the Lord. Their profile in the gospels reminds us that our natural gifts of mind and reason need never be an obstacle to faith. The magi came to recognise that the brightest star of all was Christ the Lord; he was 'light from light', in the words of the Creed.

Jesus is God's gift to all who seek the truth; he is not a gift for a select few. The figure of Herod in the gospel reading can symbolise the forces that work to prevent us finding the one for whom we long. We can encounter many obstacles on our journey towards the Lord of light and truth. Yet the gospel reading also suggests that the obstacles will not ultimately prevail if we are faithful to our search for the true light. At our baptism, the light of Christ shone upon us and remains with us to enlighten every darkness and to lead us to our eternal home.

8 January, Monday, First Week in Ordinary Time

Mark 1:14–20

Any meeting between two or more people has the potential to be a good news event. The meeting that Peter, Andrew, James and John had with Jesus in today's gospel was such a good news event, because the reign of God, the power of God, was present to them in the person of Jesus. That power of God present in Jesus to Peter, Andrew, James and John was the power of love, a love that called on them to repent, to turn towards God, a love that promised forgiveness, healing and acceptance, a love that gave them a mission in life. The kind of meeting that these two sets of brothers had with Jesus is offered to each one of us. Jesus is not just a figure of history who belongs to the past. He is a living Lord, present in his Church and in the world today. He is constantly calling us to meet with him as Peter, Andrew, James and John met with him, and each of these meetings proclaims good news for us. He meets with us and speaks to us through the sacraments, in particular the Eucharist, through the scriptures, from deep within our own hearts, through other people, through nature. Each time the Lord meets with us we will first hear from him the good news of God's unconditional love for us. Graced by that good news, we will also hear the call to mission, the call to be good news for others, to be the Lord's body in the world, his feet, his hands, his mouth, his eyes, his ears.

9 January, Tuesday, First Week in Ordinary Time

Mark 1:21–28

Prayer doesn't always have to be measured and controlled. It can be spontaneous and blunt at times. We have a good example of that kind of prayer in today's first reading. It is said that Hannah spoke to God out of the depth of her grief and resentment. Her prayer was silent; the priest Eli heard nothing and only saw her lips move. Yet it was full of emotion. As she said to Eli, she was pouring out her soul before the Lord. She was being herself before the Lord, opening up to the Lord the resentment and sadness that was in her heart and soul, because she had been childless for so long. Hannah's prayer shows us that our own prayer can be completely honest. We do not have to censure our prayer in the Lord's presence. There is nothing in our lives that is out of bounds in our prayer. The Lord can deal with whatever we throw at him in prayer. There is no such thing as uncivil prayer. The possessed man in the gospel reading addresses Jesus in the same direct way that Hannah addresses God in the first reading. He shouted, 'What do you want with us, Jesus of Nazareth? Have you come to destroy us?' We can almost sense the anger in the questions that the man hurls at Jesus. Yet, as God was comfortable with Hannah's resentment and grief, Jesus seems comfortable with this man's deep, demonic anger. Jesus responds with a word that calms the man and releases him of his demon, just as in the first reading it is said of Hannah that she was dejected no longer after her prayer. Whenever we open our hearts to the Lord, revealing to him what is there, including our darkest emotions, we too will experience the Lord's healing and calming presence.

10 January, Wednesday, First Week in Ordinary Time
Mark 1:29–39

In today's first reading, the young Samuel heard a call, but it took the older Eli to help Samuel discern that the call was coming from the Lord. We sometimes need others, people more experienced in the spiritual life than ourselves, to help us discern the call of the Lord in our lives. Eli fulfilled the very important ministry of a wise mentor. He enabled Eli to recognise the way that the Lord was calling him. In the gospel reading, we find Jesus getting up long before dawn and going off to a lonely place to pray. He may have been trying to discern the call of God in his own life. Having ministered in Capernaum, where should he go now? It seems that after his prayer, he was clear that he had to go to 'the neighbouring country towns, so that I can preach there too, because that is why I came'. However, whereas Eli acted as an enabler in Samuel's life when it came to God's call, Jesus' own disciples acted as disablers in Jesus' life when it came to God's call. They wanted to drag him back to Capernaum when Jesus was clear that God was calling him to go to other towns to preach the Gospel. We may be fortunate enough to encounter an Eli in our lives who helps us to discern God's call. We can also encounter the equivalent of the disciples, those who, although well intentioned, try to take us in directions that are contrary to where God is calling us to go. We need to pray for the grace to know who is helping us to answer the Lord's call and who is hindering us from doing so. We also need to ask the Lord to help us to play the role of Eli in the life of others rather than the role of the disciples in the life of Jesus in today's gospel reading.

11 January, Thursday, First Week in Ordinary Time
Mark 1:40–45

Making choices is something that we do every day. We try to choose well, to make the best choice possible, the choice that the Lord would want us to make. We don't always succeed in choosing well; sometimes we make choices the Lord would not have wanted us to make. In the gospel reading, a leper comes up to Jesus and says, 'If you want to – if you choose – you can cure me.' The leper could not presume that Jesus would choose to heal him, because lepers were not supposed to approach others; they were to keep out of the way, for fear they would contaminate others. However, in reply, Jesus said to him, 'Of course I want to! Be cured.' Jesus chose to do what nobody else would have chosen to do; he reached out and touched the leper and, as a result, his leprosy was healed. In the gospels, Jesus is consistently portrayed as choosing to make contact with those who are broken in body, mind or spirit, and who live on the margins because of their brokenness. The risen Lord continues to make those same choices today; he chooses to connect with each of us in our own brokenness. He will always be a healing and life-giving presence in our lives. He asks us to be the same for each other, to make the kinds of choices that bring healing and new life to others.

12 January, Friday, First Week in Ordinary Time
Mark 2:1–12

We often pray that eternal rest would be granted to those who have died. 'Rest' in that sense is not just the absence of activity, but a renewal of our spirit. The psalm, 'The Lord is my shepherd', says of the Lord, 'near restful waters he leads me to revive my drooping spirit'. The Lord wants us to experience such 'rest', not just beyond this earthly life but during our earthly lives. He is always at work to revive our drooping spirits and he wants to work through us to revive the drooping spirits of others. In today's gospel reading, a very concerned group stop at nothing to bring their paralysed friend to Jesus, even going as far as making a hole in the roof of the house where Jesus was teaching. They wanted their friend to reach a place of rest; they brought him to Jesus so that he would revive their friend's drooping spirits by healing him of his paralysis. A group of men making a hole in the roof above would normally be experienced by a teacher as an unwelcome interruption to a lesson. However, Jesus sees the faith that drove these men to take such desperate measures and he immediately responds to the plight of the paralytic. He not only heals him physically, but assures him that he is loved by God, by declaring his sins forgiven. Jesus heals the whole person, physically and spiritually. He brings him to a place of rest. The Lord works in the same healing way in all our lives. He also wants to work through us for the holistic healing of others. The Lord needs us to play the role of the paralytic's friends today, so that the broken in body, mind and spirit can experience his healing power to the full.

13 January, Saturday, First Week in Ordinary Time

Mark 2:13–17

In today's gospel reading the religious experts, the scribes, express surprise at the company Jesus kept. They ask his disciples, 'Why does he eat with tax collectors and sinners?' Someone like Jesus, a religious teacher, was expected to keep better company than that; he should be in the company of religious people like himself. However, Jesus clearly did not restrict his company to those who were seen to have measured up in some way. He was happy to keep the company of those who were considered sinners, just as doctors are normally found in the company of the sick, at least during their working hours. The gospel reading reminds us that the Lord is happy to be in our company, even when we have fallen short of what some people expect of us, even when we are far from being all that God is calling us to be. Our failings and weaknesses do not drive the Lord away or drag him down, rather his presence to us in our failings and weaknesses lifts us up. We can always come before the Lord in our brokenness and he never drives us away. His table is always set for us and there is always a place for us there, regardless of where we are on our life journey.

15 January, Monday, Second Week in Ordinary Time
Mark 2:18–22

There are many changes happening across our parishes at present, as we try to move together towards becoming larger (and fewer) parishes. There is a great deal of loss in that journey, for all of us. There is a sense in which things will never be the same. Something new is coming to birth and it can leave us feeling unsettled. The gospel reading suggests that many of Jesus' contemporaries found his way of giving expression to the Jewish faith quite disturbing and unsettling. It gave rise to all sorts of questions, such as the question we find at the beginning of the gospel reading, 'Why is it that John's disciples and the disciples of the Pharisees fast, but your disciples do not?' Jesus seemed to be showing little respect for the ancient Jewish practice of fasting. Indeed, he was criticised by some as a glutton and a drunkard. In response to that criticism, Jesus spoke of his ministry as like a wedding feast. There was something celebratory about Jesus' ministry, because, through him, God was working to renew his marriage, his loving relationship, with his people and all humanity. In the time of Jesus, weddings engaged the whole community, the whole village, and they could go on for days. No one would dream of fasting at such a time. Jesus was saying that some of the old venerable traditions had to give way because God was working through Jesus in a new way. Jesus was offering new wine, and the old wineskins simply couldn't contain it. New wineskins were needed. The Lord continues to do a new work among us. He is always moving us to work together with him in new ways, so that the Gospel can be heard afresh in our time. This will often mean letting go of structures that have served us well in the past but no longer serve the new work that the Lord is doing today. This letting go is painful, especially when we are not sure of the shape of the new structures, the new wineskins. Yet we try to remain open to what the Lord is doing among us, trusting that he is furthering his mission as the good shepherd who came that we may have life to the full.

16 January, Tuesday, Second Week in Ordinary Time
Mark 2:23–28

Both of today's readings suggest that our way of seeing can be very limited. In the first reading, when Samuel saw the first of Jesse's sons he thought, 'Surely, the Lord's anointed one stands there'. However, Samuel heard the Lord say to him, 'Take no notice of his appearance or his height … God does not see as humans see; humans look at appearances but the Lord looks at the heart.' It turned out that the son of Jesse whom God had chosen, his youngest son, David, had the least to recommend him, just going on appearances. The Lord saw something in David that no human being could see. There is another instance of limited human seeing in the gospel reading. When the Pharisees saw Jesus' disciples picking and eating ears of corn on the sabbath, they saw people who were breaking the sabbath law requiring rest from labour. When Jesus looked upon the action of his disciples, he saw a legitimate attempt to satisfy hunger. He went on to say to the Pharisees that human need will often take priority over religious law, including the sabbath law. 'The sabbath was made for humans, not humans for the sabbath.' Both readings remind us that our own way of seeing can often be very limited. We can so easily judge on the basis of appearances, rather than seeing beyond appearances to what is deepest in the person. Our calling is to grow into the Lord's way of seeing, with the help of his Spirit, the Holy Spirit. The first step on that journey of deeper seeing is to acknowledge our own blindness and our need for fuller light.

17 January, Wednesday, Second Week in Ordinary Time
Mark 3:1–6

In the gospel reading, when Jesus walked into a synagogue, he seems to have walked into a trap. It was the sabbath day. A man with a with- ered hand was there and the Pharisees were waiting to see if Jesus would cure him, thereby breaking the sabbath law. There is a sug- gestion that the man was placed there by those who wanted to catch Jesus out. Using a vulnerable person to catch out and bring down someone perceived as a threat has to be one of the darker arts in human relationships. The human tendency to use others for our own personal gain is always with us. On this occasion, it evoked two strong emotions in Jesus. 'He grieves with anger' at the hardness of heart of these religious leaders. The presence of such strong emo- tions as anger and grief within us are often a sign that something is not right with the world. Jesus directed his feelings into the healing of the man's hand. We can sometimes struggle to use our strong emotions in the service of the well-being of others. All of our emo- tions, even the most potentially destructive, can empower us 'to do good' and 'to save life', in the words of the gospel reading. If that is to happen, we may need to call upon the Spirit of the Lord to help us harness these emotions in the service of the coming of God's king- dom. There was no aspect of Jesus' humanity that did not serve

God's life-giving purpose. He shows us what a fully human life looks like.

18 January, Thursday, Second Week in Ordinary Time
Mark 3:7–12

It often happens that when someone becomes very popular it can lead to a great deal of resentment on the part of others. We find such a scenario in the first reading. The young David became extremely popular, having slain the Philistine. People were comparing him very favourably to King Saul. This left Saul enraged and seething with jealousy. Anger and jealousy can be very volatile emotions that, if left unchecked, can drive people to do terrible things. Saul determined to kill David, even though David was fighting on behalf of Saul. The popularity of Saul in the first reading is surpassed by the popularity of Jesus in the gospel reading. We are told that people came out to Jesus, not just from Galilee, but from Judea, Jerusalem, Idumea, Transjordania and the region of Tyre and Sidon, hugely impressed by his power to heal. This popularity of Jesus resulted in great resentment towards him from the religious and political leaders of the time. The verse just before our gospel reading begins says, 'The Pharisees went out and immediately conspired with the Herodians against him, how to destroy him.' They would eventually succeed in doing so. Saul, however, did not succeed in destroying David, and this was due to the intervention of Saul's son, Jonathan. He spoke up in defence of David to his father, declaring that 'what he [David] has done has been greatly to your advantage'. Jonathan allowed Saul to see David with eyes no longer distorted by anger and jealousy. Jonathan models the reconciling, peace-making role we are all called to. Jesus was the supreme reconciler, and he calls us to share in his reconciling work. One of the ways we can do that is by helping people to see those towards whom they are hostile with new eyes.

19 January, Friday, Second Week in Ordinary Time
Mark 3:13–19

In today's gospel reading, Jesus appoints twelve of his disciples to be his companions and to be sent out to preach and to heal. Firstly, they are to be Jesus' companions; they are to spend time with him; they are to enter into a personal relationship with him. Only then can they be sent out to share in his work of preaching and healing. We are all called to share in the Lord's work today in some way or another. We are to proclaim his presence by our words and his deeds. However, this sharing in the Lord's work can only flow from our personal relationship with him. Like the twelve in today's gospel reading, we need to be with the Lord before he can send us out in his name. The Lord is always with us, but we need to be with him. The Lord befriends us, but we need to receive the gift of his friendship and befriend him in return. It is above all prayer that nurtures our personal relationship with the Lord. In prayer we attend to the Lord's presence, we become present to his presence to us, we become his companions. In opening ourselves to the Lord's presence, we are empowered to live as he lived, to love as he loved. That will often mean loving even those who do not love us, just as in the first reading David is portrayed as showing goodness and kindness to Saul who wanted to kill David. The Lord needs us to be the agents of his unconditional love in the world, but if that is to happen we need the Lord. We first need to be present to him and to open ourselves to his empowering presence.

20 January, Saturday, Second Week in Ordinary Time
Mark 3:20–21

Today's very short gospel reading from Mark suggests that Jesus was misunderstood by his own family. They had come to hear that so many people were coming to Jesus for help that he and his disciples had no time even to eat. They concluded that Jesus must be out of his mind and they wanted to take him back to Nazareth. Jesus' family meant well, but they completely misinterpreted Jesus. Having set out on his mission of bringing God's merciful and healing love to all, Jesus was never going to return to Nazareth and live the hidden life he had lived before he left there. There are misunderstandings in every family. A member of a family can set out on a path that just makes no sense to other family members. Jesus' family was no different from most human families. The members of his family had to learn to let him go to God's purpose for his life, even if it made little sense to them. We often have to let go of those we care about, even if the path they are taking is very concerning to us. We sometimes just have to let them be. The members of Jesus' family were trying to control him, but we cannot control Jesus. Our calling is to surrender to Jesus and to try and go where he is leading us. Jesus once said, 'the Spirit blows where it wills'. What is true of the Holy Spirit is true of Jesus, who is full of the Holy Spirit. Far from trying to control Jesus, we invite him to control us, in the sense of becoming Lord of our lives. When Jesus becomes Lord of our lives, we don't lose our freedom. Rather, we become truly free, free to live in the fully human way for which God has created us.

22 January, Monday, Third Week in Ordinary Time
Mark 3:22–30

In the gospel reading Jesus speaks of a kingdom divided against itself not being able to stand, and likewise a household divided against itself not being able to stand. He was refuting those who claimed that the power at work in his life was the power of Satan. How could Satan, he asked, be driving out Satan? Why would the kingdom of Satan seek to be divided against itself? That would be a recipe for its collapse. It is extraordinary to think that some people were of the opinion that the power at work in Jesus was the power of evil. Here was Jesus doing good, healing the sick, seeking the lost, feeding the hungry, proclaiming God's mercy to sinners. It was the power of God that was at work through Jesus, not the power of Satan. The scribes who came down from Jerusalem and who accused Jesus of acting in the power of Satan were blind; they saw white and called it black. It is easy for any of us to see what is not there or not to see what is there. We need ongoing healing of our blindness. We need to keep coming before the Lord with the prayer, 'Lord, that I may see'. We ask to see as Jesus sees, to see with generous and compassionate eyes, recognising the good that is in people even when it is hidden.

23 January, Tuesday, Third Week in Ordinary Time
Mark 3:31–35
The bringing of the ark of God, or the Ark of the Covenant, in procession to Jerusalem was a very significant event for the people of Israel under their king, David. The ark of God was a container that held the two tablets of stone on which the Ten Commandments were written. On Mount Sinai, God had promised the people of Israel that he would be their God, and they in turn had promised God that they would be his people by living according to the Ten Commandments. This container with its contents symbolised God's covenant with his people and theirs with him. It embodied God's choice of the people of Israel in the service of all humanity. As the ark of God is brought to the citadel of David in Jerusalem, it is celebrated with elements with which we are very familiar from our own liturgy, especially the Eucharist. There is music and song, there is sacrifice and there is communion, the sharing of food. At every Eucharist, we generally have some singing. At every Eucharist, the sacrifice of Christ on the cross, his loving surrender to God and to humanity on Calvary, is sacramentally present to us. At every Eucharist, we enter

into communion with the Lord as Bread of Life and with each other as members of his body. So much of our faith has deep roots in the religion of Israel. In the gospel reading we have another element that is central to our Eucharist, the ministry of the word. Jesus is in a house in Capernaum with people sitting around him listening to him preaching, proclaiming God's word, God's will. He identifies those sitting around him as his brothers and sisters and mother, his new spiritual family. We all belong to that family, and at the Eucharist we both celebrate and consolidate our belonging to the Lord's family.

24 January, Wednesday, Third Week in Ordinary Time
Mark 4:1–20
Those who like to do some gardening are aware that not everything that is planted will survive the various assaults of weather and insects. However, what doesn't grow or what grows and doesn't last can be more than compensated for by what flourishes. It can be such a joy when something that is planted reaches its full potential, even if other plantings are much less successful. In the parable, Jesus imagines a sower scattering seed in a very liberal fashion. Much of it does not come to fruition, because of hungry birds, thin soil, thorny weeds and much else. However, some seed survived all those threats and produced an extraordinary crop. Thirty, sixty, a hundredfold is way above the yield any farmer would expect. At this point the parable loses touch a little with reality. However, perhaps that is the point. Much of Jesus' preaching has encountered unreceptive hearts. It made little or no impact. The interpretation of the parable, which may reflect the setting of the early Church rather than the setting of Jesus' ministry, suggests reasons why the preaching of the word fails to bear fruit in people's lives. Yet Jesus was saying to his disciples that whenever his word is received by hearts that are open and receptive the fruits can be wonderful. In spite of so much indifference

and failure, even a small number of receptive hearts can usher in the kingdom of God in ways that defy all normal expectations. We can easily get discouraged by the indifference of many to the message of the Gospel. The Lord is reminding us that even in times of great loss, he can nevertheless work powerfully through those whose hearts are receptive to his word. They can be the beachhead in our world for the coming of God's kingdom.

25 January, Thursday, The Conversion of Saint Paul, Apostle
Mark 16:15–18

Before the risen Lord appeared to Paul on the road outside Damascus, he was a very religious person. As a devoted Jew, he really wanted to do God's will. That is why he persecuted the members of the Church. He saw them as Jews who had gone off the rails and who could easily lead other Jews astray if they weren't stopped. Yet, in persecuting this group of Jews who believed that Jesus was the Messiah, he was actually persecuting Jesus himself who was God's beloved Son. This was the discovery he made when Jesus, the risen Lord, appeared to him in a bright light and Paul heard Jesus ask him, 'Saul, Saul, why are you persecuting me?' Jesus didn't ask Paul, 'Why are you persecuting my followers?' The risen Lord identified himself so closely with his followers that to persecute them was to persecute him. Paul was persecuting the members of Jesus' body. We are all members of the Lord's body. We are now his hands, his feet, his eyes, his ears. Later on, Paul would write to the church in Corinth, 'You are the body of Christ and individually members of it' (1 Corinthians 12:27). Earlier in that letter he wrote, 'when you sin against the brothers and sisters [the members of the church] … you sin against Christ' (1 Corinthians 8:12). Paul learned a lesson on the road to Damascus that he never forgot. We meet the risen Lord in each other. We serve the Lord by serving one another; we reject the Lord by rejecting one another. Through baptism, each of us is a member of Christ's body, which gives us a very special dignity. It also gives us a very special calling. We are to allow Jesus to come into the world through us. He wants us, needs us, to be his hands and feet and eyes and ears and mouth. 'Christ has no body now but yours', in the words of St Teresa of Avila.

26 January, Friday, Saints Timothy and Titus
Luke 10:1–9
The grandparents of the pupils had been invited to a Mass I celebrated in one of the parish primary schools. There is a reference to a grandmother in today's first reading. Paul is writing to his closest co-worker, Timothy. He tells Timothy that he is always being reminded of the sincere faith he has, and Paul goes on to acknowledge that Timothy's faith came first to live in his grandmother Lois, and then in his mother Eunice. We can all look back to the faith of our grandparents and, perhaps, to our parents as well. Grandparents continue to have a very important role today in passing on the faith to their grandchildren. They often do this by praying for their grandchildren, praying with them, taking them to church and pointing out the various images and symbols in the church and explaining their meaning. Grandparents are so often among the labourers in the harvest that Jesus mentions in the gospel reading. As he sends out the seventy-two labourers, he calls on them to keep praying to God to send more labourers into the harvest. We are all called to be labourers in the Lord's harvest, in virtue of our baptism. The Lord needs each one of us to witness to him and his Gospel in our world today. Timothy and Titus were co-workers of Paul. He had many other co-workers, women as well as men. Paul knew that the Lord's work could not get done without all these co-workers. The Lord's need is as great today as it was at the beginning of the Church, in the time

of Paul. He needs every one of us to be a labourer in his harvest, just as he needed the seventy-two and many more. The harvest of the Lord remains rich and the Lord needs all the co-workers he can get. We need to all work together to ensure that people today hear and experience the same good news that the seventy-two were called by Jesus to preach: 'The kingdom of God is very near to you.'

27 January, Saturday, Third Week in Ordinary Time
Mark 4:35–41

It is likely that Mark's Gospel was written to the church in Rome, shortly after it had come through the persecution of Emperor Nero. If so, Mark's church would easily have recognised itself among the disciples in the boat, battling a gale, with the waves breaking into the boat so that it was almost swamped. Just as Jesus was asleep as the storm howled and the disciples concluded that he didn't care for them, so Mark's church may have wondered during their own stormy ordeal whether the risen Lord was asleep, indifferent to their plight. As a church we have been through difficult times; we have taken a battering, for various reasons. We too may be tempted to think that the Lord has forgotten about us and doesn't care. The message of today's gospel reading is that nothing could be further from the truth. The reason that Jesus was asleep in the boat as the storm broke wasn't that he didn't care for his disciples but that he had complete trust that God would preserve the boat in the storm because God was stronger than the storm. He rebuked his disciples for their lack of trust: 'How is it that you have no faith?' The Lord is never asleep to our plight; he is always with us in the storm and will never allow the storm to swamp the Church. He does ask, however, that we keep faith in him while the storm is doing its worst and not just in the calm after it.

29 January, Monday, Fourth Week in Ordinary Time
Mark 5:1–20

The man who lived among the tombs could not be described as weak. He had the strength to snap the chains and break the fetters with which he had been secured. No one had the strength to control him. He seems to have had an almost superhuman strength. Yet it was a destructive strength, damaging to himself and to others. According to the gospel reading, he would gash himself with stones and was clearly a danger to the local townspeople, which is why he had been banished to the local graveyard. Here was someone who had a storm raging within him. When Jesus came within sight of him, he addressed Jesus very aggressively: 'What do you want with me, Jesus, Son of the Most High God?' His destructive strength came from his anger, and his anger was a sign of how damaged and broken he was. Yet Jesus did not run from him. He absorbed his anger and then healed his brokenness. When the townspeople saw him in the company of Jesus, he was 'in his full senses'. The story reminds us that Jesus never runs away from us, no matter how unapproachable we may be to others. He comes to us as we are, sometimes in our brokenness and anger, and, if we are open to his coming, he can calm the storm that might be raging within us, just as he calmed the storm at sea. The risen Lord is always entering our personal storms to give us a share in his strength, which is a life-giving strength that empowers us to become the person he is calling us to be.

30 January, Tuesday, Fourth Week in Ordinary Time
Mark 5:21–43

The grief of David in the first reading is very moving. Even though his son Absalom had led a rebellion against his father, he was still David's son and, on hearing the news of Absalom's death, David grieved bitter tears, as any father would for a son, even a rebellious son. In the gospel reading we hear of the death of a daughter, not a rebellious daughter but a young girl of twelve. Her death causes people to grieve, to weep and wail unreservedly, in the words of the gospel reading. The death of children is especially heartbreaking, especially for the child's parents. In the gospel reading, Jesus takes the child by the hand and restores her to life and instructs that she be given something to eat. The evangelist is showing us that the power of Jesus is stronger than the power of death. This became very evident to the early Church in the light of the resurrection of Jesus. As believers in a risen Lord, we continue to grieve when a loved one dies. Yet there is hope in our grief because we are convinced that the Lord is stronger than death. If we open ourselves in faith to the Lord, like Jairus and the woman with the flow of blood in the gospel reading, we will experience his life-giving power just as they did. Jesus remains the life-giver for all who turn to him in faith, both in the course of this earthly life and, especially, at the hour of our death.

31 January, Wednesday, Fourth Week in Ordinary Time
Mark 6:1–6
We are familiar with the saying, 'Familiarity breeds contempt.' We see this saying working itself out in today's gospel reading. Jesus returns to his home town of Nazareth. It was a very ordinary, insig-nificant, out-of-the-way kind of place, which is never mentioned in the Jewish scriptures. Jesus' family were as ordinary as all the other inhabitants of this small town. He was the son of a 'carpenter', a term that can refer to a person with a skill not just with wood but with stone. Such a skill would have been in demand but indicated noth-ing exceptional. The people of Nazareth were familiar with Jesus' family, who continued to live among them and whom they could name. Rather than rejoicing in the life-giving power of his ministry

and the wisdom of Jesus' teaching, they were scandalised by him, because, in so many ways, he was no different from themselves. We encounter here the scandal of the incarnation. God was powerfully present to them through someone who was one of their own. God comes to us all in and through the ordinary and the everyday. The great saints never ceased being amazed at the mysterious presence of God they sensed all around them. To grow in faith is to grow in our capacity to recognise the presence of the Lord in and through the ordinary and the familiar. 'Ordinary time' is filled with the mysterious presence of the Lord and every place can be holy ground.

1 February, Thursday, Saint Brigid, Abbess, Secondary Patron of Ireland
Luke 6:32–38
The tradition about Brigid that has come down to us speaks of a woman who had a great love of God and who gave her life to God in the face of family opposition. She knew herself to be a friend of God. Because she experienced God's friendship in her own life, she was able to reveal God's friendship to others. She was especially good and kind to the poor and those in greatest need. She knew that God had a special love for them. Brigid often gave away food to those who were poor and hungry. She welcomed all who visited her. She lived the kind of life that Jesus speaks about in the gospel reading when he called on us to be loving and forgiving and to give generously to others. She lived like Jesus. People soon realised that Brigid was a very special person who had a deep relationship with the Lord and she gathered a community around her. As a saint in heaven, we can pray to her. We can ask her to help us to live like Jesus as she did, to be as loving and kind as she was. Brigid gave new life to people by her kindness and generosity. Today is not only the feast of Saint Brigid, it is also the first day of spring when we begin to

notice signs of new life in nature. We speak of Brigid as one who welcomes the spring. She is the saint of springtime. Brigid not only took special care of people, she was also remembered as one who cared for animals and nature. She teaches us to care for all of God's creation. Saint Brigid's cross is her traditional symbol. It speaks to us of nature, as it is made from rushes or straw. People often place it in their homes, perhaps over the door or in the window, because they believe it brings a very special blessing to the house and to all who live there. Today, on her feast, we ask Saint Brigid to bless each one of us by helping us to be as generous and loving as she was towards all in need, and as respectful as she was towards our natural environment.

2 February, Friday, The Presentation of the Lord
Luke 2:22–40
The prayer of Simeon in today's gospel reading has become part of the Night Prayer of the Church: 'Now, Master, you can let your servant go in peace'. He is now ready to embrace death because his eyes have seen the Saviour promised by God in the Jewish scriptures. It is often said of people who are dying that they seem to hang on until some loved one who has been away arrives at their bedside. Then, having seen their loved one or heard their voice, they slip away. When a young couple came to the Temple that day with their new-born child, Simeon knew that the one he had been longing to see had finally arrived and he was now ready to depart this life. Simeon's prayer has become part of the Night Prayer of the Church because believers have recognised from earliest times that Simeon's prayer can easily become our prayer. Our eyes too have seen the salvation that God has prepared for all the nations to see. The light of God that shone upon Simeon through the child Jesus in the Temple on

that day has shone upon all of us. The risen Lord journeys with us every day as God's light, dispelling our darkness, guiding us along the right path. The candles we light on this day remind us that we have seen Jesus, the light of the world, with the eyes of faith, and that we will see him face to face in heaven, when eternal light shines upon us. The other elderly person in the gospel reading, Anna, spoke about the child of Mary and Joseph, God's light to enlighten everyone, to all those who were looking forward to the Saviour whom God had promised. She reminds us that having looked upon Christ our Light with the eyes of faith, we are called to allow his light to shine through us so that others can be drawn to him.

3 February, Saturday, Fourth Week in Ordinary Time
Mark 6:30–34
In taking his disciples away to a lonely place after their period of missionary work, Jesus highlights the value of rest and the importance of space in the midst of a busy schedule. There was much to be done, both for Jesus and his disciples, yet Jesus recognised that there were other values alongside the value of activity, even activity in the service of God. There was the value of being, of stepping back to spend time with oneself, with others and with God. Stepping back from our various activities can help to ensure that our doing, our work, is shaped by God's purpose and desire. In the first reading, Solomon had just become king of Israel. There was much to be done for the young king. Yet, in that reading, we find Solomon stepping back from his work as king to spend time with the Lord in prayer, asking the Lord for the gift of the wisdom and discernment he would need for his work as king. He recognised that if he was to rule in the way the Lord wanted, he would need the Lord's help. We all need to get that balance right in our lives between being and

doing, between, on the one hand, being really present to others and to the Lord in prayer and, on the other hand, the many activities we need to engage in, some of them essential. In the gospel reading, the prayerful rest that Jesus sought out for himself and his disciples didn't actually materialise. When they arrived at the lonely place, people were there waiting for them and, as the compassionate shepherd, Jesus set himself to teach them at great length. Thereby, Jesus was showing his disciples and us the importance of another and higher value, the value of serving in love even those who unexpectedly disrupt our legitimate search for space, rest and prayer.

5 February, Monday, Fifth Week in Ordinary Time
Mark 6:53–56

We have a wonderful image in today's gospel reading of people 'hurrying' to Jesus all through the countryside, bringing their sick on stretchers to him. He had no sooner stepped out of the boat with his disciples, having sailed through a storm on the Sea of Galilee, than people started hurrying towards him. We all have a sense today that people are in much more of a hurry than they used to be. If you drive a car, you can see it especially on the roads. Where are we all hurrying to? Today's gospel reading invites us to ask ourselves if we are hurrying to Jesus. Are we seeking him out with something of the energy and desire of the people in today's gospel reading? Are we hurrying towards him with the same sense of urgency that those people showed? The Lord is always inviting us to come to him, to seek him out. He certainly comes to us, he seeks us out. He comes to us wherever we happen to find ourselves. The gospel reading speaks of Jesus going to village, town and farm. He met people where they were. The risen Lord continues to meet us where we are today, even if we are not in a good place, for whatever reason. He seeks us out with a sense of urgency. He waits for us to seek him out with the same urgency, like the people in the gospel reading. One of the ways we do that is by turning to him in prayer, whether it is the prayer of the Eucharist or other forms of communal prayer or our own personal prayer. At such moments of prayer, we touch the Lord, like the people in the gospel reading, and we open ourselves to his healing and life-giving presence.

6 February, Tuesday, Fifth Week in Ordinary Time
Mark 7:1–13

The beginning of today's gospel reading has a contemporary feel to it. The Pharisees and scribes were complaining that Jesus' disciples were eating with unclean hands, without washing them. The handwashing that so preoccupied the Pharisees and scribes had to do not so much with physical cleanliness but ritual cleanliness, which is more difficult for us to understand today. The Bible prescribed handwashing rituals for the priests who worked in the Temple in Jerusalem, but the Pharisees wanted to extend these rituals to daily life because they held that all Israel was a priestly people. These regulations of the Pharisees for daily life were not in the Bible but were part of what they called the 'tradition of the elders'. In reply, Jesus criticises the Pharisees for giving more importance to these human traditions than to the commandment of God. Jesus is reminding us that we can be overly preoccupied with non-essentials, in religious matters as much as in other areas of life. In the religious sphere, we can easily attribute the greatest importance to something that in God's eyes is not so important, while failing to take seriously what really does matter to God. The life, death and resurrection of Jesus reveal what matters most to God, a way of life that reflects the love that is within the heart of God.

7 February, Wednesday, Fifth Week in Ordinary Time
Mark 7:14–23

In today's first reading, the Queen of Sheba praises King Solomon to the hilt. She was deeply impressed by his wisdom, but also by his palaces, the food at his table, the accommodation for his officials, the organisation of his staff, his cup-bearers, his sacrifices in the Temple, his wives, his servants and much else. As a monarch herself, she was impressed by these extraordinary trappings of monarchy and saw it all as a sign of God's everlasting love for Israel. The lavish scale of the visible expressions of monarchy took her breath away. In the gospel reading, in contrast, Jesus places the focus not on externals but on what is in a person's heart. He recognised that what lies within a person is of much greater importance because it is the source of either evil intentions or good intentions. Jesus came to transform the human heart, to create a community of disciples whose hearts were transformed by the Holy Spirit, the Spirit of God's love. He said on one occasion that he had come to cast fire upon the earth, the fire of the Holy Spirit that can burn away what is not of God in our hearts and kindle in our hearts the fire of God's love. It is only a community of people of transformed hearts who can create an opening for the coming of God's kingdom, which bears little resemblance to the kingdoms of the various Solomons of this world. We are all called to belong to such a community.

8 February, Thursday, Fifth Week in Ordinary Time
Mark 7:24–30

Most of the people who approach Jesus for help in the gospels are Jews, like himself. In today's gospel reading, however, it is a pagan woman who approaches Jesus to heal her very disturbed daughter. It seems that Jesus regarded his ministry as primarily to Jews. As he says to the pagan woman, 'The children should be fed first', the children being the people of Israel. It is only after Jesus rose from the dead that he would instruct his disciples to preach the Gospel to all nations, Jews and pagans. However, this pagan woman was not prepared to wait; her daughter was in great need. The parents of a sick child are never prepared to wait; they insist that their child be cared for immediately. When Jesus says, in a little parable, 'it is not fair to take the children's food and throw it to the house dogs', the woman identifies with the house dogs: 'But the house dogs under the table can eat the children's scraps.' In other words, the children and the house dogs can eat at the same time, with the house dogs benefiting from the children's untidy eating habits. Jesus couldn't but respond to such an ingenious response; he had to heal the woman's daughter. His timetable of a ministry to the Jews before a ministry to pagans had to give way. Jesus shows us that we need to hold our plans, our programmes and our timetables lightly. Human need takes priority over all else. God calls out to us through those in great need, even when their need disrupts our carefully laid plans. God can be speaking to us through the unexpected and unplanned event and through those who are very different from us. We need something of the freedom that Jesus displayed, the freedom of the Spirit, to go where God is leading us and to do what God is asking of us.

9 February, Friday, Fifth Week in Ordinary Time

Mark 7:31–37

According to the Book of Genesis, Adam and Eve hid from the Lord among the trees of the garden. Having eaten from the one tree in the garden that God said was out of bounds, they couldn't face God. In the gospel reading, in contrast, far from hiding from the Lord, the people of the Decapolis sought him out, bringing to him a deaf man who had an impediment in his speech. The Decapolis was a region that was occupied mostly by pagans rather than Jews. These people recognised that God was working in a healing, life-giving way through Jesus. There was no reason to hide from such a person. Indeed, Jesus went looking for those who were considered religious outsiders by the religious leaders of the time, sharing table with them. In the setting of a meal, he wanted to convey to them the merciful and unconditional love of God. We need never hide from the Lord in fear, regardless of what we have done or failed to do. His love for us is perfect and complete, and as Saint John says in one of his letters, 'perfect love drives out fear'. The Lord is always coming towards us to heal us of our brokenness, just as he healed the deaf man with the speech impediment who was brought to him. Sometimes we too need the Lord to open our ears so that we listen more attentively to one another, and to the Lord speaking to us through one another and especially through the scriptures. The better we hear, the more likely we are to speak well, to speak a word that is helpful to others, just as the man spoke plainly after his deafness was healed. When we allow the Lord to open our ears, we can proclaim the Lord to others by the way we speak. When the risen Lord joined the two disciples on the road to Emmaus, he listened carefully to what they had to say before speaking to them, and, when he did finally speak to them, their hearts began to burn within them. The risen Lord shows us how good listening can bear fruit in good speaking.

10 February, Saturday, Fifth Week in Ordinary Time
Mark 8:1–10

In today's first reading, King Jeroboam of the northern kingdom of Israel is portrayed as, in a sense, starting his own religion to consolidate his power. Political leaders can often be tempted to use religion to serve their own purposes. We don't have to look far to find contemporary expressions of this phenomenon. It was the very close association of religious and political authority that resulted in Jesus being crucified. He exercised authority in a very different way from the way in which the religious and political authorities of his day exercised it. He once declared to his own disciples, who were tempted to follow the way that authority was usually exercised, 'Whoever wishes to become great among you must be your servant, and whoever wishes to be first among you must be slave of all.' In today's gospel reading, we find Jesus exercising this form of servant leadership, in spite of the protestations of his disciples. When he declared to his disciples that he had compassion for the hungry crowd and was reluctant to send them home hungry in case they collapsed on the way, the disciples asked the somewhat dismissive question, 'Where could anyone get bread to feed these people in a deserted place like this?' It was a question that showed a degree of self-concern on the part of the disciples. Jesus, however, asked a question that revealed a concern for the hungry crowd, 'How many loaves have you?' That question created a space for Jesus to feed the crowd, with the help of his initially reluctant disciples. Jesus' compassion for the hungry crowd found a way to feed them. When we allow the Lord's compassion to shape our own lives, we too will create spaces for the Lord to exercise his servant leadership in our own place and time.

12 February, Monday, Sixth Week in Ordinary Time
Mark 8:11–13

In Mark's Gospel, from which we are reading these weeks, strong emotion is often ascribed to Jesus. We find an example of that in today's gospel reading. The Pharisees had asked Jesus for a sign, in order to test him. Jesus responded in a very emotional way, 'with a sigh that came straight from the heart', with a kind of inward groan, which found expression in his question, 'Why does this generation ask for a sign?' The Pharisees were looking for some kind of proof that Jesus was who he said he was. However, faith is not faith if it must ask for proof. The letter to the Hebrews says that 'faith is the assurance of things hoped for, the conviction of things not seen'. It is an act of the will; it is not a mental assent to a set of proofs. Saint Paul was a man of very deep faith, but he says in his first letter to the Corinthians, 'now we see in a mirror dimly, but then we will see face to face' (1 Corinthians 13:12). Believing always entails an element of seeing dimly. We cannot demand signs or proofs from the Lord as a condition of our believing. Yet the Lord does give us signs of his presence if we have ears to hear and eyes to see. When the Pharisees asked Jesus for a sign, they were failing to see that Jesus himself was the sign, if only they would open their hearts and minds. His whole life was the powerful sign of God's presence. The Lord continues to give us signs of his presence today. Such signs are to be found in the people whose lives are shaped by the Holy Spirit, people who journey with us when we need support, who care for us when we are ill. These are the living signs the Lord sends us. We are all called to be such living signs of the Lord in our world.

13 February, Tuesday, Sixth Week in Ordinary Time
Mark 8:14–21
Immediately prior to the gospel scene in today's gospel reading, Jesus had fed a crowd of four thousand people with seven loaves and a few small fish. Yet, as they cross the Sea of Galilee in a boat, the disciples are fretting because they have only one loaf with them. They completely misunderstood Jesus' warning about the leaven of the Pharisees and the leaven of Herod as a reference to the scarcity of bread present among them. Jesus didn't intend his reference to 'leaven' to be taken literally. Leaven was a traditional image for a hidden

element of moral corruption. Jesus is portrayed as being totally frustrated with his disciples, asking a series of eight questions, like a schoolteacher who feels he will never get through to his pupils. Jesus, however, remained faithful to them to the end, even though they would go on to desert him. Even after they deserted him, he appeared to them as risen Lord and renewed their calling. The portrayal of the disciples in the Gospel of Mark can be of some consolation to us. Their inability to hear what Jesus is saying, to see what he is showing them, and their self-protective flight at the end, shows up all the more the faithful love of the Lord for them. The Lord who was faithful to the first disciples is faithful to us, even though we get it wrong from time to time. He keeps coming towards us, inviting us to renew our response to his call to become his faithful followers in today's world, and also promising us that, if we strive to respond to his call, he will give us the spiritual resources that we need.

14 February, Ash Wednesday
Matthew 6:1–6, 16–18

The word 'Lent' comes from an old English word meaning 'season of spring'. Lent always coincides with the season of spring. Spring is a season of renewal of nature. The trees, shrubs and plants that look rather dead during winter start to come to life again in a wonderful way. Lent is a season of spiritual renewal in our own lives. It is a time when we try to renew our friendship, our relationship, with Jesus. Jesus' friendship with us never dies; it never withers. His love for us never changes, regardless of what we do or fail to do. He is completely faithful to us. However, our friendship with him, our response to his friendship, can die back; it can wither. Lent in our lives can be like the season of spring in nature. It is a time when our friendship with the Lord can come more fully to life. In today's gospel, Jesus puts before us three ways of renewing our friendship with him: prayer, fasting and almsgiving. In prayer we become aware that the Lord is present to us and we become present to him. We need to be present to our friends if our friendship is to grow, and the same is true of our friendship with the Lord. Lent is a season when we give a little more time to prayer. When we hear the word 'fasting' we think mostly of giving up some food or drink. However, it could be understood as giving up and letting go of whatever is holding back our friendship with Jesus. What is it that is causing us to turn away from the Lord, to take a different path from the one he shows us in the gospels? In Lent we look at what may be damaging our spirit, weakening our faith, and we try to fast and step back from it. Almsgiving can be understood as any form of loving service of others. During Lent we look at ways we can give ourselves more generously to those in need, after the example and in the Spirit of Jesus. These are three paths we can take that will help to renew our friendship with Jesus. Lent is seven weeks long, so we are given plenty of time to take these paths. If we turn aside from any one of them during that time, we needn't get discouraged. We just start again. Lent finishes with Easter, and on Easter Sunday we are invited to renew our baptismal promises. As we work to renew our friendship with Jesus during the seven weeks of Lent, we are preparing ourselves to say a renewed 'yes' at Easter to our baptism and its calling.

15 February, Thursday after Ash Wednesday
Luke 9:22–25
On this second day of Lent, the gospel reading points us ahead to the story of Holy Week. Jesus declares to his disciples that he is 'destined to suffer grievously, to be rejected by the elders and chief priests and scribes and to be put to death', and then 'to be raised on

the third day'. In this gospel, Jesus speaks these words just before he sets out on his final journey to Jerusalem. This will be a journey to suffering and death on a Roman cross, but, ultimately, it will be a journey to glory, as Jesus passes through death into the hands of his loving Father. In the following scene in Luke's Gospel, Jesus' transfiguration on the mountain, Luke tells us that Moses and Elijah, who appeared alongside him, were speaking with him about his 'departure', or 'exodus', his leaving this world and going to his heavenly Father. Because this exodus entails his passion and death, Jesus will soon have to 'set his face to go to Jerusalem' (Luke 9:51). He will have to steel himself for this journey. In the gospel reading, Jesus suggests that his disciples will also need a certain steeliness if they are to be faithful to him. As Jesus had to renounce himself, empty himself, to remain faithful to God's call, so his disciples will often have to renounce themselves to be faithful to his call. Giving ourselves in faithful love to the Lord means giving ourselves in loving service to those whom the Lord loves, which is all humanity. Such self-giving service of others will often mean renouncing our own selves in some way. We die to ourselves so as to live to others. In the gospel reading, Jesus assures us that in taking this path we will save our lives, we will become more alive, more fully the person God created us to be.

16 February, Friday after Ash Wednesday

Matthew 9:14–15

In the gospel reading, Jesus affirms the value of fasting for the time after his death and resurrection, the time of the Church. 'The time will come for the bridegroom to be taken away from them, and then they will fast.' Only Ash Wednesday and Good Friday remain as days of fast and abstinence, but the whole season of Lent has traditionally been understood as such a time. We deny ourselves something so that we can give ourselves more fully to the way of the Lord. The saying 'no' that fasting involves is always in the service of a greater 'yes' to the Lord and his people. This is what the prophet Isaiah stresses in today's first reading. He makes a firm connection between fasting and the service of the Lord through the care of the most vulnerable, breaking unjust fetters, letting the oppressed go free, sharing our bread with the hungry, sheltering the homeless poor, clothing the naked. Jesus declares in the gospels that whatever we do for those in greatest need we do for him, and whatever we do for him we do for God, because he, Jesus, is God-with-us. Within the Christian tradition, Lent, the season of fasting, is also the season when we give ourselves in a special way to those in greatest need. The Trócaire Lenten campaign is one expression of that dimension of Lent. Showing hospitality to the refugees of war is another expression of the care of the needy that both Isaiah and Jesus stress so strongly. Isaiah declares to the people in that first reading that if they care for the vulnerable, those who are wounded in some way, their own wound will be healed over. We ourselves are healed when we work for the healing of others. As Jesus declares in the gospels, when we give to others, a full measure will be poured into our lap.

17 February, Saturday after Ash Wednesday
Luke 5:27–32

The opening words of today's first reading from the prophet Isaiah suggest that if the people of Israel behave in certain ways, such as doing away with the yoke, the clenched fist, the wicked word, and feeding the hungry, then the Lord will be their guide and will give them relief in desert places. Jesus' ministry seems to have taken a different shape. He revealed God's unconditional love to people before they changed for the better, thereby empowering them to become the person God was calling them to be. In today's gospel reading, Jesus called Levi, a tax collector, before he gave up his tax collecting. Such people were very unpopular because the payments they exacted from others often included large contributions for themselves. Certainly, the religious leaders of the time regarded people like Levi as 'sinners'. Yet the Lord called Levi to become one of his intimate disciples, thereby empowering him to leave his lucrative trade and become a follower of the one who had nowhere to lay his head. In gratitude, Levi invited Jesus to be his guest at a meal at which other tax collectors were present. This was the kind of company Jesus loved to keep because he knew that such people, who were marginalised because of their profession, needed to know that God was calling out to them in his love, inviting them and empowering them to live in ways that were more in keeping with his desire for them and that would be truly life-giving for them. Like a doctor, Jesus knew his place was among the broken in body, mind and spirit. The risen Lord continues to relate to us all in the same way. He continues to pour his love, God's unconditional love, into our hearts so that we are empowered to become the new creation God needs us to be, if his kingdom is to make a breakthrough into our world.

19 February, Monday, First Week of Lent
Matthew 25:31–46
In one of the Beatitudes Jesus declares, 'Blessed are the merciful, for they will receive mercy'. In today's gospel reading, Jesus outlines what being merciful entails. It means standing with the most vulnerable and responding to their need for the basic necessities of life such as food, water, welcome, clothing, healing and companionship often termed the six corporal works of mercy. A seventh has been added in the tradition of the Church, burying the dead. These works of mercy open us up to receive God's mercy. Jesus makes the striking statement that whenever we perform such works of mercy for

someone, we are performing them for him, and whenever we fail to perform them for someone we fail to perform them for him. He identifies himself completely with those in greatest need. Jesus has both a special relationship with God – he is Emmanuel, God-with-us – and a special relationship with the most vulnerable. It is God, God-with-us, whom we meet in those whose great need calls out to us. Even the smallest act of service done for someone in need has enormous significance, because it is God with whom we are engaging. The here and the now is what matters, because so often the here is holy ground and the now is holy time, the place and the time where God meets us and calls out to us. We don't have to search for 'Sacred Space'; it is all around us.

20 February, Tuesday, First Week of Lent
Matthew 6:7–15

In today's gospel reading, Jesus says, 'Your Father knows what you need before you ask him.' Whereas Jesus encourages us to petition God for our needs, he is saying that our prayers of petition are not about making God aware of something of which God is ignorant. In that sense, our prayer of petition does not change God, giving him information he doesn't have, prompting God to do something he was not intending to do. Our prayer of petition changes us. It makes us more receptive to what God wants to give us. By naming what we need to God, we become more aware of what we need from God and become more open to what God wants to give us. In the prayer that has become known as the Lord's Prayer, Jesus names for us what it is we really need. We often pray for what we want, but what we want does not always correspond to what we need. According to Jesus, in the prayer he has given us, we need to acknowledge in our thoughts, words and deeds, the priority of God's kingdom over all earthly kingdoms. When the promotion of earthly kingdoms is the priority, the result is very often destructive conflict. We are to pray for the coming of God's kingdom, which Jesus identifies with the doing of God's will, as Jesus reveals it to us in his teaching and by his life. According to Jesus' prayer, we need 'daily bread'. We need sustenance for body and soul, and when others are deprived of such sustenance, we need to provide for them out of our resources. According to Jesus' prayer, we need to pray for forgiveness for our sins against God and God's people, while being ready to pass on that forgiveness to those who sin against us. Finally, we need to pray for the grace to remain faithful to the Lord's way, especially when we are tempted to take a path that is not God's will for us. We pray this prayer so often that we can fly through it. It is worth praying slowly and meditatively because it brings us in touch with our deepest needs before God.

21 February, Wednesday, First Week of Lent
Luke 11:29–32

Today's responsorial psalm is one of the great penitential psalms in the Book of Psalms. It is a Jewish prayer but it has spoken to Christians from the earliest days of the Church. It is a prayer any one of us could pray when we feel the need for God's forgiveness. The psalm acknowledges that what pleases God more than the sacrifices that were carried out in the Temple in Jerusalem is what the psalm calls a 'humble, contrite heart'. What speaks most powerfully to God is what is in our heart. That is why in the parable of the Pharisee and the tax collector, it was the prayer of the tax collector that was pleasing to God. His simple prayer, 'God, be merciful to me a sinner', revealed a humble and contrite heart. In today's first reading, the preaching of Jonah touched the hearts of the people of Nineveh. Their humble and contrite heart expressed itself in a period of fasting and in putting on sackcloth and ashes. In the gospel reading, Jesus laments the failure of his own contemporaries to allow their hearts to be touched by his preaching, even though he is greater than Jonah, and greater than

Solomon. 'There is something greater than Solomon ... than Jonah here.' We continue to live in the presence of this greater one, now risen Lord. He continues to proclaim his Gospel to us, the gospel of God's unconditional and faithful love for us all. When we open ourselves to this wonderful gift of the Lord's love, we cannot but realise that we haven't always loved him in return. We haven't made a return for all he has given us. That is why today's responsorial psalm is a prayer that we can always pray. Such a prayer, prayed with a humble and contrite heart, is a prayer that will always be heard by God and will leave us at peace with God.

22 February, Saint Peter's Chair
Matthew 16:13–19
In the world of Jesus and the early Church, teachers used to sit to teach and pupils gathered around them. The chair of Peter is a symbol of the teaching role of the Bishop of Rome, the Pope of the Universal Church. It is this teaching role that Jesus gives to Peter in today's gospel reading when he says, 'I will give you the keys of the kingdom of heaven: whatever you bind on earth will be considered bound in heaven; whatever you loose on earth shall be considered loosed in heaven.' Keys are a symbol of authority and the language of loosening and binding suggests that teaching authority is intended. Peter is being given the authority to declare which elements of the teaching of Jesus are binding and which elements can be interpreted more loosely. The early Church understood that Peter had a special role in interpreting the teaching of Jesus for the emerging Church. Within our own Roman Catholic tradition, we understand that this teaching authority, given by Jesus to Peter, has always resided with the Bishop of Rome, the Pope of the Universal Church. It is a claim that is disputed by other traditions within the Christian family. The Lord speaks to the Church in a whole variety of ways, but as Catholics we

believe that the Lord speaks in a unique way through the one we call 'Our Holy Father', which is currently Pope Francis. Yet he is very aware that the Lord speaks to him through the whole Church, every member in every part of the world. That is why he is calling on the Church throughout the world to come together in a synodal way, to gather to listen to each other and in doing so to listen to what the Holy Spirit is saying to the Church today. All good teachers are also good pupils and that is especially true of teachers of the faith. Pope Francis, without compromising his teaching authority, is showing us that he has much to learn from all the faithful. It is to be hoped that this synodal pathway will help us all to appreciate the ways that the Holy Spirit can speak to us through all the members of the Church.

23 February, Friday, First Week of Lent
Matthew 5:20–26

In today's gospel reading, Jesus calls his disciples to a virtue that goes deeper than the virtue of the scribes and Pharisees. One of the ten commandments of the Jewish Law was 'You shall not kill'. However, the call of Jesus goes deeper than that; it looks beyond the action of killing to the underlying attitudes and emotions that lead people to kill or injure each other. Jesus invites us to look below the surface of what we do to why we do it. He calls for a renewal of the heart and mind; that is what we mean by 'repentance' or 'conversion'. That deep-seated renewal that Jesus calls for is not something we can bring about on our own. We need the Holy Spirit to work that kind of deep transformation within ourselves. A prayer that has been traditional within the Church acknowledges that very clearly: 'Come Holy Spirit, fill my heart, and kindle in me the fire of your love.' It is a prayer I have always found myself drawn to. It calls on the Holy Spirit to recreate deep within us the love that shaped the person of Jesus; it calls on the Spirit to form in us the roots of that deeper virtue that Jesus speaks about in today's gospel reading. This is a virtue that enables us to channel in life-giving ways those powerful emotions, such as anger, that we all experience.

24 February, Saturday, First Week of Lent
Matthew 5:43–48

When we say of someone that they are a perfectionist, we probably mean that they like everything to be just right. It is a compliment, but it can also imply a slight criticism. We sometimes think of perfectionists as people who can be intolerant of those who don't measure up to their high standards. We can be slightly anxious around them. However, when Jesus says in the gospel reading that 'your heavenly Father is perfect', it is not with a view to making us anxious. On the contrary, to say God is perfect is to say that God is perfect in love. God loves us with a complete love, regardless of what we have done or failed to do. As Jesus says in the gospel reading, 'he causes his sun to rise on bad people as well as good, and his rain to fall on honest and dishonest people alike'. When the sun shines here in our parish, it shines on everyone, and when the rain falls it falls on everyone. The sun and the rain do not discriminate. Likewise, God's love does not discriminate; it embraces all humanity. There is no more or less in God's love, because, as Saint John says in one of his letters, 'God is love'. God loved us into life at our birth; God's love sustains us during our earthly lives; God will love us into eternal life at the end of our earthly lives. God's gracious love is pure gift; it does not have to be earned or deserved. It is not a reward for a good life. Rather, a good life flows from knowing in our hearts that we are loved unconditionally by God. If we open our hearts to God's love, if we allow God to love us unconditionally, then we will begin to reflect something of God's love to others to love others in the same indiscriminate way that God loves

us. We might even find ourselves loving those who have persecuted or harmed us in some way. At the very least, we might find
ourselves praying for the grace to love them. When Jesus calls on
us to be perfect as God is perfect, he is calling on us to be loving
as God is loving. However, before we can love others as God loves
them, we must first allow ourselves to be embraced by God's perfect love.

26 February, Monday, Second Week of Lent

Luke 6:36–38

There is a striking image of God in today's first reading, which is a
prayer asking God for forgiveness: 'Integrity, Lord, is yours ... To
the Lord, our God, mercy and pardon belong.' It is because the one
praying believes so strongly that it is in the nature of God to be merciful and forgiving that he can be so honest about his own failings
and those of the people: 'We have sinned, we have done wrong, we
have acted wickedly.' We can be totally honest about our failings
only with those we know will accept us and love us as we are, without judging us. The Lord accepts and loves us as we are, which is
why we can be totally honest with him about our failings. The Lord,
who loves us as we are, also loves us enough to keep calling us
beyond where we are, to live in ways that are true to what is best
and deepest in us. The Lord wants us to be holy, as God is holy, to
be loving, as God is loving, or, in the opening words of today's
gospel reading, to be compassionate as God is compassionate. We
are made in the image of God, and only a life that, in some way,
reflects the life of God is worthy of us and will bring us true joy.
Jesus reveals the life of God to be a life of self-giving love. To live
a life that reflects the life of God is to be giving as God is giving. In
the gospel reading, Jesus assures us that in living in this self-giving
way, we will receive more than we give: 'Give, and there will be

gifts for you: a full measure, pressed down, shaken together, will be poured into your lap.' I like that expression, 'full measure'. When we give of ourselves as fully as we can in loving service of the Lord and his people, in return we will receive a full measure from the Lord. We pray for the grace to live in such a way that we come to experience the Lord's full measure.

27 February, Tuesday, Second Week of Lent
Matthew 23:1–12
In this gospel reading Jesus is very critical of those religious leaders who impose unnecessary burdens on an already burdened people through their strict interpretation of the Jewish Law. Jesus had earlier called on those who were overburdened to come to him, promising them rest, declaring that his teaching, his interpretation of God's will for our lives, was not burdensome. Most people carry burdens of one kind or another, very often imposed by others. Jesus is clear in this reading that our relationship with God is not intended to be another burden on a burdened people. Jesus allowed himself to be burdened by the constraints of the human condition. Among the burdens he carried was that imposed by those who were hostile to all he stood for. Jesus was at his most burdened as he hung from the cross. He carried that burden so that he could help us to carry our own burdens. Through his life, death and resurrection, he released into the world the power of God's love, the power of the Holy Spirit, which is not an oppressive power but a life-giving, enabling power. Saint Paul was very burdened as he wrote to the church in Philippi from his prison cell. Yet he could say to that church, 'I can do all things through him who strengthens me' (Philippians 4:13). The Lord strengthens us to carry our burdens so that we can help to carry the burdens of others. As Paul writes to the churches of Galatia, 'Bear one another's burdens, and in this way you will fulfil the

law of Christ' (Galatians 6:2). The law of Christ, which is the law of love, the fruit of the Spirit, is not about imposing burdens but about lifting them.

28 February, Wednesday, Second Week of Lent

Matthew 20:17–28

It is natural for mothers to want the best for their children. In today's gospel reading, the mother of James and John asks Jesus if her sons could have the best seats in his kingdom, one at his right and the other at his left. Jesus had been proclaiming the nearness of the king-dom of God and she seems to have imagined that God's kingdom would be like an earthly kingdom, such as the kingdom of Rome, or the Roman Empire, as it is usually called. She wasn't alone in think-ing this. Her sons thought as much, along with the ten other members of the twelve. These ten were indignant with the two brothers for trying to get the best seats in God's kingdom ahead of them. Jesus must have been rightly fed up with the lot of them! He had just announced that his mission would lead to him being mocked, scourged and crucified. He would end up on a Roman cross with the mocking title over his head, 'Jesus of Nazareth, king of the Jews'. Some king! It was his self-emptying love for all of God's children, whether Jew, Samaritan or pagan, religious or sinner, that put him on a cross. The kingdom of God was present when he healed the sick, touched lepers, shared table with sinners, allowed women to wash his feet, fed the hungry in the wilderness and released the oppressed from their demons, even on the sabbath. As he said at the end of the gospel reading, he had come not to be served, like the kings of this world, but to serve. If his disciples want to belong to God's kingdom that is the mindset they must have. If they want to be great they must become a servant. They can forget about honour and privilege. Whenever any one of us serves others without looking for anything in return, the kingdom of God is present in our world, and heaven draws nearer to everyone.

29 February, Thursday, Second Week of Lent
Luke 16:19–31
In the time of Jesus only a tiny number of people would have had the excessive wealth of the rich man in the parable. He is described as dressed in purple and fine linen, the most expensive cloth of the day. He feasted magnificently every day. The vast bulk of the population in the place and time where Jesus lived never feasted at all. To feast magnificently every day is a vulgar display of wealth in that culture. In contrast to the rich man, Lazarus would have been a familiar figure to people. There were many people who depended on the generosity of others to survive, which is why almsgiving was such an important value in the Jewish religion. Lazarus seems to have been extremely destitute. He had so little that he longed to eat the scraps that fell from the table of the rich man who lived just the other side of the gate. Yet, even though Lazarus was physically close to this extremely wealthy man, he was invisible to him. The rich man walked past Lazarus as if he wasn't there. However, Lazarus was not invisible to God. When Lazarus died he received the hospitality that was denied him in this life. He was given a place of honour beside Abraham at the banquet of eternal life. The rich man had the opportunity to reveal something of God's hospitality to Lazarus before Lazarus died but he failed to do so. We are all called to reveal something of God's hospitable and welcoming love to each other in the here and now. Individuals and whole groups whose need is great can become invisible to us. They may be physically near us, but we don't see them. It is the Lord who calls out to us through those in greatest need, just as God was calling out to the rich man through Lazarus.

1 March, Friday, Second Week of Lent

Matthew 21:33–43, 45–46

People who communicate their dreams to others can become very unpopular. Some find their dreaming to be too disturbing and they can belittle their dreams. Joseph, one of the twelve sons of Israel/ Jacob, is described by his brothers in today's first reading as a 'man of dreams'. They wanted rid of this 'man of dreams', saying to one another, 'Come on, let us kill him and throw him into some well ... we shall see what becomes of his dreams.' In the end, they didn't kill him, because of the intervention of Reuben, one of the brothers. They threw him into an empty well alive, and then sold him to some merchants passing on their way to Egypt. They wanted rid of this dreamer. Having sold him on, they never expected to see him again. However, God worked in a life-giving way through their hostile actions. Joseph went to Egypt as a slave but he won favour with Pharaoh and was eventually put in charge of Egypt's grain reserves. When famine struck the land of Canaan where his brothers lived, along with Jacob their father, the brothers went to Egypt for food and it was Joseph who provided them with the food they needed. Joseph's brothers ended up going to Egypt to live, taking their father with them. God brought great good out of the harm the brothers did to Joseph. In the gospel reading, Jesus tells a parable that portrays the harm that would soon be done to himself. In the parable, when the landowner sent his son to collect the produce of the vineyard, the tenants seized his son, threw him out of the vineyard and killed him. Jesus would turn out to be the stone rejected by the builders. Yet God brought great good out of the harm that was done to his son. The cross, the instrument of the death of God's Son, became the tree of life. Jesus' death allowed God to reveal all the more the extent of his love for all humanity. God works in every human situation, no matter how dark, how sinful, to bring to life some good for everyone involved. We believe in a God who is always at work in a life-giving way, even in those situations that seem devoid of his presence.

2 March, Saturday, Second Week of Lent
Luke 15:1–3, 11–32

In about four weeks' time we will be celebrating the great feast of the death and resurrection of Jesus. We celebrate the good news that Jesus, who was crucified, who was dead, was brought back to life by God. That language of death followed by new life is to be found in today's parable. To the servants the father said, 'this son of mine was dead and has come back to life'; to his elder son he says, 'your brother was dead and has come back to life'. There is more than one form of resurrection. The resurrection to new life that we long and hope for beyond this earthly life can be anticipated in various ways in the course of our earthly lives. In the parable, resurrection for the younger son took the form of a journey from a self-imposed isolation to an experience of community, and from a sense of guilt to an experience of loving acceptance. It was the father's unconditional love that allowed his younger son to make his journey, to rise from the dead. The father's emotional response to his son was one of compassion. The father in the parable is an image of God. The parable suggests that God's compassionate love is always at work, bringing people from some form of death to a new life. In contrast to the father, the elder son considered his brother ('this son of yours') dead and was happy to see him remain in his self-imposed tomb. Whereas the father's response to his son was one of compassion, the elder brother's response to him was one of anger. The parable challenges us to embody in our own ways of relating to others the life-giving presence of the father's compassion rather than the deadening presence of the elder son's anger.

3 March, Monday, Third Week of Lent

Luke 4:24–30

It is said in today's gospel reading that in response to Jesus' preaching in Nazareth 'everyone in the synagogue was enraged'. What was it that enraged people so much? Jesus had the nerve to suggest that God was as concerned with the enemies of Israel as with the people of Israel. Jesus identifies himself with Elijah when he was sent to minister to a widow of a town near Sidon in Phoenicia, and with Elisha when he ministered to a commander in the Syrian army. The Phoenicians and the Syrians were perceived by the people of Israel as enemies because of the past history of the relationship between them and Israel. It can be very dangerous to speak well of enemies, especially in time of war. The great anger that Jesus generated has been replicated all through history by those who have tried to show that life is more complex, less black and white, than we may think. Jesus was revealing to the people of Nazareth that God was not a national God, fighting on the side of Israel against everyone else. Rather, the heart of God embraced all humanity, and he was as concerned for widows in Phoenicia as for widows in Israel, and for lepers in Syria as for lepers in Israel. God sent his Son to show the length and breadth and depth and height of God's love, a love that surpasses knowledge, in the language of Saint Paul (Ephesians 3:19). It is very tempting to make God in our own image, our own personal image or our own image as a nation. Jesus reveals a God who has no favourites. He cares for the suffering and broken of the world, regardless of where they live or what their nationality. Jesus has sent the Spirit of God, the Holy Spirit, into our lives, so that we may be empowered to love others with the all-inclusive, non-discriminatory love of God that Jesus revealed to the full by his teaching, his life, his death and resurrection.

5 March, Tuesday, Third Week of Lent

Matthew 18:21–35

When the servant who owed the king a staggering amount of money discovered that he and all his family and possessions were to be sold into slavery to pay the debt, he asked the king for time to pay the debt: 'Give me time and I will pay the whole sum.' The king agreed to his servant's request. When the servant subsequently met a fellow servant who owed him a very small amount of money, his fellow servant made the same request of him that he had made of the king: 'Give me time and I will pay you.' However, the servant was not prepared to grant his fellow servant the precious gift of time, the time he needed to pay off the debt. For him, time was money. Time can symbolise money but it can symbolise so much else as well. It can also symbolise forgiveness. Giving time to someone can be saying, 'I withhold judgement for now.' One of the greatest gifts we can give to another is the gift of time. One of the messages of today's parable may be that the Lord is much more generous with the gift of time than we are. The Lord gives us time to put things right, to return to him with all our heart, to give him the place in our lives that he deserves. As one of the letters of the New Testament puts it, 'with the Lord, one day is like a thousand years' (2 Peter 3:8). The parable calls on us to give this gift to others with the same generosity with which the Lord gives this gift to us.

6 March, Wednesday, Third Week of Lent

Matthew 5:17–19

In today's first reading, Moses is portrayed as asking the question, 'What great nation is there that has its gods so near as the Lord our God is to us whenever we call upon him?' Even though the people of Israel had a very strong sense of the otherness of God, God's distance from them, they also had a sense of God's nearness to them, God's presence in the midst of their lives. As followers of the Word who became flesh, we have an even stronger sense of the nearness of God to us, through his Son. Jesus came among us as Emmanuel, God-with-us, and he promised to be with us until the end of time. Even more than Moses, we can ask the question, 'What great nation is there that has its gods so near as the Lord our God is to us whenever we call upon him?' It is because Jesus knew himself to have a unique relationship with God, to be God-with-us, that he claimed the authority to reveal God's will for our lives fully. Up until the time of Jesus, it was believed that the Jewish Law revealed God's will for the lives of his people. However, Jesus claimed to be a fuller revelation of God's will for our lives than the Jewish Law. That is why Jesus says in today's gospel reading, 'Do not imagine that I have come to abolish the Law or the Prophets. I have not come to abolish them but to fulfil them.' Jesus would complete the role of the Jewish Law by revealing God's will for our lives more clearly and completely. That is why we stand up for the reading of the gospel. Because we believe that God is speaking to us through Jesus in a uniquely complete way, we spend our lives taking the word of Jesus to heart, so that it shapes all of our living.

7 March, Thursday, Third Week of Lent
Luke 11:14–23
Jeremiah is a prophet who is known for his complaints. He regularly complains to God because of the hostile way in which people are responding to the message that God had asked him to proclaim. In today's first reading, he complains to God that nobody is listening to the message that God gave him to speak: 'They have not listened to me, have not paid attention … Here is a nation that will not listen to the voice of the Lord its God.' Jesus could have made the same complaint as Jeremiah, to an even greater degree. In today's gospel reading, people are not only not listening to Jesus, they are not seeing

either. Indeed, their seeing is completely skewed. When they see Jesus healing the broken, they claim that the power at work in Jesus' life is the power of Satan. This is a very good example of what has come to be known as fake news in a most extreme form, calling the life-giving power of God the evil power of Satan. Jesus confronts his accusers, these peddlers of fake news, declaring that it is through the finger of God that he casts out devils and heals the broken. It is a striking image, 'the finger of God'. It suggests that through Jesus God attends to the details of people's lives. God is not just concerned with people in general, but with the unique situation of each and every person, in all its very personal detail. If we are open to see, we will recognise God's involvement in the detailed care many people show to those who are broken in body, mind and spirit. Each of us is called to be an instrument of the finger of God in the way we relate to others.

8 March, Friday, Third Week of Lent
Mark 12:28–34
Today's first reading is very striking in many ways. The Lord, speaking through the prophet Hosea, calls on his people to come back to him, and if they do the Lord promises to love them with all his heart. The Lord goes on to say to his people, 'I am like a cypress ever green, all your fruitfulness comes from me.' Because the Lord alone loves us with all his heart, he alone is the source of true life for us. The Lord calls out to us in love, pleading with us to keep turning to him as the one who can allow our lives to bear rich fruit, the fruit of the Spirit. God's life-giving love for us is the basis of Jesus' call to us in the gospel reading to love the Lord with all our heart, soul, mind and strength. If we can open ourselves to the Lord's love for us, then we will be moved to love the Lord in return. God always loves us first and our love for God is a response to this love for us. The good news of God's faithful, unconditional love for us is the foundation

of what Jesus calls the first commandment, to love the Lord our God with all our being, with a love that is worthy of his love for us. Our loving relationship with God in turn is the foundation of what Jesus calls the second commandment, to love our neighbour as ourselves. The more we open ourselves to God's love for us and respond to his love by loving him, the more we will be empowered to love others with God's own love. At the heart of our life as people of faith is love, God's love for us, our love for God in return and the outpouring of God's love through us onto others. When love becomes central to our lives in that sense, Jesus will say to us what he said to the scribe in today's gospel reading, 'you are not far from the Kingdom of God'.

9 March, Saturday, Third Week of Lent

Luke 18:9–14

The parable in today's gospel reading begins, 'Two men went up to the Temple to pray.' Both men did pray. The Pharisee prayed a prayer of thanksgiving, 'I thank you, God … .' The tax-collector prayed a prayer of petition, 'God, be merciful to me, a sinner.' Yet, only one prayer was acceptable to God. Only one person 'went home at rights with God'. The difference between the two men's prayer was what was in their heart when they prayed. The prayer of the Pharisee revealed a heart that looked down in judgement on a fellow worshipper. He thought of himself as morally better than the tax collector. The prayer of the tax collector revealed a heart that was humble and contrite before God. He knew that he had nothing to offer God and everything to receive from God, especially mercy. In the first reading, speaking through the prophet Hosea, the Lord declares, 'What I want is love, not sacrifice; knowledge of God, not holocausts'. The journey to the Temple was an act of love for God, for both men. However, the heart of the Pharisee revealed a lack of love for the worshipper who stood close to him in the Temple. He considered him less acceptable to God than himself. The Pharisee was right to regard the tax collector as a sinner, but he failed to recognise that he too was a sinner. Both men went up to the Temple in need of God's mercy, but only one of them recognised that reality. We all stand before the Lord as sinners. We all come before him in our poverty. None of us can get into the business of deciding who is less, or more, of a sinner than me. That is best left to God. All we can do is open ourselves to the Lord in our poverty and allow him to enrich us in his love, in other words, to pray the prayer of the tax collector.

11 March, Monday, Fourth Week of Lent
John 4:43–54

In the first reading the Lord, speaking through the prophet Isaiah, says of the city of Jerusalem that had been besieged some years before, 'No more will the sound of weeping or the sound of cries be heard in her; in her, no more will be found the infant living a few days only, or the old man not living to the end of his days ... They will build houses and inhabit them, plant vineyards and eat their fruit.' This is God's desire for the ruined city of Jerusalem. It is hard not to think of the many cities ruined by today's wars when we hear those words. God's desire for Jerusalem is also God's desire for every city, yet so often what the powerful desire for the cities of the earth is far removed from God's desire. When the powerful of the world seek to promote their own kingdom, it usually inhibits the coming of God's kingdom to earth, a kingdom where God's justice and peace reign. The God in whom we believe is a God of life, not a God of death. Jesus was the fullest revelation possible in human form of the God of life. He was the supreme life-giver. In today's gospel reading, he declares to an official at the court of Herod Antipas, who came to him pleading for his seriously ill son, 'Go, your son will live'. The official trusted in Jesus' word of promise and his trust was vindicated; his son recovered from his life-threatening fever. Jesus will declare in this Gospel of John that he came so that we may have life and have it to the full. Fullness of life is our ultimate destiny, a sharing in God's own life. Yet Jesus intends that we have a foretaste of eternal life in this present earthly life; his deepest desire is that something of the kingdom of heaven would come to earth. He looks to us his followers to be channels of his life-giving presence in the here and now. They will often mean standing up to those who are intent on inflicting death on others.

12 March, Tuesday, Fourth Week of Lent
John 5:1–3, 5–16

The question Jesus puts to the man who had been paralysed for thirty-eight years sounds strange to our ears: 'Do you want to be well again?' Why would he be near to a pool known for its healing properties if he didn't want to be well again? However, perhaps he had begun to lose all hope of ever being well again. He may have lost the will to be better, the will to live. By his question, Jesus wanted to arouse in him the hope for healing that he once cherished. He had obviously been disappointed many times. As he said to Jesus, 'I have no one to put me into the pool when the water is disturbed; and while I am still on my way, someone else gets there before me.' If people are disappointed often enough, they can easily lose hope. By asking, 'Do you want to be well again?' Jesus was inviting him to recover his desire to be well. We can all be tempted to lose hope. We can easily get despondent, lose our zest for life, our hope of something better, for a whole variety of reasons. The Lord is always at work among us to renew our hope, to help us recover our desire for that fullness of life the Lord desires for us all. By asking his question, Jesus sought to heal the man's despondency before he could really heal him physically. Even when we are physically well, we can all need that deeper healing, that renewing of our hopes. The risen Lord is always at work among us renewing our hope, our desire for all of humanity to be well again. Hope is more than optimism; it is the work of the Spirit of the risen Lord among us and within us. As Paul says in his letter to the Romans, 'Hope does not disappoint us, because God's love has been poured into our hearts, through the Holy Spirit that has been given to us' (Romans 5:5).

13 March, Wednesday, Fourth Week of Lent
John 5:17–30

In answer to the religious authorities' question as to why Jesus works on the sabbath by healing people, he replies, 'My Father goes on working, and so do I'. God never ceases to do God's saving, reconciling, healing, life-giving work, not even on the sabbath. Because of Jesus' unique relationship with God, his Father, he too must go on working, day after day. A line in one of the Psalms says of God that he neither slumbers nor sleeps. God is always awake and alert to us, always working for our present and ultimate well-being. The same is true of Jesus, our risen Lord. Even when he seems to be asleep, as he was in the storm at sea, he is alert to us. God never forgets us, just as a woman never forgets her baby at the breast, in the language of today's first reading. We forget God from time to time. We are not always alert to God. We don't always work on God's behalf. We can be faithless. Yet God and his Son are always faithful. They go on working among us and within us. Likewise, the Holy Spirit works away within us. According to Saint Paul, even when we do not know how to pray, the Spirit 'intercedes with sighs too deep for words' (Romans 8:26). God began a good work in our lives the moment we were created and enhanced that good work at our baptism. God is always working to bring that good work to completion, through the agency of his Son, our risen Lord, and the Holy Spirit.

It can be reassuring to remember this good news, when we are tempted to cry out like the people of Israel in the first reading, 'The Lord has abandoned me, the Lord has forgotten me.'

14 March, Thursday, Fourth Week of Lent

John 5:31–47

The figure of Moses is to be found in both readings today and in the responsorial psalm. In the first reading, Moses intercedes with God on behalf of his rebellious people, and God listens to the prayer of Moses. The responsorial psalm, reflecting on this incident, says that 'Moses, the man God had chosen, stood in the breach before him.' Moses stood in the breach between God and his people; he helped to keep God's relationship with his people alive. In the gospel reading, Jesus declares that Moses was writing about him. What Moses said and did point ahead to the person of Jesus. Yet Jesus was greater than Moses. He brought a fuller revelation of God than Moses ever did. Jesus stood in the breach between God and his people in a much more profound way. Whereas Moses is depicted as standing between an angry God and his people, Jesus stands between a loving God and his people, and, indeed, all humanity. Jesus reveals God to be Love. Jesus casts a greater light upon God than Moses. It is because of Jesus that we can say that God loved the world so much that he gave his only Son so that we may have life and have it to the full. In the gospel reading, Jesus says that the works God his Father gave him to carry out testify to God, reveal God. The works Jesus refers to are all his deeds that brought life in its various forms to those he encountered. The death and resurrection of Jesus was an even fuller revelation of the God of love and life. We have much to be grateful for, because of all that Jesus has revealed to us about God, all that Jesus has brought to us from God. As the opening chapter of John's Gospel says, Jesus came full of God's grace and truth, and from his fullness we have all received, grace upon grace.

15 March, Friday, Fourth Week of Lent

John 7:1–2, 10, 25–30

As we approach Holy Week the gospel readings have more of an ominous tone to them. Jesus is spoken of in today's gospel reading as the man they want to kill. Yet, in spite of that, he is described as 'speaking freely'. The reading suggests that Jesus did not allow the hostility of some people towards him to deter him from doing what he had been sent to do. Twice in that gospel reading Jesus speaks of himself as having come from God and of God as having sent him. Jesus was faithful to his God-given mission, even when that mission made people very hostile towards him. Jesus teaches us to be faithful to our own calling, regardless of the environment in which we find ourselves. The environment in which we live has not been all that supportive of a life of faith. We could easily get very discouraged as people of faith who are trying to grow in our relationship with Jesus. The portrait of Jesus in today's gospel reading teaches us to keep living out our baptism and witnessing to the Gospel even when it is difficult to do so. Just as Jesus knew the support of his heavenly Father, we will know the support of Jesus. As Paul says in his first letter to the Corinthians, God 'will not let you be tested beyond your strength, but with the testing he will also provide the way out so that you may be able to endure it' (1 Corinthians 10:13).

16 March, Saturday, Fourth Week of Lent

John 7:40–52

At the end of the gospel reading, the religious leaders say, 'Prophets do not come out of Galilee'. Earlier in this Gospel of John, Nathanael had asked, 'Can anything good come out of Nazareth?' Both the statement and the questions reveal a certain prejudice relating to a particular place. There is another example of prejudice in the gospel reading. The religious authorities declare, 'this rabble knows nothing about the Law – they are damned'. There is a presumption here that that those who have not had a certain kind of religious training are incapable of sound judgement when it comes to the ways of God. It can often be tempting to prejudge someone or some group on the basis of where they live or where they come from or their level of education. The corrective to prejudice or prejudging is suspending judgement on some individual or group until sufficient evidence can be gathered that enables an informed judgement to be made. This is the attitude displayed by Nicodemus in the gospel reading. Although he was a Pharisee, a member of a group normally hostile to Jesus of Nazareth, he was devoid of prejudice, declaring, 'surely the Law does not allow us to pass judgment on a man without giving him a hearing and discovering what he is about'. The corrective to prejudice is to give people a hearing, to be open to the presence of truth and goodness in someone or some group, even when we might least expect it. Giving people a hearing with a view to really understanding who they are and where they are coming from can head off unnecessary conflict. Such unprejudiced listening is needed today more than ever. As people of faith, especially, we have to be open to the presence of God's Spirit where we might not expect to find it.

18 March, Monday, Fifth Week of Lent

John 8:1–11

The story of Jesus and the woman caught in the act of adultery is one of those gospel stories that we find ourselves drawn to. The portrayal of Jesus in the story is one that stays with us. We are struck by the contrast between the way the scribes and the Pharisees relate to the woman and the way that Jesus relates to her. The religious leaders have condemned her of a serious breach of the Jewish Law, one that is worthy of the prescribed punishment, death by stoning. Jesus, however, refuses to condemn her: 'I do not condemn you.' As the evangelist John says a little earlier in his gospel, 'God did not send the Son into the world to condemn the world, but in order that the world might be saved through him.' Rather than condemning the woman, Jesus pardons her and calls her to a way of life more in keeping with God's purpose for her life. We may not have sinned in the way the woman sinned, but we are all sinners. We all come before the Lord as people who have not lived in accordance with God's will and purpose for our lives. The reading assures us that when we come before the Lord in our sinfulness, we will not hear a word of condemnation, but a word of forgiveness – 'I do not condemn you' – and also an invitation: 'Do not sin any more.' Condemnation comes easily to human nature. Thankfully, it is not in the nature of Jesus or of the God whom he reveals. Forgiveness for our past and empowerment through the Spirit to live more loving lives are the Lord's gifts to us.

19 March, Tuesday, Saint Joseph

Matthew 1:16, 18–21

One of the gospel readings for the feast of Saint Joseph is the story of the birth of Jesus, according to Matthew. It is a little less familiar to us than the story of the birth of Jesus as we find it in Luke's Gospel, which we read on Christmas night. The gospel reading portrays Joseph at a moment of crisis. It could be termed a crisis of intimacy. Joseph tends to be depicted in religious art as an elderly man, more like Jesus' grandfather than father. In reality, at the time of Jesus' birth, he must have been a vigorous young man, perhaps still in his teens. The gospel reading describes him as betrothed to Mary. Betrothal is more than what we refer to as an 'engagement'. As betrothed, he and Mary were legally husband and wife, but they would only live together as husband and wife after their marriage ceremony. The future happiness of this young man is suddenly clouded by an event of which he can make little sense, Mary's pregnancy. What is he to do in this unexpected and confusing situation? The Jewish Law would have required him to take a course of action that went against all his natural feelings for Mary. In that moment of personal crisis, according to the gospel reading, Joseph experienced God as Emmanuel, God with him. God communicated with Joseph at this difficult time in his life and Joseph was open to hearing God's word to him, a word that directed him beyond what the law required, prompting him to marry his betrothed, to take her home as his wife. The story of Joseph reminds us that God continues to communicate with us in the challenging situations of our own lives, including crises of intimacy. There is no personal dilemma that need cut us off from God. God speaks a word of love and wisdom to us even in the most unpromising moments of our life's journey. Jesus reveals God to be Emmanuel, God with us, and God is with us, guiding us and supporting us, especially in our own difficult family experiences. The gospel reading also suggests that Joseph was not only open to God's presence but revealed God's presence to Mary, showing her great care and sensitivity in a disturbing and unsettling moment. Joseph inspires us not only to be open to God's presence in difficult family moments, but to reveal God's loving and tender presence to each other, to look out for one another, when events come along that are disruptive and disturbing. Joseph's care for the pregnant Mary, and later for Mary and his young son when faced with exile, is an inspiration to us all.

20 March, Wednesday, Fifth Week of Lent
John 8:31–42
There is a line in the prophet Isaiah where God, addressing his people in exile, says through the prophet, 'When you walk through fire, you

will not be burned, and the flame shall not consume you' (Isaiah 43:2). That divine promise is expressed in story form in today's first reading. Shadrach, Meshach and Abednego have been thrown into the fiery furnace but it does not consume them. The angel of the Lord is with them in the furnace to protect them. Modern-day Jews may well ask where God was when millions of people were thrown into the furnace of the gas chambers during the Second World War. Jesus' disciples may well have asked where God was when Jesus, his anointed one, was being crucified. The scriptures suggest that God is suffering when those who are precious in his sight suffer. God weeps with those who weep, as Jesus wept with Mary and Martha when their brother died. The weeping, suffering God also brings new life out of the terrible suffering and death inflicted on his beloved sons and daughters. When human evil and sin destroy God's beloved creatures, God works to recreate them, just as God recreated his crucified Son. According to the gospel reading, the Son whom God sent into the world 'makes you free'. God works through his Son, now risen Lord, to free us from the suffering and death inflicted by those, like King Nebuchadnezzar in the first reading, who would destroy others to uphold their own power. We may not experience this freedom that God desires for us in the course of our earthly lives. Yet our ultimate destiny, according to Paul, is to enjoy 'the freedom of the glory of the children of God' (Romans 8:21).

21 March, Thursday, Fifth Week of Lent
John 8:51–59

We would all probably acknowledge that we have limited insight into others, and even into ourselves. We certainly have limited insight into God. We would be rightly wary of someone who claimed to know God well. We are suspicious of those who seem too sure of themselves when it comes to God. Yet, in today's gospel reading,

Jesus states very clearly that he knows God. 'I know him, and if I were to say, 'I do not know him', I should be a liar … But I do know him, and I faithfully keep his word.' The opening fourteen verses of this Gospel of John is often called the Prologue to the gospel, and the last verse states, 'No one has ever seen God. It is God the only Son, who is close to the Father's heart, who has made him known.' Because Jesus has the most intimate relationship with God, close to the Father's heart, he knows God in the fullest possible way, and, therefore, he can make God known to us. That is why we keep turning to Jesus, because we recognise that he alone can show us the face of God. In the setting of the Last Supper in this Gospel of John, Philip turns to Jesus and asks him, 'Show us the Father, and we shall be satisfied', and Jesus replies, 'To have seen me is to have seen the Father'. We all have that longing of Philip to see God, to know God, not just with our mind but with our heart. Like Philip we sense that we will never be fully satisfied until we see God, know God, in this deep sense. It was Saint Augustine who said that our hearts are restless until they rest in God. It is only Jesus who can satisfy this restless longing we all have to see and know God. We need to keep turning towards Jesus, who comes to us in his Word, in the Sacraments, in the community of believers, so that we can begin to experience in the here and now something of that rest, that resting in God, which is our ultimate destiny.

22 March, Friday, Fifth Week of Lent

John 10:31–42

In the first reading, the prophet Jeremiah cries out in response to all who are opposing him, 'Terror from every side.' I am sure those in besieged and shelled cities today could cry out 'Terror from every side!' They could equally say in the words of today's responsorial psalm, 'The waves of death rose about me; the torrents of destruction assailed me; the snares of the grave entangled me; the traps of death confronted me.' The forces of death are bringing anguish to many in conflict zones at present. The same forces of death are ranged against Jesus in the gospel reading. Some people want to stone him because of the claim he makes to be the Son of God. 'You are blaspheming,' they say. In time, Jesus would be put to death, not by stoning but by the Roman form of execution reserved for certain kinds of criminals, crucifixion. Jesus, now risen Lord, identifies with all who are being terrorised and brutalised. He continues to travel his way of the cross through them. He cries out to us through them. He is crying out to those who are inflicting the violence and terror, but his cries are falling on deaf ears. He cries out to all of us to do whatever we can to support and help the victims of violence. These cries are not falling on deaf ears as many people from nations throughout Europe and elsewhere open their homes to refugees and support fund-raising efforts to help those in greatest need. In the gospel reading, Jesus refers to his 'many good works'. The Lord's many good works continue today through all who are doing what they can to respond to the cries of those who are being brutalised by war. These many good works are what Jesus refers to in that reading as 'my Father's work'. It is God's work. In the face of all death-dealing aggression, God needs us all to do his life-giving and life-saving work. Our good works are a sign that God and his Son are at work in and through us.

23 March, Saturday, Fifth Week of Lent
John 11:45–56
In the first reading, the Lord, speaking through the prophet Isaiah, promises to gather the people of Israel from everywhere they have been scattered and bring them home to their own soil. The people of Ukraine and of other war-torn nations have been scattered to many

nations and most of them long to be brought home to their own soil. This is also the Lord's longing for them. In the gospel reading, the evangelist declares that Jesus died to gather together in unity not just the people of Israel but the scattered children of God, all of humanity. Jesus died to reveal God's love for the world, a love that seeks to draw all people together. As Jesus says elsewhere in this Gospel of John, 'when I am lifted up from the earth, I will draw all people to myself'. In drawing all people to himself, he wanted to draw all people together around himself. The risen Lord wants to continue working through all of us to draw all people together in unity. This gathering work of the Lord is being undone by those who are dividing people, who are treating whole nations as their enemy, invading their land, killing innocent civilians. In the face of such divisive aggression, we all have to do whatever we can to further the Lord's work of bringing people together in harmony, so that, in the words of today's responsorial psalm, 'the young girls will rejoice and dance; the men, young and old, will be glad'.

25 March, Monday in Holy Week
John 12:1–11
The scene in today's gospel reading is placed six days before the Jewish feast of Passover, the time of Jesus' final journey, his passion and death. On that journey he would be brutally treated by political and religious leaders and by their military forces. In our gospel reading, however, Jesus is cared for in a very loving way by the family of Lazarus, Martha and Mary, in appreciation for Jesus having restored Lazarus to life. We are told that 'Martha waited' on him, playing a leading role in serving him a meal, in a way that seems to have been typical of her. Her sister Mary served Jesus in a different way, anointing his feet with very costly ointment and wiping them with her hair. It was an extravagant gesture that Judas, who was about

to betray him, considered a waste of money that could have been better spent on the poor. Yet Jesus recognised the timeliness of Mary's extravagant gesture; it was an anointing to strengthen him for the difficult journey ahead: 'she had to keep this scent for the day of my burial'. In the language of the first reading, there was something of the 'crushed reed' and 'wavering flame' about Jesus at this moment in his life, and he deeply appreciated Mary's costly and loving gesture, which strengthened him for the journey ahead. Mary's gesture is being replicated in our own times in the costly and loving gestures towards so many of the crushed reeds and wavering flames in our world today. The Lord considers such loving gestures for those who have been rendered vulnerable as done for him personally. Such costly and loving gestures are expressions of what today's responsorial psalm calls 'the Lord's goodness'. Hopefully, such gestures will allow those in greatest need to say, in the words of today's psalm, 'Though an army encamp against me, my heart would not fear. Though war break out against me, even then would I trust.'

26 March, Tuesday in Holy Week
John 13:21–33, 36–38
In today's gospel reading, Jesus dips a piece of bread in the main dish and gives it to Judas. In the culture of the time to take a morsel of food and dip it into sauce and hand it to a guest would have been considered a gesture of honour and affection. Jesus had already washed the feet of the disciples, including the feet of Judas. He now offers Judas a final gesture of affection. As the evangelist stated earlier, Jesus loved his own to the end, including Judas. Yet even divine love, present in Jesus, is powerless before the human refusal to receive such love. According to the gospel reading, when Judas received the bread, Satan entered him. He left the company of Jesus,

God's light in the world, and went out into the night. Jesus could not prevent Judas from betraying him, yet Judas' betrayal came to serve God's purpose for the world. God worked powerfully through the betrayal and the resulting death of Jesus to reveal his love for the world. God loved the world so much that he gave his only Son, even when that giving meant the death by crucifixion of his Son. The Lord may be powerless before human resistance to his self-emptying love, but he can work in a life-giving way for all, even in and through the human refusal to receive his love. Jesus reveals a God who does not desire death but who can bring new life out of death. There is much death in our world as a consequence of some people's refusal to receive the Lord's love into their lives. The events of this holy week allow us to trust that God is at work bringing light into this darkness and bringing forth new life out of this death.

27 March, Wednesday in Holy Week
Matthew 26:14–25

In today's responsorial psalm the person praying declares, 'I have become a stranger to my brothers, an alien to my own mother's sons.' He had reached the end of his strength and the very people from whom he would have expected support, his blood brothers, look upon him as an alien and a stranger. When the members of our own family abandon us when we are at our lowest, it is a painful and devastating experience. This was the experience of Jesus on the night of the Last Supper. He had left his blood family in Nazareth and had started to form a new family of disciples, the inner core of which was the twelve disciples he had chosen to share in his ministry in a special way. Yet, on that evening of the Last Supper, Jesus was well aware that one member of this inner core was about to betray him. He had become a stranger, an alien, to Judas Iscariot, who had already agreed to betray Jesus to the religious authorities for thirty pieces of silver.

When Jesus announced to the twelve at the Last Supper, 'One of you is about to betray me', everyone present wondered if it could be them: 'Not I, Lord, surely?' It is a question we can all ask because any one of us is capable of betraying the Lord by living in ways that are contrary to his desire for our lives. How does the Lord want us to live? There is a very good portrayal of the disciple in today's first reading. The disciple is one who has learned to listen to the word of the Lord, and, as a result, knows how to reply to the wearied. As disciples, we are all called to listen attentively to the Lord and out of that listening to speak in ways that sustain and strengthen the wearied, those who say to themselves or to others, in the words of today's psalm, 'I have reached the end of my strength.'

Easter Triduum, 28–30 March

1 April, Easter Monday
Matthew 28:8–15
There is a strong contrast in today's gospel reading between the actions of a group of women and the actions of a group of men. The women fall down before the risen Lord and clasp his feet; they then respond immediately to the Lord's command to go to the disciples and announce to them that he is going to meet them all in Galilee. Matthew portrays them as worshipping the Lord and then going out as his messengers in response to his call. They model for us our own Easter calling. We gather to worship the Lord, to fall down before him like the women. We go forth from our worship to proclaim the good news that the Lord is risen and wants to meet us not just in Galilee but in all the places where we live and work. In contrast to the women, the group of men, both soldiers and elders, conspire between them to spread a false story about Jesus' disciples stealing his body. They are not open to the good news that Jesus is risen; they

cannot take seriously anyone who says, as Mary Magdalene said, 'I have seen the Lord'. There are versions of that false story around to this day, pouring scorn on the central core of our faith, 'the crucified one has been raised from the dead'. It is a counter story to the story of the gospels, the women's story in today's gospel reading, the story of Peter, the story of the two disciples on the road to Emmaus, the story of Paul. It is in and through those stories that we continue to meet the risen Lord. It is to those stories we give our minds and hearts and souls, so that we may have life and have it to the full.

2 April, Easter Tuesday

John 20:11–18

I have often been struck by those words of the risen Jesus to Mary Magdalene in today's gospel reading, 'I am ascending to my Father and your Father, to my God and your God.' The God of Jesus is also our God, the Father of Jesus is also our Father. Because of Easter, we have come to share in Jesus' own relationship with God. The risen Jesus gives us the gift of the Holy Spirit and that Spirit draws us into a sharing in Jesus' relationship with God. Writing to the churches of Galatia, Paul expresses this conviction in his own way: 'God has sent the Spirit of his Son into our hearts crying, "Abba! Father!"' The Spirit of the risen Lord within us moves us, inspires us, to address God in the same intimate way that Jesus did. In a sense, because of the presence of the Holy Spirit in our lives, the risen Lord prays his own prayer to God in us. Perhaps we don't often think of the Lord as praying to God within us. Yet that is the depth of the Lord's communion with us that Easter makes possible. When Jesus says to Mary Magdalene, 'Do not cling to me', he was saying that it was not necessary for her to cling to him as if she was in danger of losing him. Through the Holy Spirit, he would come to her and be in a deeper relationship with her than he had ever been, his God becoming her God, his Father becoming her Father. This was the message that she was to go and proclaim to the other disciples, to all of us. She becomes the first and primary preacher of the Gospel. This is the Easter Gospel that continues to be proclaimed to us through her. The risen Lord is always in a deeply personal relationship with us, even in those times when we feel we have drifted from him. He doesn't drift from us. Because of Easter, we can all make our own what Paul says elsewhere in his letter to the Galatians, 'It is no longer I who live, but it is Christ who lives in me' (Galatians 2:20).

3 April, Easter Wednesday

Luke 24:13–35

There is a very striking example of eye contact in today's first reading. We are told that Peter and John looked straight at a beggar who had been crippled from birth and then said to him, 'Look at us'. Before going on to heal him they wanted to make very clear eye contact with him. The eye contact created a kind of communion between the beggar and the apostles, which allowed Peter and John to be channels of the Lord's healing presence to him. It is said that the eyes are the windows to the soul. We can use our eyes not only to look at someone but to see into their soul, to sense what lies in their heart of hearts. Eye contact can be the basis of a life-giving communion between us and the other. A lack of eye contact, a refusal to make eye contact, can suggest an unwillingness to get too close to someone. Good eye contact can be enhanced by what could be termed good ear contact, a willingness to listen carefully to someone, not just to the words they speak but to what lies behind the words. In the gospel reading, Jesus shows himself to have good ear contact in that sense. When he joined the two sorrowful disciples on the road to Emmaus, he invited them to share with him what they had been discussing along the way. He listened attentively to the story they told him. His careful listening inspired the words he went on to speak to them, which led to their hearts burning within them, to their invitation to him to share their table and eventually to their recognising him for who he truly was in the breaking of bread. Jesus' listening created a strong communion between himself and the two disciples which was the basis of all that followed. Our own careful listening, as well as our considered eye contact, can have life-enhancing consequences for others that we might not have anticipated at the time.

4 April, Easter Thursday

Luke 24:35–48

The Stations of the Cross have been an important part of our Catholic tradition for many years. Recently, I came across the expression 'The Stations of Light'. These stations are the various appearances of the risen Lord to his disciples as recorded in the gospels. The whole of the Easter Season between now and Pentecost Sunday is an invitation to reflect on those Stations of Light. Today's gospel reading puts before us one of those Stations of Light, Luke's account of the appearance of the risen Lord to the disciples as a group. According to the beginning of that gospel reading, the two disciples who had met the Lord on the road to Emmaus and at table in Emmaus were sharing their story with the other disciples. It was while they were sharing their story that the risen Lord stood among them and declared, 'Peace be with you'. Luke is reminding us that whenever we share our faith stories the risen Lord is there in our midst. Sharing our faith with others creates an opening for the Lord to stand among us. In that gospel reading the disciples struggle to believe that the Lord was present to them. According to Luke, even after Jesus spoke to them, 'their joy was so great that they still could not believe it and they stood there dumbfounded'. They presumed that the crucifixion of Jesus had brought to an end the story of their relationship with him. Yet the presence of the risen Lord among them revealed that the Lord of love and life was stronger than the powers of hatred and death. The first Easter shattered all their expectations. Easter continues to shatter our expectations. The risen Lord continues to take us by surprise. He stands among us even when all hope seems lost; he touches us with his presence when we are least expecting it. When we are most aware of our failure to follow him, he speaks his word of peace to us, because even when we are faithless, he remains faithful. Easter announces that the story of our relationship with the Lord never ends, because his relationship with us never ends. He continues to stand among us, assuring us of his presence, offering us his gift of peace and sending us out as his messengers of hope.

5 April, Easter Friday
John 21:1–14

I always find striking the sentence in the gospel reading, 'There stood Jesus on the shore.' The phrase can be understood as Jesus standing on the shore of our lives. When Jesus stood on the shore of the Sea of Galilee, the disciples did not realise that it was Jesus, just as the two disciples on the road to Emmaus did not realise that the stranger who joined them was Jesus. Jesus can be standing on the shore of our lives without our realising it. Sometimes the trials and struggles of life can blind us to the presence of the Lord alongside us. In the gospel reading, the disciples had gone back to their fishing business in the wake of Jesus' crucifixion. They seemed to have lost their skill because they had gone out at night, the best time to catch fish in the Sea of Galilee, and had caught nothing. In this moment of despondency and failure, the Lord stood on the shore close by them, even though they failed to recognise him. Yet they had enough energy to respond to the invitation of this stranger on the shore to set out again and this time to throw their nets to starboard. The resulting enormous catch led one of the disciples, the beloved disciple, to recognise that the stranger was none other than the Lord. 'It is the Lord,' he said to Peter. Sometimes when we refuse to let a difficult situation get the better of us, and set out again, perhaps in response to some invitation, we too come to recognise that the Lord is with us, standing on the shore of our lives. We come to see that he had been there all along, when all seemed dark, but we hadn't recognised him. The Lord who stood on the shore of the Sea of Galilee wanted to enter into a personal communion with the disciples. He invited them, 'Come and have breakfast', and then went on to take bread and give it to them, which is suggestive of the Last Supper, when Jesus took bread, broke it, blessed it and gave it to his disciples. The risen Lord who stands on the shore of our lives wishes to be in a personal communion with his disciples today, all of us, and he does this in a special way when we gather to celebrate Eucharist.

6 April, Easter Saturday

Mark 16:9–15

The impression today's gospel reading gives is that the first disciples found it very difficult to believe reports that Jesus who had been crucified was now alive. When Jesus appeared to Mary Magdalene and she went and told the disciples what had happened, they were in such deep mourning that they did not believe her. When Jesus appeared to the two disciples on the road to Emmaus and they went and told the disciples their news, they did not believe them either. It was only when the risen Lord appeared to the group of disciples themselves that they finally believed that Jesus who was crucified was now living with a new quality of life. On that occasion, the risen Lord rebuked them for refusing to believe the witness of those to whom he had appeared. We are asked to do what the original disciples failed to do, to believe that Jesus is risen on the basis of the witness of those to whom the risen Lord appeared. We find this witness in the gospels and in the letters of Paul. Our belief in the risen Lord is also based on his coming to us personally. He may not appear to us in the way he appeared to the first disciples, but he touches our own lives in a very personal way. We are to believe on the basis of the written testimony of the first eyewitnesses, and on the basis of our own personal experience of the risen Lord's presence in our lives. The risen Lord who comes to us sends us out in the same way he sent out the disciples in today's gospel reading, to 'proclaim the good news [of Easter] to all creation'.

8 April, Monday, The Annunciation of the Lord
Luke 1:26–38

The question of Mary in today's gospel reading, 'How can this come about?' is a very human one. It is the kind of question that is asked by others in the gospels. When Jesus was with his disciples in the wilderness in the presence of a hungry crowd, they asked him, 'How can one feed these people with bread here in the desert?' When we stand before a situation that seems beyond our resources to deal with, we all find ourselves asking the same kind of question, 'How can this be?' 'How will I deal with this?' The angel Gabriel's answer to this question of Mary invited her to trust not in herself but in God. 'The Holy Spirit will come upon you and the power of the Most High will overshadow you.' A lot was being asked of Mary and it would make great demands on her, but she was not being asked to take on this task of being mother to God's Son on the strength of her own resources alone. With this reassurance, she surrendered to the demanding role that God was giving her. 'Let what you have said be done to me.' Mary has often been described as a model disciple. In today's gospel reading, she models a faith that trusts in God's power and, because it trusts in God's power, stands ready to do what God asks. Asking 'How can this be?' 'How will I get through this?' can inhibit us, hold us back, but, as in the case of Mary, it can also open us up to the working of the Holy Spirit in our lives.

9 April, Tuesday, Second Week of Easter

John 3:7–15

The first reading gives us an insight into how the members of the early Church looked out for one another. If a member of the community had more than was needed, it was presented to the apostles, who distributed it to those who were in greater need. As a result, none of the members of the community were ever in want. This tradition of sharing from our surplus to give to those in greater need has been an essential feature of the life of the Church since its earliest beginnings. One expression of it today is the work of the Vincent de Paul Society. The monthly collection that is taken up outside the church allows them to help people who find themselves in a once-off need or perhaps in a situation that requires a more sustained response. This is one manifestation of the presence of the Holy Spirit in the life of the Church, what Saint Paul calls a fruit of the Spirit. In the gospel reading, Jesus compares the Spirit to the wind. Just as we cannot see the wind as such but can experience its impact on ourselves, on others, on nature, so we cannot see the Holy Spirit directly, but we can see the impact of the Holy Spirit in our lives and the lives of others. Just as the wind blows wherever it pleases, so the Spirit works where it pleases. We will often see the impact of the Spirit in people and in places where we didn't expect to find it. We can delight in wherever we happen to find the fruit of the Spirit. As people born of the Spirit through baptism, we have a special calling to allow the Spirit to blow through us and to shape what we say and do.

10 April, Wednesday, Second Week of Easter
John 3:16–21

The first reading suggests that no human power can block the preaching of the Gospel, not even the imprisonment of the apostles, Jesus' closest associates. The risen Lord will always find a way for the Gospel to be proclaimed, in spite of people's best efforts to silence it. That is because, in the words of today's gospel reading, 'God so loved the world'. God sent his Son into the world so that everyone may have eternal life. For God, it is a matter of the greatest urgency that the Gospel that was proclaimed and lived by his Son, now risen Lord, be announced to as many people as possible. God will stop at nothing to ensure that the world of humanity hears the Gospel of God's saving love for all. The light of God's love shines through the Gospel and God passionately desires that this light would shine upon all, in every time and place, just as the earthly sun shines on all. Yet the gospel reading also states that people need to be open to this light, to come out into the light, to love the light of God's enduring love. In the words of today's psalm, we need to look towards the light so that we can be radiant. Nothing we do or fail to do will prevent the light of the Gospel of God's love from shining upon us, but we can choose to turn away from the light, to block it out, just as, at the Last Supper, Judas went out into the night. The good news is that even when we turn from the light and choose darkness, the light shines in the darkness and, if there is even the smallest opening in us to the light, the darkness will not overcome it.

11 April, Thursday, Second Week of Easter
John 3:31–36

The words of Peter and the apostles to the high priest, 'Obedience to God comes before obedience to men', was a conviction that shaped the life of the first believers. It often brought them into conflict with the religious leaders, who thought of themselves as the mediators of God's word. For us as Christians, obedience to God is obedience to his Son, Jesus, our risen Lord, because, as today's gospel declares, 'he whom God has sent speaks God's own words'. The Greek word that translates as 'obedience' suggests attentive listening. We are called to listen attentively to the word of God, especially as proclaimed and lived by Jesus, who is God's Word in human form. As the Word of God, Jesus is the Bread of Life because his words can satisfy the deepest hunger in our hearts, our hunger for truth and for an assurance of God's love. In the words of today's responsorial psalm, we are invited to 'taste and see that the Lord is good'. The gospel reading declares that 'God gives him [Jesus] the Spirit without reserve', and in this Fourth Gospel Jesus declares that his words are 'spirit and life'. When we listen attentively to the Lord's word, we are opening ourselves to Holy Spirit, and in the power of that Spirit we will be able to witness to our faith in the Lord with something of the courage shown by Peter and the apostles in today's first reading.

12 April, Friday, Second Week of Easter
John 6:1–15
The speech of Gamaliel in today's first reading is thought-provoking. The Jewish Sanhedrin were worried about the growing popularity of the disciples of Jesus. Gamaliel said, in effect, that if this new movement is not from God, it will disappear, like so many other movements. If it is from God, the Sanhedrin are powerless to destroy it. God alone endures; he is the Alpha and Omega, the beginning and the end. What is of God will also endure. The Church has endured for over two millennia because it is from God. However, many aspects of Church life have not endured because they were not of God. In these changing times for the Church, we have to trust that

what is of God will endure and that what isn't will pass away. In the gospel reading, after Jesus fed the multitude in the wilderness, the people wanted to take him by force and make him king. However, Jesus knew that this impulse was not from God and he fled from it, and the impulse passed away for the moment, even though the impulse to make the Church an earthly kingdom would rear its head more than once in the following centuries. What doesn't pass away, because it is of God, is Jesus' capacity to work powerfully through humble human resources in the service of God's people, such as feeding a large crowd with five barley loaves and two fish. The risen Lord continues to work among us in this way today, as power in weakness. We can be tempted to ask the somewhat despairing question of Andrew in today's gospel reading, 'What is that between so many?' We sense that there is much for us to do as the Lord's disciples and our resources seem so small at times. Today's gospel reading encourages us to trust that if we are generous with the resources we have, small as they may seem to us, the Lord will work powerfully through them in ways that will surprise us.

13 April, Saturday, Second Week of Easter
John 6:16–21

According to the verse before our gospel reading (John 6:15), Jesus had withdrawn to the mountain by himself, in response to the crowd wanting to make him king. The suggestion is that Jesus needed to be in communion with God in prayer. Jesus' prayer did not remove him from the struggles of his disciples. It was while he was at prayer that he became aware of the disciples in the boat on the Sea of Galilee struggling with a strong wind and a rough sea. He immediately came to them, speaking a reassuring word, 'It is I. Do not be afraid.' The literal translation would be 'I am. Do not be afraid.' In this Fourth

Gospel, the words 'I am' on the lips of Jesus suggest the name of God revealed to Moses at the burning bush. Jesus comes to his disciples as God in human form. Once the disciples show a willingness to take Jesus into the boat with them, they reach the shore. The prayer of Jesus created a space for him to be present to his disciples in a very troubling moment. The first reading puts before us a troubling moment in the life of the Church, conflict between Greek-speaking and Aramaic-speaking Jewish Christian widows over the distribution of food. This conflict in the Church required the Twelve to clarify for themselves and for the other members of the Church what their priorities were to be. 'We will continue to devote ourselves to prayer and to the service of the word.' The clarity with which the apostles could identify their priorities amid competing claims on their time is admirable. They understood, as Jesus did, that prayerful attentiveness to God's word would allow their lives to be shaped by God's purpose and would best serve the life of the believing community. Today's readings remind us that prayerful attentiveness to God's word needs to be at the heart of the Church's life, and of our own lives as individual disciples.

15 April, Monday, Third Week of Easter

John 6:22–29

In times of conflict and war, truth is often the first casualty. The aggressor in particular will often bend the truth to try to justify what they are attempting to do. The Jewish religious leaders who were hostile to Jesus were equally hostile to his followers, who were proclaiming that God had raised Jesus from the dead. In today's first reading, we hear of their antagonism to Stephen, a gifted preacher. They procured people to falsify what Stephen had said: 'We heard him using blasphemous language against Moses and against God …

This man is always making speeches against this Holy Place and the Law. We heard him say that Jesus the Nazarene is going to destroy this Place.' Although such accusations were essentially false, they would be a significant factor in the eventual death of Stephen by stoning. Jesus once said of himself, 'I am the truth.' He revealed to us the truth about God, about what it is to be human, about creation. His followers are to be people of truth, who live by the truth that Jesus proclaimed and lived. Because he is the truth, he can satisfy the deep hunger in our hearts for truth. In the gospel reading, Jesus challenges the crowd to come to him not just as someone who can satisfy their physical hunger, which he had done recently, but as someone who can satisfy their deeper hungers, their hunger for truth, for a love that is faithful, for a life that is eternal. 'Do not work for food that cannot last, but for food that endures to eternal life.' Jesus offers himself to them, and to us all, as one who can satisfy the deepest hungers of our heart. Such hungers will only be fully satisfied at the banquet of eternal life, but insofar as we keep coming to the Lord and opening our hearts to him, our deepest hungers will begin to be satisfied in the course of our earthly lives.

16 April, Tuesday, Third Week of Easter
John 6:30–35
More than once in the gospels, people come to Jesus asking him to perform a sign before they will take him seriously. In today's gospel reading people ask Jesus, 'What sign will you give to show us that we should believe in you? What work will you do?' This is immediately after Jesus had done the work of feeding a large crowd with five barley loaves and two fish. Here was a work that was a sign for those with eyes to see. This work pointed beyond itself to Jesus' true identity. His feeding of the crowd with bread and fish was a sign that Jesus was 'the bread of life', in the language of today's gospel

reading. The real significance of Jesus' miraculous work of feeding the crowd lay in what it has to say about who Jesus is for all those who believe in him. The crowd who were fed would become hungry again, but Jesus remains the bread of life for all who come to him, not just during his public ministry, but for all future generations who will come to him as risen Lord. Jesus is our bread of life today. The promise he makes in today's gospel reading is made to each one of us: 'Those who come to me will never be hungry; those who believe in me will never thirst.' The risen Lord promises to satisfy the deepest hungers and thirsts in our heart, the hunger and thirst for love, for forgiveness, for justice, for peace, for communion, for life to the full. Here and now, in our own place and time, he is the bread of life for all who believe in him and for all who come to him. We encounter the Lord as bread of life in a special way at the Eucharist. Yet the Lord's invitation to come to him as the bread of life is not limited to the Eucharist. He can be our daily bread of life wherever we find ourselves.

17 April, Wednesday, Third Week of Easter
John 6:35–40
In Luke's Gospel, Jesus had tried to preach the Gospel to a Samaritan village, but the Samaritans rejected him. In Luke's second volume, the Acts of the Apostles, the risen Lord preaches the Gospel again to the Samaritans through Philip, as described in our first reading, and on this occasion the Samaritans 'united in welcoming the message Philip preached'. The Lord does not take an initial 'no' to him as final. He continues to offer the Gospel to those who initially reject it. In today's gospel reading Jesus declares, 'Whoever comes to me, I shall not turn away.' Even though we may have turned away from him in the past, he does not turn away from us. If we come to him, having initially turned away, he will not turn us away because, as he declares in the gospel reading, it is his Father's will that

'whoever sees the Son and believes in him shall have eternal life'. There is a time for every matter under heaven, according to the Book of Ecclesiastes. According to Luke, the public ministry of Jesus wasn't the time for the Samaritans to respond to the Gospel (contrary to the Gospel of John!) but the preaching of Philip in the period after Pentecost was that time. Like the father in the parable of the prodigal son, the Lord knows how to wait on us. Although his time is always 'now', he is prepared to wait on our timing, just as he waited on the timing of Saul who, according to our first reading, 'worked for the total destruction of the church' before becoming the great apostle to the pagans in response to the Lord's call.

18 April, Thursday, Third Week of Easter
John 6:44–51

In the gospel reading, Jesus declares that all who come to him have been drawn to him by the Father,: 'No one can come to me unless drawn by the Father who sent me.' God is always drawing us towards his Son, who says of himself in the gospel reading, 'I am the bread of life'. God often draws us to his Son in and through other people of faith. In the first reading, God initially draws the Ethiopian to his Son through the scriptures. When the Ethiopian reflects on a passage from Isaiah, he begins to ask questions: 'Is the prophet referring to himself or someone else?' He needed the help of a person of faith to answer this question, the help of the deacon Philip. God, who began to draw the Ethiopian to his Son through the scriptures, now draws him fully to his Son through the spiritual accompaniment of Philip, the preacher of the Gospel. Philip's ministry to the Ethiopian led the Ethiopian to take an initiative of his own: 'Look, there is some water here; is there anything to stop me being baptised?' It is as if the final step of God drawing the

Ethiopian to his Son was through the medium of creation, water. Having allowed God to work through him to bring the Ethiopian to Jesus, Philip moved on from him, and the Ethiopian continued on his way rejoicing. God will find many ways of bringing us to his Son, if we allow ourselves to be drawn.

19 April, Friday, Third Week of Easter
John 6:52–59

The question that people ask in today's gospel reading is a perfectly understandable one: 'How can this man give us his flesh to eat?' The notion of eating's someone's flesh is abhorrent. Yet Jesus does not qualify what he says but, rather, he goes on to say something even more shocking. He not only calls on people to eat his flesh but to drink his blood. It is evident that Jesus is not speaking literally. His way of speaking reflects what he said at the Last Supper where, having taken, blessed and broken bread, he gave it to his disciples and said, 'This is my body.' Then, having taken and blessed wine, he gave it to his disciples and said, 'This is my blood.' Jesus identified himself, body and blood, flesh and blood, with the elements of bread and wine. He went on to instruct his disciples at the Last Supper to 'do this in memory of me'. Ever since, the Church has repeated the actions and words of Jesus at the Last Supper. In today's first reading we have the dramatic story of the call of Paul. Paul will later declare in his first letter to the Corinthians, 'The cup of blessing that we bless, is it not a communion in the blood of Christ? The bread that we break, is it not a communion in the body of Christ?' This was the faith of the early Church and of the Church ever since. The Lord wishes to enter into communion with us in a very profound way at the Eucharist so that we can draw life from him. The Eucharist is a celebration of life. We are then sent out from the Eucharist to nurture and protect life in all its forms.

20 April, Saturday, Third Week of Easter
John 6:60–69

We don't often think of churches, communities of believers, in the land where Jesus lived and worked, what today's first reading refers to as 'Judea, Galilee and Samaria'. Jesus was from Galilee and spent most of his public ministry in Galilee, but he also entered Samaria and his ministry concluded in Judea, although he may also have travelled to Judea from Galilee in the course of his ministry, as the Fourth Gospel suggests. Luke speaks of the churches in these areas as 'building themselves up, living in the fear of the Lord, and filled with the consolation of the Holy Spirit'. This is the wonderful fruit of Jesus' ministry. Today's gospel reading, from the Fourth Gospel, is set in Galilee and, in contrast, it highlights a moment of crisis for the original group of disciples that Jesus had gathered about himself. Jesus had been revealing himself to them as the bread of life and declaring that 'those who eat my flesh and drink my blood have eternal life'. Some of the disciples declare, 'This is intolerable language. How could anyone accept it?' The evangelist goes on to state, 'many of his disciples left him and stopped going with him'. This is a very different picture from that of the vibrant church in Galilee given to us by Luke in the first reading. There is often an ebb and flow to the life of the Church in a region. When the tide seems to be going out, we shouldn't get discouraged. The risen Lord is with us in the lean times as much as in the times of flourishing. In crisis times, it is important that some believers hold firm. This is what we find happening in the gospel reading. When many of Jesus' disciples left him (and he may not have had too many), he turns to the twelve and asks them, 'What about you, do you want to go away too?'

It is one of those questions of Jesus that hangs in the air for us all. Where do we stand when it seems easier to join the stampede heading for the exit? We are all invited to make our own Peter's response to Jesus' question, 'Lord, to whom shall we go? You have the message of eternal life.'

22 April, Monday, Fourth Week of Easter
John 10:1–10

In today's gospel reading Jesus declares that it is only the one who enters the sheepfold through the gate who is to be given access to the sheep. Those who try to get into the sheepfold some other way, such as over the wall when no one is looking, are not to be trusted. Jesus then goes on to identify himself as the gate. Jesus' flock, his disciples, are to be approached through him. We go towards each other through Jesus. In other words, our relationship with Jesus is the basis of our relationship with each other. Jesus, who says of himself in today's gospel reading, 'I am the gate', elsewhere in this Gospel of John says of himself, 'I am the way'. There is a close relationship between the images of the gate and the way. When we go through Jesus, taking him as our way in life, then we are more likely to approach one another in the loving way that the Lord desires. We see that happening in today's first reading. It was because of Peter's close relationship with the Lord, nurtured by prayer, that he was able to respond in a loving way to the invitation of the pagan centurion Cornelius to come to his house. A law-abiding Jew like Peter would not normally have entered the house of a pagan. However, because Peter had taken Jesus as his gate, as his way, on a daily basis, he knew that the Spirit was moving him to go with this little pagan group to their household. There Peter saw for himself the work of the Holy Spirit in their lives, in response to his preaching of the Gospel. Our relationship with the Lord will always move us and inspire us to relate to others, especially those very different from us, in the same accepting and welcoming way as he himself related to people during the course of his earthly ministry.

23 April, Tuesday, Fourth Week of Easter
John 10:22–30

The first reading describes a significant moment in the life of the early Church, the preaching of the Gospel to pagans for the first time, in the city of Antioch. Up until that moment, all the disciples of Jesus were Jews. The leaders of the church in Jerusalem had to discern whether this new development in Antioch was the work of the Holy Spirit, or just a human aberration. As part of their discerning, they sent one of their members, Barnabas, to check out what was happening in Antioch. He was sent because he was known to be a good man, filled with the Holy Spirit and faith. A person filled with the Holy Spirit was likely to discern whether or not this novelty was the work of the Spirit. Barnabas immediately recognised that God was at work here. He not only gave them all every encouragement, he set out for Tarsus to bring Paul to Antioch, because he could see that this new development in Antioch was ripe for Paul's gifts. Paul and Barnabas went on to spend twelve months together in that church. According to the reading, it was in Antioch that the followers of Jesus were first called 'Christians'. People began to see that this movement wasn't just a particular branch of Judaism. The Lord is always doing something new among us, and we all need to discern the ways the Lord is leading the Church, especially in these times. To do that well, we need a listening ear, an ear that is open to the surprising ways of the Spirit. As Jesus says in the gospel reading, those 'who belong to me listen to my voice'. People like Barnabas who are in tune with the working of the Spirit among us are an invaluable asset as we try to discern where the Lord is leading us. The Lord will always provide such people at times of transition, like the present time. Indeed, he invites each of us to become such a person.

24 April, Wednesday, Fourth Week of Easter
John 12:44–50

In today's gospel reading Jesus refers to 'the Father who sent me'. In the Fourth Gospel Jesus is the 'sent one'. One of the most memorable verses of this gospel declares, 'God did not send the Son into the world to condemn the world, but in order that the world might be saved through him'. Jesus personalises this statement in today's gospel reading: 'I have come not to condemn the world but to save the world.' In the language of the Fourth Gospel, God sent his Son into the world so that we may have life and have it to the full. There is another sending in today's first reading. The church in Antioch, under the guidance of the Holy Spirit, sent two of their leading members, Barnabas and Saul, on mission to places where the Gospel had not been preached, resulting in the expansion of the Gospel westwards. This was a costly sending, because Barnabas and Saul had been central to the life of the church in Antioch. God's sending of his Son into the world was also costly because it entailed a giving of his Son over to death, death on a cross. Yet both the sending of Jesus and the sending of Barnabas and Saul were life-giving for those to whom they were sent. This is supremely true of the sending of Jesus, without which there would have been no sending of Barnabas or Saul. The Church in every age is called to send, to let go of precious resources, so that others may flourish. The dynamic of sending is vital today as parishes learn to journey together, sharing resources, learning to become poor so that others may become rich, and, in the process, discovering that all are enriched.

25 April, Thursday, Saint Mark, Evangelist
Mark 16:15–20

Mark was the first to write a gospel. It always strikes me as strange
that the gospel reading for his feast is taken from the longer ending
of Mark, which was probably a later addition to his gospel! According to early tradition, Mark was a disciple of Peter, which accounts
for the first reading being from the first letter of Peter. Mark's Gospel was the primary written source for the Gospels of Matthew and
Luke. In the early centuries the Church seems to have found Matthew's Gospel in particular more helpful for the life of faith because
of the large amount of the teaching of Jesus it contains, relative to
Mark's Gospel. As a result, Mark's Gospel was overshadowed somewhat in the early centuries by its larger relations, especially Matthew, and also John. Yet without Mark's Gospel the Church would
not have had the Gospels of Matthew or Luke in the form that they
have come down to us. In time, Mark came to be appreciated on its
own terms, and not just as a poorer version of Matthew. It is now
recognised for the wonderful literary and theological masterpiece it
is. Mark portrays Jesus as the suffering Son of Man who came not
to be served but to serve, and who was ready to lay down his life in
the service of all. Mark's portrait of the disciple mirrors that of Jesus.
As disciples we are called to walk in the way of Jesus' self-emptying
service of God and God's people, even when that means travelling
the way of the cross. Mark is often unsparing in his portrayal of the
failure of the disciples to imbibe this vision of Jesus and to live by
it. Jesus struggles to open their eyes. As the gospel progresses, their
failure becomes more pronounced, until, at the end, 'they all deserted
him and fled'. Yet the gospel ends (the shorter ending) with the young
man calling on the faithful women to tell the other disciples that Jesus
is going ahead of them to Galilee where they will see him. The risen

Lord remains faithful to his failed disciples and his faithfulness finally allows them to see clearly and to go out afresh to preach the Gospel. This faithfulness of the Lord is well expressed in today's gospel reading: 'the Lord working with them confirming the word by the signs that accompanied it'. This message of Mark's Gospel that the Lord continues to work with his disciples, in spite of past serious failings, is a message the Church needs to hear today.

26 April, Friday, Fourth Week of Easter
John 14:1–6
Many of us find departures difficult, especially when the person departing from us is significant for us in some way. The words Jesus speaks in today's gospel reading are set by the evangelist within the context of the Last Supper on the evening before Jesus was crucified. Jesus is about to leave his disciples. Yet in leaving them he also assures them that he is not abandoning them. He will in fact come back to them. That is the promise of Jesus to the disciples in today's gospel reading: 'I shall return to take you with me.' That promise is generally heard as a promise that at the end of our earthly lives Jesus will come and take us to the many-roomed house of his Father, which is why this reading is so often chosen for the funeral liturgy. However, Jesus goes on to assure his disciples that we don't have to wait until the end of our lives to experience his coming. He will come to us in and through the Paraclete, the Holy Spirit, 'whom the Father will send in my name', and who 'will teach you everything, and remind you of all that I have said to you'. Through the Spirit, the Lord comes to us here and now, today, and his coming through the Spirit is a foretaste, an anticipation, of his coming to us at the end of our lives. That is why Saint Paul refers to the Spirit as the first fruit of the final harvest, eternal life.

Our present calling is to allow the first fruit of the Spirit to bear the rich fruit of love in our lives.

27 April, Saturday, Fourth Week of Easter
John 14:7–14
You often hear parents say to children, 'You are never satisfied'. There is a sense in which that is probably true of all of us. We are never satisfied. Saint Augustine said that our hearts are restless until they rest in God. In today's gospel reading, Philip is clearly not satisfied. He says to Jesus, 'Lord, let us see the Father, and then we shall be satisfied.' He understood that it is only in seeing God that all the longings of his heart would be satisfied. Jesus replies to Philip's words with the statement, 'To have seen me is to have seen the Father'. Jesus reveals the Father; he is the way to the Father. We won't see God the Father in this life, but God has sent us his Son. Although we cannot see Jesus in the way Philip and the other disciples saw him, we can see him with the eyes of faith in this life. We can see him in his Word, in the Eucharist, in the other sacraments, in each other. Such 'seeing' of the Lord won't fully satisfy us but it gives us a glimpse of what awaits us. As we journey towards our seeing of the Lord 'face to face', we try to heed the invitation of the letter to the Hebrews: 'Let us run with perseverance the race that is set before us, looking to Jesus, the pioneer and perfecter of our faith.'

29 April, Monday, Saint Catherine of Siena
Matthew 11:25–30
Born in 1347, Catherine entered the Dominican Third Order at the age of eighteen and spent the next three years in seclusion, prayer and austerity. Gradually, a group of followers gathered around her, men and women, priests and religious. An active public apostolate grew out of her contemplative life, working with the sick, the poor,

prisoners and plague victims. In 1378, the Great Schism began, splitting the allegiance of Christendom between two, then three, popes. She spent the last two years of her life in Rome in prayer, pleading on behalf of the cause of Pope Urban VI and the unity of the Church. She offered herself as a victim for the Church in its agony. She died surrounded by her followers and was canonised in 1461. A contemplative, her life of prayer expressed itself in the loving service of those in need. A mystic, she involved herself as a peacemaker and a reconciler in the great affairs of Church and state of the day. In the words of today's first reading, she lived her life in the light, in God who is light, and brought the light of God's reconciling love to her broken church and world. Today's gospel reading gives us an insight into the prayer of Jesus. 'I bless you, Father, Lord of heaven and earth.' Jesus' communion with God in prayer directs him to those who labour and are overburdened, inviting them to come to him and receive the gift of rest, the revival of their drooping spirits. This twofold dynamic of prayerful communion with God and loving service of the broken and needy, which shaped the life of Jesus, also shaped the life of Catherine. It is to shape all of our lives.

30 April, Tuesday, Fifth Week of Easter

John 14:27–31

In the first reading we find Paul and Barnabas putting fresh heart into the disciples, encouraging them to persevere in the faith. One of the ways they put fresh heart into the disciples was by calling forth pastoral leaders from among them, 'elders', whom they commended to the Lord with prayer and fasting. The ministry of encouragement, of putting fresh heart into one another as people of faith, remains a vital ministry today. The temptation to discouragement can be quite strong in these times, so this ministry of encouragement is all the more vital. In the gospel reading we find Jesus exercising this ministry of encouragement in the setting of the Last Supper. Jesus' disciple are troubled and afraid, aware as they are that Jesus is about to be taken from them. Jesus reassures them that he is going to the Father, the one who sent him into the world. This journey to the Father is an expression of his love for the Father. His journey there will enable him to serve his disciples in a new and more powerful way. As a result of his return to the Father, he will be able to share his own peace with his disciples, the peace of Easter, a peace the world cannot give. Jesus is showing them that his leaving them is to their advantage, a reason for encouragement. It will result in his putting fresh heart into them. Today's readings invite us to share in this ministry of encouragement that Jesus, Paul and Barnabas so powerfully exercise. The gospel reading also shows us that leavetakings can be sources of new life for all. In the midst of loss, signs of the Lord's encouraging presence are always to be found.

1 May, Wednesday, Fifth Week of Easter

John 15:1–8

In today's gospel reading, Jesus speaks frequently about the importance of the disciples bearing fruit. From what Jesus goes on to say, it is clear that the fruit Jesus is referring to is the fruit of love, a life of love that reflects Jesus' love for his disciples, for all of us, and for humanity. Jesus makes clear in our gospel reading that such a life of love flows from our communion with him, just as fruit on the branches of a vine is due to the branches being in communion with the vine. If the branches are separated from the vine, the fruit will wither. In the same way, Jesus says, 'cut off from me you can do nothing'. Jesus stresses the importance of a certain way of life, a life of love, but he suggests that even more important is our communion with him and his communion with us. His primary call is not to bear the fruit of love but to make our home in him, as he makes his home in us. In becoming flesh, Jesus made himself at home with us; he looks to us to make ourselves at home with him. As he has cultivated his communion with us, we are to cultivate our communion with him. It is this intimate relationship with the Lord that empowers our lives to bear the fruit of love. It is only in and through our communion with the Lord that we can come to love one another as he has loved us, and it is such a way of life that gives glory to God the Father.

2 May, Thursday, Fifth Week of Easter

John 15:9–11

In today's first reading Peter argues that the Church, which was composed of Jews almost exclusively, should not make things more difficult than is necessary for pagans who want to join the Church, by insisting they submit to the Jewish practice of circumcision. Peter seems to be touching on a good pastoral principal, namely, not to make it more difficult for people to come to the Lord than is necessary. The Lord is always drawing people to himself, sometimes in ways that may surprise us. Peter suggests that we must be careful not to get in the way of the Lord's work of drawing people to himself by imposing conditions that the Lord himself would not impose. Very often, the best thing we can do is get out of the Lord's way and let the Lord work. People's journey to faith is ultimately the Lord's work. The Lord is always engaged in his work of drawing people to himself. He wants to work through us, but we have to be careful that we don't become a hindrance to him rather than a help by complicating the Lord's work. In the gospel reading, Jesus suggests that we serve his work best by remaining in his love, opening ourselves to the gift of his love: 'As the Father has loved me, so I have loved you.' If we open ourselves to the Lord's love we will begin to experience the Lord's own joy. 'I have told you this so that my own joy may be in you and your joy be complete.' When we open ourselves to the Lord's love and his joy fills our lives, then the Lord will be able to work through us more freely so as to draw others to himself.

3 May, Friday, Saints Philip and James, Apostles
John 14:6–16

There are several people by the name 'James' in the gospels. The James of today's feast is the one referred to as the brother or cousin of Jesus. In today's first reading, Saint Paul lists James as one of those to whom the risen Lord appeared: 'Then he appeared to James, and then to all the Apostles.' James would become a leading member of the church in Jerusalem. In his letter to the Galatians, Paul refers to him as one of the pillars of the church in Jerusalem. Paul and James did not see eye to eye on the contentious issue of the grounds for admitting pagans to the Church, with James insisting that they needed to be circumcised and Paul adamant that their faith in Christ was sufficient. Paul was on the right side of Christian history there. James was a man of deep faith, but he had much to learn. According to the opening chapter of John's Gospel, Philip was from the town of Bethsaida, on the northern shore of the Sea of Galilee, and it was he who found Nathanael and called him to Jesus, with the invitation to 'Come and see.' In today's gospel reading, Philip says to Jesus, 'Let us see the Father and then we shall be satisfied.' Philip had already come to Jesus and seen him. Yet he did not yet realise that in seeing Jesus he was seeing the Father, which is why Jesus says to him, 'To have seen me is to have seen the Father.' Philip had responded to the call of Jesus and had gone on to bring Nathanael to Jesus, yet, like James, he too had much to learn; he was still on a journey of discovery with regard to Jesus. Even though he saw Jesus with the eyes of faith, there were greater things he had yet to see, namely, that the Father was living in Jesus and working through Jesus, so to see Jesus was to see the Father. Like James and Philip, we are all on a journey of discovery with regard to Jesus. There are always 'greater things' in regard to Jesus that we have yet to see. Through the Holy Spirit the Lord works in our lives to lead us to the complete truth. All he asks is that we be open and responsive to his guiding, like Philip and James.

4 May, Saturday, Fifth Week of Easter

John 15:18–21

We are given a sense in today's first reading of Paul's mission being directed by the Holy Spirit, the Spirit of the Lord. They travelled in response to the promptings of the Spirit. At the end of the reading, the Spirit communicates with Paul through the medium of a vision. One night, while Paul was in Troas on the northwest coast of modern Turkey, he had a vision. Someone from the Roman province of Macedonia (northern Greece today), appeared to him and appealed to him in these words, 'Come across to Macedonia and help us.' Paul promptly responded to this invitation and it resulted in the Gospel being preached on the continent of Europe for the first time. The Spirit continues to guide the Church today. We are aware that we are in a time of great transition in the Church. It can be an unsettling time, but it is also an exciting time. We can be sure that the Spirit will direct us in these days. The Spirit is always at work in the life of the Church, and in our own personal lives, bringing new life out of death, opening up new opportunities when past opportunities seem to have run their course. In the gospel reading, Jesus alerts us to the likelihood that his disciples, the Church, will experience the same hostility and persecution as he did. As he says, 'A servant is not greater than his master.' We are all trying to be the Lord's servants, and Jesus says plainly that if they persecuted him they will persecute his servants. Yet, just as the Spirit was with Jesus in his moments of struggle, so the same Spirit is with his Church, all of us, in our moments of struggle, and we can trust the Spirit to bring us to where the Lord wants to take us. What the Lord needs from us is a willingness to be brought where the Spirit is leading us. This is something we all need to pray for at this time.

6 May, Monday, Sixth Week of Easter
John 15:26–16:4

Today's first reading describes a significant moment in the spread of the Gospel in the early Church. For the first time, Paul preaches the Gospel in the equivalent of modern-day Greece, which is on the continent of Europe. The first people to hear the Gospel on European soil from Paul, according to our first reading, were a group of devout women who gathered for prayer on the sabbath outside the gates of the city of Philippi. One member of that group, a woman named Lydia, responded wholeheartedly to Paul's preaching of the Gospel. She was clearly a woman of some means, involved in the purple dye trade. Purple cloth was the most expensive cloth at the time. She had the financial means to offer Paul hospitality and she insisted that Paul accept her offer; it was her way of giving thanks to God for what she had received through Paul. People who get involved in parish ministry often say that they want to give something back. They are conscious that they have received a great deal in life and they want to give from what they have received. Lydia had no sooner received the Gospel than she engaged in the ministry of hospitality. This was her way of bearing witness to her faith, of giving back. In the gospel reading, Jesus calls on his disciples to become his witnesses and he promises to send them the Holy Spirit who is Jesus' primary witness. It is the Holy Spirit who empowers us to witness to our faith. It was the Holy Spirit who moved Lydia to witness to her new-found faith by offering hospitality to Paul and his companions. The Holy Spirit will always be inspiring us to witness to our faith in various ways. We need to be attentive to the ways in which the Holy Spirit may be inspiring us to be the Lord's witnesses in the world.

7 May, Tuesday, Sixth Week of Easter
John 16:5–11

In today's gospel reading, Jesus, on the night before he died, addresses himself to the sadness of the disciples. They are sad because they have heard him talk about going away. On this evening, full of foreboding, they sense that he is referring to his imminent death. We always experience sadness when someone who has been significant for us, someone we have loved and valued, is taken from us in death. We need to grieve the loss of our loved ones. Yet Jesus wants to bring some light into the sadness, the darkness of spirit, of his disciples. He does so by assuring them that, in going from them, he will be able to do something for them that he would not otherwise be able to do. In returning to the Father, he will be able to send them the Advocate, the Paraclete, the Holy Spirit. In and through this Spirit, Jesus will be present to his disciples in a new and very intimate way, and he will be present in this manner not just to his disciples gathered with him that evening but to all future disciples, including ourselves gathered here. Jesus' death and his resurrection from the dead leads to the outpouring of the Holy Spirit, the Spirit of the risen Lord, upon us all, and, in and through the Spirit, Jesus is within us and among us. That same Spirit is with us in all our dark and difficult times, in all our times of painful loss. The Spirit assures us of the Lord's loving presence at such moments, so that even in our sadness we can experience something of that joy which is the fruit of the Spirit.

8 May, Wednesday, Sixth Week of Easter

John 16:12–15

In the first reading, Paul addresses the people of Athens as seekers after truth. He declares that God wanted all nations to seek the deity and, by feeling their way towards him, to succeed in finding him. Moreover, he says that God, who wants all people to seek and find him, has drawn close to them, because it is in him that we live and move and have our being. Paul is able to announce to the people of Athens that the God whom they have been seeking has been fully revealed in the life, death and resurrection of Jesus, who is God's beloved Son. We have come to believe in Jesus as the full revelation of God, but that doesn't mean that our seeking has come to an end. Those of us who celebrate Jesus as the truth remain seekers after truth, because we recognise that faith is not perfect vision. As Paul says in his first letter to the Corinthians, 'now we see as in a mirror, dimly' (1 Corinthians 13:12). Even as people of faith, we remain on a journey towards what Jesus in the gospel reading calls 'the complete truth'. None of us, no matter how strong and deep our faith, has the complete truth. Jesus declares that one of the roles of the Holy Spirit is to lead us to the complete truth, by calling to our minds all that Jesus has said and done. As Jesus declares in our reading, 'all he tells you will be taken from what is mine'. We are on a shared journey led by the Holy Spirit, and while we may be further on that journey than the people of Athens in the first reading we still have a way to go. Every day, as people of faith we set out again, calling on the Holy Spirit to lead us ever closer to the complete truth.

9 May, Thursday, Sixth Week of Easter

John 16:16–20

When sadness overcomes us for whatever reason, it can be difficult to believe that we will ever be joyful again. Our sadness can drain us of the hope that better times will come. Speaking in the setting of the Last Supper, Jesus says to his disciples in today's gospel reading, 'You will be weeping and wailing.' He acknowledges the sadness and sense of loss that will engulf his disciples when he is put to death on a Roman cross. The onset of such overwhelming sadness will drain them of hope. Yet Jesus immediately announces to them that their sadness will not last for ever: 'Your sorrow will turn to joy.' The killing of Jesus will not be the final act in the drama of Jesus' life. Rather, God's raising Jesus to new life will be the final act of that drama. As Jesus' death gives way to his new risen life, so the sorrow of his disciples will give way to Easter joy, a sharing in the Lord's own joy. The risen Lord continues to say to us that death, our own death and the death of our loved ones, will not be the final act in the drama of our lives. Rather, as God brought Jesus through death to new life, so God will bring us through death to a sharing in the Lord's own risen life. The sorrow associated with death will not be the final emotion. Sorrow will give way to joy, for our loved ones who have died and, in time, for all of us who mourn the death of our loved ones. As followers of a risen Lord, we can sing the words of today's responsorial psalm with an awareness that those who composed it could not possibly have possessed: 'Sing a new song to the Lord, for he has worked wonders.'

10 May, Friday, Sixth Week of Easter
John 16:20–23

In the gospel reading, Jesus reflects upon a woman's experience of giving birth to a child to cast light for his disciples on his forthcoming passion and death. The pain a woman experiences in giving birth is the necessary prelude to the unique joy of holding her newborn child for the first time. In the joy experienced at holding this new life the pain of childbirth is, at least momentarily, forgotten. Jesus is saying that the pain of his coming passion and death for himself and his disciples is the prelude to the new life of Easter in which he and his disciples will rejoice within three days of his death. For the disciples, the sadness of death, of Jesus' departure, will give way to the joy of his new life, his coming to them again. Whereas the sadness of Calvary will be overcome by the joy of Easter, the joy of Easter will never be overcome: 'That joy no one shall take from you.' From the first Easter Sunday onwards, they will continue to live in the light of Easter and there will be a joy in that experience, even in the difficult and troubling moments that lie ahead, of which there will be many. The Lord is reminding us that we always walk in the light of Easter, even when we are experiencing some dark valley or other. We can taste something of the joy of Easter, the Lord's own joy, even when deep sadness comes over us, because the risen Lord is always with us. This light and joy of Easter, which cannot be taken from us, is the foretaste of the eternal light and unending joy of the kingdom of heaven. The light and joy of Easter in the here and now can empower us to be channels of the Lord's light and joy to others, especially to those who struggle to find it.

11 May, Saturday, Sixth Week of Easter
John 16:23–28

Today's first reading from the Acts of the Apostles gives us an insight into how people in the early Church supported one another in faith. We are introduced in that reading to a man called Apollos. By all accounts he was a very impressive figure; he had a sound knowledge of the scriptures; he spoke with great eloquence, and had been given instruction in the faith, in the Way of the Lord. Yet it is clear that he needed further instruction in the faith and that was given to him by a married couple, Priscilla and Aquila. Apollos obviously had gifts that this married couple did not have, yet they had something that he didn't have; they had a fuller understanding of the way of the Lord. Apollos had a great deal to offer but he also had something to receive from this married couple. That is how it is in the Church. We need each other's faith if we are to grow in faith. We need the believing community if we are to grow in our relationship with the Lord. Within the community of faith we have an opportunity to give from our own faith and to receive from the faith of others. As members of the body of Christ, we all have something to offer and we all have something to receive. When it comes to our relationship with the Lord we are always interdependent. We need the Church, the living community of faith; we cannot go it alone. The gospel reading suggests that above all we need the Lord, who comes to us in and through the members of the Church. We need to pray, to ask the Lord for the help that he alone can give us, the help that enables us to do his work, and, indeed, as he says, to do even greater works than he has done. Jesus almost seems to rebuke the disciples when he says in the gospel reading, 'until now you have not asked for anything in my name'. He encourages us to ask, to live our lives as his followers not on our own resources but in union with him, recognising our dependence on him.

13 May, Monday, Seventh Week of Easter

John 16:29–33

When Paul asked the disciples in Ephesus, 'Did you receive the Holy Spirit when you became believers?', they answered, 'No, we were never even told there was such a thing as a Holy Spirit.' It was a very honest acknowledgement of ignorance. The first step in coming to know is often the acknowledgement that we don't know. We are approaching the feast of Pentecost, the feast of the Holy Spirit. Perhaps there is a sense in which we all have a lot to learn about the Holy Spirit. The Holy Spirit was spoken of in the past as the forgotten person of the Blessed Trinity. We can picture God the

Creator and Jesus his Son more easily than we can picture the Holy Spirit. We find images of the Holy Spirit in the scriptures – the dove, fire, the wind – yet we sense that they all fall very far short of the reality. The Holy Spirit is the life presence of God the Father and the risen Lord. It is through the Holy Spirit that the Father and the Son make their home within us and among us. When the Holy Spirit is alive in us, it shows itself in a way of life that reflects the life of God, the life of Jesus, a life of self-giving love. Saint Paul speaks about the fruit of the Spirit. Just as a healthy tree bears good fruit, so a spiritually healthy person, who is alive with the Holy Spirit, will bear the good fruit of the Spirit, what Paul calls 'love, joy, peace, patience, kindness, generosity, faithfulness, gentleness and self-control' (Galatians 5:22–23). When Jesus says to his disciples in today's gospel reading, 'I have told you all this so that you may find peace in me', he is referring to the fruit of the Spirit. He is promising to pour out the Holy Spirit into the lives of his disciples, all of us, the Spirit of God's love, of his own love, and this experience of being unconditionally loved will bring peace, even though, as Jesus says in the gospel reading, the world will bring us trouble of various kinds. As we approach the feast of Pentecost, we pray for a fresh growth of the rich fruit of the Spirit in our lives.

14 May, Tuesday, Saint Matthias, Apostle
John 15:9–17

It is likely that Matthias never expected to find himself a member of the group of twelve that Jesus had formed around himself. The betrayal of Judas and his resulting death created an opening that needed to be filled. Jesus had chosen the twelve personally. How was a replacement for Judas going to be chosen, now that Jesus was no longer present in bodily form? It is clear from the first reading that the members of the early Church believed that Jesus was indeed present, as risen Lord. That is why they turned in prayer to the Lord and asked him to show them which of two possible candidates, Matthias or Barsabbas, he wanted to replace Judas. The disciples understood that Judas's replacement had to be the Lord's choice. Just as he had chosen the original twelve, he would have to choose Judas's replacement. At the same time, the disciples recognised that they also had a role to play. They narrowed the possible candidates down to two, then asked the Lord to show which of the two he had chosen. They used their own judgement, while recognising that the final choice was the Lord's. The disciples' prayer, 'Lord, show us which of these you have chosen', is a prayer we all need to make in some shape or form. We always need to seek what the Lord wants, and not just what we want. We have to draw upon our own human resources in order to make a good decision, like the disciples who narrowed the field down to two candidates. Yet we recognise that any good decision has to be the Lord's decision. His choice has to prevail, and only if our choice corresponds to his choice will it be of any value. The Lord's choice is primary. As Jesus says in the gospel reading, 'You did not choose me, no, I chose you.' Every day we seek to live in accordance with the Lord's choice, the Lord's will for our lives. In that gospel reading, Jesus sums up his choice for us, his will for our lives, very simply: 'Love one another, as I have loved you.'

15 May, Wednesday, Seventh Week of Easter

John 17:11–19

The theme of 'truth' links both readings today. Paul, addressing the elders of the church of Ephesus, declares, 'Even from your own ranks, there will be men coming forward with a travesty of the truth on their lips to induce the disciples to follow them.' There is an acknowledgment there that not every interpretation of the Gospel by the Lord's followers is faithful to the Gospel received from the

Lord. In the gospel reading Jesus prays that God would protect his disciples from the evil one. More positively he prays that God would consecrate them in the truth, in other words, set them apart for the mission of bearing witness to the truth. Earlier in this gospel Jesus had said of himself, 'I am the truth', because he is the full revelation of God's truth in human form. The calling of the disciples, of all of us, is to bear witness to the truth Jesus proclaimed, lived and embodied. Both readings suggest that there will be pressure put upon us to deviate from this truth in some way. Elsewhere in the gospel Jesus promises to send us the Advocate, the Holy Spirit, to lead us to the complete truth. What Jesus refers to in the gospel reading as 'the evil one' leads us away from the truth of Jesus, whereas the Holy Spirit leads us towards the truth Jesus revealed. We spend our lives trying to open ourselves to the leading of the Holy Spirit so that, in the words of Jesus in this Gospel of John, 'You will know the truth and the truth will make you free.'

16 May, Thursday, Seventh Week of Easter
John 17:20–26
Today's gospel is the final part of the prayer of Jesus for his disciples. It is a very striking prayer. In the very last line, Jesus expresses his desire, his prayer, that the love with which God the Father loved him may be in his disciples, so that he, Jesus, may be in them. There is a powerful vision there of the life of the disciple, as one in whom God's love for his Son is alive, and, therefore, Jesus himself is alive. If that became a reality, then the earlier part of Jesus' prayer would come to pass: 'Father, may they be one in us ... may they be one as we are one.' To the extent that God's love is alive in us, to the extent that Jesus is alive in us, we will become one, as God the Father and Jesus are one. It is only the risen Lord living in his disciples who can bring about the quality of unity among his

disciples that Jesus prays for. There is another prayer of Jesus in that reading which shows that allowing the Lord to live in us is a fore-taste of our eternal destiny. Jesus prays, 'Father, I want those you have given me to be with me where I am, so that they may always see the glory you have given me.' Therein lies our ultimate destiny, to be with Jesus where he is, in the many-roomed house of God his Father, so that we may see his glory. If our ultimate destiny is to be with Jesus in heaven, our present calling is to allow Jesus to be with us, to live in us, to allow God's love to live in us. The Lord's com-munion with us and ours with him is what is common to our present and future state. The prayer of Jesus shows that if the Lord's com-munion with us is genuine, it will find expression in our communion with one another, in our becoming one as he and his Father are one.

17 May, Friday, Seventh Week of Easter

John 21:15–19

At the Last Supper, according to the Gospel of John, Jesus announced to his disciples that he loved them as the Father loved him. Jesus went on to call on his disciples to remain in his love. Jesus would love them to the end; his love for them would be faithful. He asked in return that their love for him would be faithful. However, Peter did not remain in Jesus' love; his love for Jesus did not turn out to be faithful, as he denied Jesus three times. That is the context for the risen Lord asking Peter the question three times, in today's gospel reading, 'Simon, son of John, do you love me?' Jesus was giving Peter the opportunity to renew his love, to come home to the Lord's love, and remain in his love once more. Only then could Peter be given the responsibility of the pastoral care of the Lord's flock, the other disciples. Jesus made no mention of Peter's denials. He simply invited him to renew his love. The Lord does not hold our failings against us. When we drift out of his love, when we deny him by our way of life, he always gives us the opportunity to renew our love for him. He personally asks us the same question he asked Peter, 'Do you love me?' and, in prayer, we can give the answer Peter gave, 'Lord, you know I love you.' The Lord then asks us to express our love for him by taking care of others, by acting as a good shepherd to those who need our pastoral care. The Lord needs us all to share in some way in his work of pastoral care, but first, he needs us to keep renewing our own personal love of him. It is our loving communion with the Lord that allows him to work through us.

18 May, Saturday, Seventh Week of Easter
John 21:20–25

The final verses of the Acts of the Apostles, from which we have been reading for the seven weeks of Easter, portrays Paul under house arrest in Rome. The one who had been travelling thousands of miles to preach the Gospel since his call on the road to Damascus now has to stay put for two years. Yet, even in these restricted circumstances, he remains true to his vocation, 'proclaiming the kingdom of God and teaching the truth about the Lord Jesus Christ'. Whether a free man or a prisoner of Rome, Paul remained true to his deepest identity. The circumstances of our own lives may not be all we desire them to be, but we can still remain true to what is deepest and best in us, to the Lord's call, 'Follow me', in the words of today's gospel reading. Just prior to our gospel reading, Jesus had commissioned Peter to shepherd his flock. This was how Peter was to follow Jesus. In the gospel reading, Peter seems preoccupied by the Lord's plans for the beloved disciple: 'What about him, Lord?' Jesus had to bring Peter back to basics: 'Follow me'. The beloved disciple's way of following Jesus would be different from Peter's way. The preaching and teaching of this disciple would become the basic source for the gospel that we now know as John's Gospel. 'This disciple is the one who vouches for these things and has written them down', or has caused them to be written down. We are each called to follow the Lord in accordance with our own unique temperament and set of gifts and limitations. We spend our lives trying to be true to that calling, no matter how unfavourable the circumstances of our lives, declaring with Saint Paul, 'I can do all things through him who strengthens me' (Philippians 4:13)

20 May, Monday, Mary, Mother of the Church
John 19:25–34

Pope Francis inserted the Memorial of the Blessed Virgin Mary, Mother of the Church, into the Church's liturgical calendar, to be celebrated on the Monday after the feast of Pentecost. Pentecost celebrates the birth of the Church and today's feast celebrates Mary as Mother of the Church. According to Luke in the Acts of the Apostles, Mary was present at Pentecost when the Holy Spirit came down upon the disciples. According to John, in today's gospel reading, Mary was present at the foot of the cross as Jesus gave up his spirit, in the sense of his bodily spirit, but also the Holy Spirit. In our gospel reading, the only male disciple at the foot of the cross is the disciple whom Jesus loved, often referred to as the beloved disciple. He is never given a name in this Gospel of John, perhaps to encourage us all to place our own names upon him. The beloved disciple represents us all, because we are all beloved disciples. What Jesus said to his disciples at the Last Supper in this Gospel of John, he says to disciples in every generation: 'As the Father has loved me, so I have loved you.' The beloved disciple stands in for us all at the foot of the cross, and Jesus' words to this disciple are addressed to us all: 'This is your mother'; and Jesus' words to his mother relate to us all: 'Woman, this is your son [or daughter].' Jesus shares his mother with all his disciples, making himself a brother to us all. We are all invited to relate to Mary as our spiritual mother, as one who can lead us to her Son and help to keep us open to the promptings of the Holy Spirit in our lives. Jesus gives us Mary as a wonderful spiritual resource. As she stood by the cross while her Son was dying, so she stands by us as we travel the way of the cross in its various forms. As she joined in prayer with the disciples prior to Pentecost, so she prays with us and for us. It is with confidence that we can turn to her, saying, 'Pray for us, sinners, now and at the hour of our death.'

21 May, Tuesday, Seventh Week in Ordinary Time
Mark 9:30–37

In today's first reading, James declares that conflict between people starts with self-serving desires and ambitions in the human heart. 'You have an ambition that you cannot satisfy, so you fight to get your way.' The truth of what James says is played out in our gospel reading. The disciples of Jesus are at odds with one another, arguing among themselves, because of the self-serving desires and ambitions in their hearts. They all want to be considered the greatest. A little later in Mark's Gospel, James and John will ask for the best seats in Jesus' kingdom, one at his right and the other at his left, which creates more conflict among the twelve. We may have experienced similar situations, where people's self-serving ambition leads to conflict and rows. The response of both James and Jesus to this all-too human phenomenon is very similar. James says, 'Humble yourselves before the Lord, and he will lift you up.' Rather than lifting ourselves up at other people's expense, we 'give in to God', as James says. We allow God, rather than our own self-serving ambitions, to have first place in our lives, allowing God to lift us up. Jesus says that those who want to be first must make themselves last of all and servant of all, including being the servant of those considered at the time the least important and influential members of society, such as children. Allowing God to have first place in our lives is, for Jesus, allowing others to have first place in our lives, especially the most vulnerable. Both James and Jesus show us the kind of ambition that our faith encourages us to cultivate.

22 May, Wednesday, Seventh Week in Ordinary Time
Mark 9:38–40

In one of the episodes of the 1980s' BBC television series, *Yes, Prime Minister*, the leading civil servant, Sir Humphrey Atkins, was shocked to discover that 'one of us', a fellow civil servant, had turned out to be a Russian spy. It was presumed that 'one of us' couldn't do such a thing. Tightly knit groups can generate a certain blindness to the failings of their members, and, sometimes, a disdain for those who are not 'one of us'. In today's gospel reading, the disciples try to stop someone doing good in Jesus' name 'because he was not one of us'. However, in a mild rebuke to his disciples, Jesus declares that he has no objection to someone 'who works a miracle in my name'. Such a person, he says, is unlikely 'to speak evil of me'. We are to rejoice in the good work done by others, regardless of where they stand in relation to our own community of faith. In the words of the Fourth Gospel, 'the Spirit blows where it chooses' (John 3:8). Towards the end of his letter to the Philippians, Paul writes, 'whatever is true, whatever is honourable, whatever is just, whatever is pure, whatever is pleasing, whatever is commendable, if there is anything worthy of praise, think about these things' (Philippians 4:8). Paul draws a very broad circle there. In today's first reading, Saint James writes, 'You never know what will happen tomorrow.' It is also true that you never know what will happen today. Like the disciples in the gospel reading, any day we can come across people who live the Gospel, without, perhaps, having any conscious relationship with the Lord. The Lord speaks powerfully to us through all who do whatever is true, honourable, just and commendable. There is something here to rejoice in. The Lord's work on our behalf is always so much bigger than our work on his behalf.

23 May, Thursday, Seventh Week in Ordinary Time
Mark 9:41–50

When it comes to our relationship with the Lord we are all very much interdependent. We don't come to the Lord on our own. We need the support of other people of faith. We bring each other to the Lord. However, today's gospel reading also recognises that we can lead each other away from the Lord. In the language of the gospel reading, we can be 'an obstacle to bring down one of these little ones who have faith'. The 'little ones' suggests people of faith who are not fully mature in their faith, which is really all of us. We are all on a journey towards a fuller and deeper faith in the Lord and we all need each other's support on the journey. We can also hinder each other, becoming obstacles to each other, on that shared journey, and that is the concern of Jesus in today's gospel reading. As often with Jesus, he speaks in stark, exaggerated language, not to be taken literally, in order to draw attention to an important message. He declares that if anyone proves an obstacle to others on their journey of faith, it would be better if a millstone were hung around their neck and that they were then thrown into the sea. He further declares that those who are an obstacle to the faith of others would be better off without a physical part of the body rather than put their own eternal salvation and that of others at risk. The word 'synod', which we are hearing a lot about, comes from two Greek words, 'with' and 'way', or 'journey'. It means journeying together. The word reminds us that we are on a shared journey towards the Lord and that we have a responsibility to support one another on that journey.

24 May, Friday, Seventh Week in Ordinary Time
Mark 10:1–12

In today's first reading, Saint James refers to 'the patience of Job'. It is one of those biblical phrases that has made its way into day-to-day conversation. We often speak about someone having the patience of Job. Certainly, Job started off being very patient. Everything was taken from him, property, children and home. His wife wanted him to curse God. He refused and instead blessed God, 'The Lord gave; the Lord has taken away. Blessed be the name of the Lord.' However, as we read on in the Book of Job, it is clear that Job soon loses his patience. He rails in anger against God for all that has happened to him and is angrily dismissive of his friends who are trying to support him. Perhaps the biblical author wants us to recognise that admirable patience and explosive anger often reside within the one person, including the person of faith. We know that from our own experience. Patience is a virtue, whereas anger is an emotion. The more we cultivate the virtue of patience, the more we can channel our anger in ways that are creative and life-giving for others. Anger directed by the virtue of patience can be a positive energy that helps to build communion between ourselves and others. In the gospel reading, Jesus speaks about the communion between a husband and wife, a very unique form of communion whereby, as he says, two become 'one body'. Yet we are all called to build communion with others, to help form communities that reflect the community that is God. If we are to do that, we will need to cultivate the virtue of patience so that the potentially divisive emotions, like anger, can be harnessed for a creative purpose. If patience is a virtue, Saint Paul reminds us that it is also the fruit of the Holy Spirit. Becoming a patient person is not primarily down to willpower on our part. It has more to do with a greater openness to the working of the Holy Spirit in our lives.

25 May, Saturday, Seventh Week in Ordinary Time
Mark 10:13–16

Why would Jesus' disciples have tried to stop parents from bringing their children to Jesus for him to bless them? They seem to have
been acting as Jesus' minders. However, Jesus did not appreciate
their efforts to protect him. They have forgotten that a short time
ago Jesus had put his arms around a child and declared to his disciples, 'Whoever welcomes one such child in my name welcomes
me and whoever welcomes me welcomes not me but the one who
sent me.' In turning the children away from Jesus, they were turning Jesus away, and turning God, whom Jesus represented, away.
The disciples must always allow children to come to Jesus, because
Jesus wants children to experience the gift of the Kingdom of God
here and now. Jesus' words are a reminder to us that, as people of
faith, we need to do all we can to introduce children to Jesus. They
have a right to hear the good news and to experience God's unconditional love for them through Jesus. Just as Jesus goes on to put his
arms round the children, to hug them, and to lay his hands on them
in blessing, so the risen Lord today wants to show his love for today's
children, in and through each one of us. Jesus also declares to his
disciples, and to us all, that children have something vitally important to teach us. If they are introduced to God's love for them through
Jesus, they instinctively welcome Jesus, and all that Jesus brings,
into their lives. We all need to have something of that welcoming
attitude of the child towards Jesus. In the words of the gospel reading, we need to welcome the kingdom of God like a little child if
we are to enter it. That means receiving it as a pure, unmerited gift
from God who is so generous as to give the kingdom and all the
blessings it entails freely and without measure to all who are open
to receive it.

27 May, Monday, Eighth Week in Ordinary Time
Mark 10:17–27

In the gospel reading, a nameless man runs up to Jesus and asks him one of the most important questions of life, 'What must I do to inherit eternal life?' He wanted to know which path he should take to bring him to a share in God's life. It is a question for us all. What path must we take to reach the goal that God has destined for us? Jesus answered initially by quoting some of the Ten Commandments, the ones that concern our relationship with others. Jesus was suggesting that the path of life was through others. The way we relate to others will determine whether or not we reach the ultimate destiny of fullness of life that God desires for us. When Jesus saw that this man was already living these commandments, out of love for him he invited him to take another step: 'Jesus looked steadily at him and loved him.' The particular call Jesus gave to this man was very challenging, to sell all his possessions, give his money to the poor and follow him, in the way that Peter, Andrew, James, John, Matthew and others had done. Unfortunately, it was a step too far for the man. Because of his excessive attachment to his great wealth, he wasn't free to take the path that would have been truly life-giving for him, so he walked away sadly. The Lord has a special call for each one of us, beyond the general call of the Ten Commandments. His personal call will be unique to each one of us. We spend our lives trying to discern what the Lord is calling us to do in the here and now. Sometimes, excessive attachments can hold us back from answering the Lord's call. We lack the freedom to go where he is leading us, and that can leave us sad. We need to keep praying for the freedom of the Holy Spirit, so that we can go where the Lord is leading us and live in a way that corresponds to what is deepest and best in us.

28 May, Tuesday, Eighth Week in Ordinary Time

Mark 10:28–31

In today's first reading, Saint Peter says that the prophets were looking and searching hard for the grace that was given to us with the
coming of Jesus. He goes on to say that 'even the angels long to catch
a glimpse of these things'. The author is reminding us of how greatly
we have been blessed and graced through the coming of the Lord.
We can take for granted the gospel that we have heard because it
is so familiar to us. However, it is worth constantly renewing our
appreciation for all that God has revealed to us and given us through
the life, death and resurrection of Jesus. In giving us his Son, God
has given us the greatest gift he could give us. He alone is worth
following and giving our lives to, because he is the way, the truth
and the life. In the gospel reading, Jesus promises that if we do give
our lives to him, if we allow him to shape and direct our lives, then
we will receive much more from the Lord than we will give to him.
Peter had the honesty to say to Jesus in that gospel reading, 'What
about us? We have left everything to follow you.' Having given up
so much, he was wondering what they would gain. Even though it is
a slightly self-serving question, Jesus takes it seriously, declaring
that those who forego personal gain in their efforts to follow him
will receive a hundred times over, not just in eternal life but in the
present time. The way the Lord calls us to take is often the road less
travelled because it is seen as the more difficult road, but if we take
it Jesus assures us we will find life to the full both in the here and
now and in eternity.

29 May, Wednesday, Eighth Week in Ordinary Time

Mark 10:32–45

Sometimes when someone speaks to us about a matter we find difficult to deal with, we can be tempted to move the conversation

on to an easier topic. Today's gospel reading seems to reflect that situation. Jesus was letting his disciples know that in the city of Jerusalem towards which they were journeying he would be condemned and put to death. It had already been said by the evangelist that the disciples were apprehensive as they travelled with Jesus to Jerusalem. What Jesus said could only have made them more apprehensive. Two of the disciples, James and John, immediately strike a very different note from the one Jesus had just struck. They ask him for places of honour when Jesus enters his glory. Jesus had spoken of the cross and shame, and they immediately speak of glory and greatness. He has to bring them back to the painful reality of what lies ahead with the question, 'Can you drink the cup that I must drink or be baptised with the baptism with which I must be baptised?' Jesus will drink the cup of suffering, not because he is in love with suffering, but because suffering will be the inevitable outcome of his life of loving service of God and humanity. As he says of himself at the end of the gospel reading, he is the Son of Man who came not to be served but to serve, and to give his life as a ransom for all. His loving service of us all was a service unto death. Jesus goes on to teach his disciples that within the circle of his followers glory and greatness consist in self-emptying service of others. The Lord wants to continue his mission of loving service of others through each one of us. Whenever we give of ourselves in some way in the service of others, we are making present in the world the Lord's self-emptying love and we will be considered great in the eyes of the Lord.

30 May, Thursday, Eighth Week in Ordinary Time
Mark 10:46–52
I have always admired the tenacity of the blind man of Jericho in today's gospel reading. Hearing that Jesus was passing by, he cried

out, 'Son of David, Jesus, have pity on me.' When some of the crowd around Jesus gave out to him and told him to be quiet, he only shouted out his prayer all the louder. He was determined to make contact with Jesus and would not succumb to the pressure of others to hold his tongue. He strikes me as a good model for us today. It is not always easy to bear witness to our faith in Jesus in today's world. Like the blind man by the roadside in today's gospel reading, we can feel a certain pressure to keep quiet, to become invisible with regard to our faith in the Lord. Yet this tenacious man encourages us to keep the Lord in view, regardless of the pressure to do otherwise. In the gospel reading, Jesus' response to the man was very different from the crowd's response to him. They wanted to silence him. In contrast, Jesus asked the very people who were trying to silence the man to call him over. In the midst of the hostility towards him, the Lord called him. In a similar way, the Lord keeps calling out to us even in those contexts that are not supportive of our relationship with him. If we try to respond to the Lord's call as generously as Bartimaeus did, the Lord will be as generous with us as he was with him.

31 May, Friday, The Visitation of the Blessed Virgin Mary
Luke 1:39–56

The gospel reading for today's feast highlights the value of a certain way of being present to others. It invites us to ask ourselves, 'What is the quality of our presence to others?' Mary went on a journey from Nazareth in Galilee to the hill country in Judea to be present to her cousin Elizabeth. The quality of Mary's presence to Elizabeth is evident in the impact her presence had. The gospel reading says that when Elizabeth heard Mary's greeting, the child leapt in her womb and Elizabeth herself was filled with the Holy Spirit. Elizabeth's being filled with the Holy Spirit immediately resulted in Elizabeth pronouncing a beatitude upon Mary: 'Blessed is she who believed … '. Mary's way of being present to Elizabeth brought out what was best and deepest in Elizabeth. The quality of Elizabeth's presence to Mary also had a profound impact on Mary, drawing forth from Mary her great prayer of praise to God that has come to be known as the Magnificat, after the Latin translation of its opening word. The meeting between these two women, their way of being present to each other, is a commentary on the call of Saint Paul to the church in Rome in today's second reading: 'Have a profound respect for each other'. More important than what we do for each other is the way in which we are present to one another. Even if we don't have the energy or the health to do something for others, our way of being present to them can bring to the surface all that is good, all that is of God, in them.

1 June, Saturday, Eighth Week in Ordinary Time
Mark 11:27–33

Jesus was a person of great authority. He derived his authority from his special relationship with God. He recognised the Temple in Jerusalem as his Father's house and that gave him the authority to cleanse the Temple, disturbing the money changers and those selling pigeons. Because of what he did there, the religious leaders in today's gospel reading come up to him and ask him, 'What authority have you for acting like this? Who gave you this authority?' We know the answer to that question. Jesus had the authority to do what he did because he was God's Son and God was at work in and through him. That is why we take Jesus as our authority today. We recognise him as Lord of our lives. We take our lead from him. We invite him to shape our lives, to direct what we say and do. We invite his Spirit into our lives and we try to open ourselves to the promptings of his Spirit. The Lord is our authority and we know that his authority is a life-giving authority, an authority that sets us free from sin and the fear of death. Earlier in Mark's Gospel, Jesus said he had authority on earth to forgive sins. We gladly submit to the Lord's authority because it is an authority that renews us, heals us and will eventually lead us to eternal life.

3 June, Monday, Ninth Week in Ordinary Time
Mark 12:1–12

The parable that Jesus speaks in today's gospel reading paints a realistic picture of the human tendency towards violence. The response of the tenants to the messengers of the vineyard owner is one of escalating violence. The first two messengers are beaten up; the third messenger is killed; the fourth messenger, who is the son of the vineyard owner, is not only killed but thrown out of the vineyard without any proper burial, a horrifying insult in that culture. The tenants are depicted as knowing full well what they were doing. They recognised the fourth messenger as the owner's son and, therefore, his rightful heir, and in killing him they were intending to gain his inheritance. Jesus saw in this figure of the 'son' a reference to himself and the fate that awaits him. The parable shows human nature at its worst. Yet Jesus' own comment on the parable includes a quotation from one of the Psalms which draws attention to God's good work: 'It was the stone rejected by the builders that became the keystone. This was the Lord's doing and it is wonderful to see.' There was nothing in the story itself that was wonderful to see. Yet Jesus suggests that God can work in a wonderful way even in situations that reveal the worst of human nature. Jesus was crucified by sinners, but God raised him from the dead and made him the keystone of a new community, the Church, where sinners could find the grace of forgiveness and renewal. The gospel reading reminds us that there is no situation so dire as to prevent the Lord from working within it in a life-giving way for others.

4 June, Tuesday, Ninth Week in Ordinary Time
Mark 12:13–17

Today's first reading from the second letter of Peter says, 'Think of our Lord's patience as your opportunity to be saved.' The Lord's patience is our opportunity. When I was young, I used to hear a little jingle, 'Patience is a virtue, keep it if you can, always in a woman, never in a man.' Perhaps there is some truth in that little saying! Patience is certainly a virtue and one we appreciate when we are shown it. Patience is the ability to wait on people. Jesus once spoke a parable about a barren fig tree that the landowner wanted to cut down. However, the landowner's gardener was a much more patient man. He persuaded his master to leave the fig tree for another year, during which he would tend to it to ensure that it bore fruit the following year. Jesus might have seen something of himself in that gardener. He was patient with people, including his own disciples. So many times, they failed to grasp what he was trying to say to them, but he never gave up on them. Even when Peter, the leading disciple, denied him, he didn't give up on him. In today's gospel reading, Jesus' patience is put to the test. The Pharisees and the Herodians asked him what seemed like a serious question: 'Is it permissible to pay taxes to Caesar or not?' In reality, they were not looking for information but, as the gospel reading says, they were trying to catch Jesus out. They weren't being sincere and, according to the gospel reading, Jesus saw through their hypocrisy. Yet he was patient with them, asking them for a coin from their pockets and declaring that Caesar should be given back what belongs to him, but, more importantly, God should be given what belongs to God. What belongs to God, according to Jesus? Just a few verses later in Mark's Gospel, Jesus will answer that question: 'You shall love the Lord your God with all your heart, and with all your soul, and with all your mind, and with all your strength.' It is only God, and God's Son Jesus, who is worthy of our total loving loyalty, certainly not Caesar. Jesus' patience towards his opponents on this occasion was their opportunity to learn a vital lesson for life. The Lord's patience is always our opportunity.

5 June, Wednesday, Ninth Week in Ordinary Time
Mark 12:18–27
The question of the afterlife is one that has intrigued people from very earliest times. In today's gospel reading, Jesus is approached by the members of a Jewish group, the Sadducees, who did not believe in life after death. They approach Jesus as someone whom they know has a different view from theirs on this issue. The question the Sadducees put to Jesus about the woman with seven husbands suggests that they understood life beyond death as simply an extension of this earthly life. However, Jesus' reply suggests otherwise. 'When they rise from the dead, men and women ... are like the angels in heaven.' Life in heaven is not a mirror image of life on earth; it is qualitatively different. Saint Paul speaks about this life beyond death in terms of transformation. 'We shall all be changed,' he says. For one thing, it will be a life with no trace of death in it. Today's first reading declares that Christ has 'abolished death and has proclaimed life and immortality through the Good News'. We would, of course, like to know more about this transformed life. In the Lord's Prayer Jesus refers to heaven as the place where God's will is done to the fullest possible extent. We are invited to pray, 'Thy will be done on earth as it is in heaven'. The transformation that awaits us is all that God wills for us, which, according to Paul, is our being fully conformed to the image of Christ himself.

6 June, Thursday, Ninth Week in Ordinary Time
Mark 12:28–34

I am struck by something Paul says in today's first reading. He refers to himself as 'being chained like a criminal'. Yet he immediately goes on to say, 'but they cannot chain up God's news'. Paul was aware that the Gospel had a power of its own; its impact didn't depend on whether he was free to preach it or not. Even if Paul was chained up and couldn't work, the Lord was at work. Even if Paul could not preach the Gospel, the Gospel was continuing to touch the hearts and lives of many people. Paul was aware that the preaching of the Gospel didn't all depend on him. Even though he was the great apostle to the Gentiles and the Lord needed him, the Lord could work without him. The Lord is bigger than any of us. His Gospel is more powerful than any of us. At the end of the day, we are all only servants of the Lord. He needs us to be his servants, but if there comes a time when we cannot serve for whatever reason, when we are 'chained' in some way, the Lord continues his good work without us. That doesn't mean that we just down tools. Indeed, we can work all the more freely, all the more generously, in the service of the Lord, when we know that it doesn't all depend on us. When we meet with failure of whatever kind, we know the Lord's good work continues. He can even turn our failures to a good purpose. As Paul says in that reading, 'we may be unfaithful, but he is always faithful'. Because we know that the Lord is always faithful to us, our own moments of unfaithfulness or failure do not leave us demoralised. All the Lord asks of us is that we keep striving to love him with all our being, all our heart, soul, mind and strength, in the words of the gospel reading. When we love the Lord in this way, we will begin to love others with the Lord's own love. That is a goal worth seeking; it gives meaning and direction to our lives.

7 June, Friday, The Most Sacred Heart of Jesus
John 19:31–37

In the traditional image of the Sacred Heart, Jesus reveals a heart that has been pierced. That image is probably inspired by today's gospel reading, where a soldier pierced the side of Jesus, and immediately a flow of blood and water came forth. In that culture, blood and water were, in different ways, symbols of life. Through this scene, the evangelist is saying that the death of Jesus has been life-giving for all. We know from experience that truly selfless human love is always life-giving for those who receive such love. Jesus' death on the cross revealed to the full his self-emptying love for us all. It is because his death was an expression of his love, God's love, that it brings us life, symbolised by the flow of blood and water. Earlier in this Gospel of John Jesus had said that no one has greater love than to lay down one's life for one's friends. On the cross, Jesus revealed that greater love to the fullest possible extent. That is why we look upon the cross not just as an instrument of death but as a source of life. Earlier in John's Gospel Jesus had said that he came that we may life and have it to the full, and he completes that life-giving mission on the cross. Jesus was full of God's love throughout his ministry, but especially so on the cross. He calls on us to receive from his fullness, to open our hearts to the love that filled his heart. In the language of Saint Paul in today's second reading, our lives are to be planted in the Lord's love and to be built on his love. Today's feast calls on us to be receptive to the fullness of God's love poured out upon us through the life, death and resurrection of Jesus. In receiving this 'greater love', we will become more alive, and we will be empowered to love one another as the Lord has loved us, thereby becoming the same life-giving presence for others that the Lord is for us.

8 June, Saturday, Ninth Week in Ordinary Time

Mark 12:38–44

In today's gospel reading, the scribes, regarded as experts in the Jewish Law, are identified by Jesus as 'men who swallow the property of widows, while making a show of lengthy prayers'. They have the visible trappings of piety while exploiting others to enrich themselves, stealing the property of the most vulnerable in society, such as widows. One of those widows reveals an extraordinary generosity of spirit in the presence of Jesus and his disciples. In contrast to the mean-spirited scribes, in the words of Paul in today's first reading, she 'chose the right course'. She gave alms to the Temple treasury, only two small copper coins. It was what we used to call a 'pittance', but it was all she had to live on. If generosity is measured not in terms of how much we give but in terms of what we have left after we give, then this widow's generosity knew no bounds. She gave until she had nothing left to give. In a sense, she anticipates the giving of Jesus, who would give himself to others until there was nothing left for him to give; he gave his all on the cross. Perhaps this is why it was only Jesus who noticed this widow and then immediately called over his disciples so that they too would see this woman's extraordinary generosity, a living parable of the kingdom of God. There are times in our lives when we may seem to have little to give, little in the way of material resources, or, perhaps, little in the way of time or energy or imagination. Yet the widow shows us that we can be just as generous, if not more so, at such times than when we seem to have a great deal more to give. Just as Jesus noticed the widow's generosity when most others would have ignored her, the Lord notices our generosity at those times in our lives when we seem to have very little to give, when our tank has run dry. In giving the little we have, the equivalent of two copper coins, when it is all we have to give, we are walking in the footsteps of the one who came not to be served but to serve and we are helping to make the kingdom of God present on earth.

10 June, Monday, Tenth Week in Ordinary Time
Matthew 5:1–12

In today's gospel reading, Jesus declares blessed or fortunate those who embrace a certain way of life. He is saying that those who live according to these values and attitudes are blessed not primarily because of their present situation but because of a future situation that will come about for them through the power and fidelity of God. Those who live according to these values are blessed because of the future that God has in store for them. In the present they may not seem blessed to others. How can it be said that those who mourn are fortunate or blessed? Jesus is saying that those who experience sadness because of the present state of the world and who, as a result, have a passionate commitment to justice, who hunger and thirst for what is right, and are prepared to be persecuted in the cause of right, will be comforted, will be satisfied, in the kingdom of heaven. The attitudes and values that Jesus espouses in the Beatitudes make people vulnerable in the eyes of the world, such as being poor in spirit, gentle, merciful to others, pure in heart. They are not a recipe for getting on in the world. They are the opposite of the competitive and grasping spirit that stops at nothing to get ahead, that will allow no one to stand in the way of reaching the top. Yet these are all attitudes and values that give space to God in one's life, thereby promoting the coming of God's kingdom, the doing of God's will in the world. God in Jesus looks upon such people and says to them, 'Congratulations! You are indeed blessed, because you are living as I intended, as sons and daughters of God, and you will know a happiness that this world cannot give.' Jesus is saying that this is the path to happiness not just in the next life but in this life too.

11 June, Tuesday, Saint Barnabas, Apostle
Matthew 10:7–13

In the gospel reading, Jesus sends out the twelve apostles on mission within Galilee, to proclaim the good news that the kingdom of heaven was at hand. In the first reading, the church of Antioch sends out Paul and Barnabas on mission to places far beyond Antioch, to Cyprus and parts of modern-day Turkey. Paul and Barnabas were leading lights of the church in Antioch and yet the members of the church were happy to share these two leaders with others, far beyond their shores. Of the two, Paul is better known to us because of his extraordinary missionary journeys and the many letters that have come down to us from him. Yet Barnabas was very significant in another way. It was Barnabas who created an opening in the early Church for Paul, when others were still suspicious of him because of his past persecution of the Church. As today's first reading says, it was Barnabas who went looking for Paul in Tarsus, his native city, and brought him to Antioch, because he saw that there was a great opening for Paul's gifts in this city where the Gospel had been preached to pagans for the first time. Barnabas was what we call today an 'enabler'. It is not surprising that his nickname in the early Church, according to the Acts of the Apostles, was 'son of encouragement'. That role of enabler or encourager remains a vital one in the Church today. We all have the capacity to create openings where the gifts of someone else can flourish for the service of the whole Church. It takes a certain humility to create a space where others can flourish to their potential in the service of the Lord. It is the attitude of John the Baptist, expressed in his comment with regard to

Jesus, 'He must increase, but I must decrease'. The feast of Barnabas invites us to ask, 'What can I do for someone so that Jesus may increase today?'

12 June, Wednesday, Tenth Week in Ordinary Time
Matthew 5:17–19

Jesus was a Jew and he appreciated all that was good and valuable in his own religious tradition. That is why he says in today's gospel reading, 'I have come not to abolish [the Law or the Prophets] but to complete them.' He wanted to take what was good in his own religious tradition and lift it up to an even higher level. In his teaching, he interpreted the Jewish Law in a way that made clearer what God was saying through the Law. As someone who was closer to God than any human being who ever lived, Jesus was able to show what really mattered most to God in the Jewish Law, namely, love of God and love of neighbour, the hunger and thirst for God's justice, and mercy towards all in need. That is why we, as followers of the risen Lord, read the Jewish scriptures, the law, the prophets and the writings, in the light of all that Jesus said and did. Indeed, we try to read, to interpret, the whole of life in the light that Jesus has given us. The great spiritual writer, C. S. Lewis, wrote, 'I believe in Christianity as I believe that the sun has risen; not only because I see it, but because by it I see everything else.' Our calling is to see everything in the light of the Lord's presence, which shines through his Word, the sacraments and the community of believers.

13 June, Thursday, Tenth Week in Ordinary Time
Matthew 5:20–26

Behaviour was very important to Jesus and to his Jewish tradition. Yet, in today's gospel, he focuses on what resides in the human heart, the source of our behaviour. Only a small proportion of the human race commits murder. However, we are all familiar with the emotion of anger. Sometimes our anger is a sign that some injustice is being done. Our anger can be a signal that all is not well with our world. The gospels show that Jesus himself was angry at times. Jesus channelled his anger in a way that was beneficial for the disciples. Many people's commitment to working for justice is motivated by anger at the injustices being done to others. Although anger can be a force for good, Jesus was well aware that it can also be a force for harm. We all need to be reflective about our anger. In the gospel reading, Jesus is inviting us to look below the surface of what we do to what is within. How do we speak about others? What emotions do we have towards them? He calls for a deeper virtue than that of the scribes and Pharisees. He wants to renew the human heart, knowing that it is only such deep-seated renewal that can give rise to a way of living that conforms to God's will for our lives. The ultimate source of the deeper virtue that Jesus calls for is the Holy Spirit because it is only the Spirit who can truly change our hearts, our depths. As Saint Paul declares in our second reading, 'the Spirit reaches the depths of everything', including our own depths.

14 June, Friday, Tenth Week in Ordinary Time
Matthew 5:27–32

Today's responsorial psalm is the prayer of the seeker: 'It is your face, O Lord, that I seek.' We can perhaps easily identify with that psalm, because we are all seekers, to some extent. What we are ultimately seeking and searching for is none other than the Lord. 'Our hearts are restless until they rest in God,' according to Saint Augustine. It is the seeker in us that makes all of us pilgrims, people on a journey towards the Lord. Elijah, the prophet, in today's first reading, was clearly such a seeker. He set out on a journey, on a pilgrimage, to the mountain of God, Mount Sinai, or Mount Horeb, as it was also called.

When he reached that mountain, he met with the Lord, but not in the way he might have expected. Within that biblical culture, it was expected that God would reveal himself in the more extraordinary phenomena of nature, in fire or storm or earthquake. However, on this occasion, God revealed himself to Elijah in a much more subtle and more humble way, in what the reading calls 'the sound of a gentle breeze'. Another well-regarded modern translation of the Bible expresses it somewhat differently, as a 'sound of sheer silence'. I prefer that translation. 'Sheer silence' is not easy to come by in the times in which we live. Yet it is there that the Lord often reveals himself to us most clearly. Because silence is not a feature of our culture, we often have to seek it out. To seek silence is, in a very real way, to seek the Lord, because it is in silence that we become most attuned to the Lord's passing by. Our attentive listening to the Lord in the sound of sheer silence empowers us to live out the call of the Sermon on the Mount as expressed in today's gospel reading.

15 June, Saturday, Tenth Week in Ordinary Time
Matthew 5:33–37
Today's gospel reading is one example of the teaching of Jesus that has not generally been taken literally. In the history of Christianity, only radical groups have taken Jesus' injunction not to swear an oath seriously. Does this gospel have anything to say to us today, then? The ruling assumes that, within the community of disciples, people's word should be trusted to such an extent that the taking of oaths is rendered unnecessary. It can be assumed that when people say 'Yes', they mean 'Yes', and when they say 'No', they mean 'No'. We all know from our own experience that this is not always the case. Like the son in the parable of the two sons, to be found only in Matthew's Gospel, we sometimes say 'Yes', although our subsequent action, or lack of action, shows that we were really saying 'No'. In recent

decades, the value of transparency has come to the fore, in response to individuals and institutions declaring one thing and doing another. In the Gospel of John, Jesus says of Nathanael, 'Here is truly an Israelite in whom there is no deceit.' As they say nowadays, 'What you see is what you get.' It was above all Jesus who was incapable of deceit. As he said to Annas, the father-in-law of Caiaphas, again in the Gospel of John, 'I have spoken openly to the world … I have said nothing in secret.' Jesus was the ultimate transparent one, because the light of God's loving presence shone fully through him, without the darkness of deceit blocking it in any way. We may never be transparent in the way Jesus was, yet we would all welcome Jesus being able to say of us, 'Here is truly a disciple in whom there is no deceit.'

17 June, Monday, Eleventh Week in Ordinary Time
Matthew 5:38–42

Those in positions of power can be very tempted to seize land that doesn't belong to them, often with deadly consequences for others. The war in Ukraine is a very obvious example of such behaviour. We find it again in our first reading. King Ahab wanted a vineyard that belonged to Naboth to use as a vegetable garden because it lay alongside the landholding of the king. Understandably, Naboth refused the request of the king. This was land that had been in his family for generations. People who fight to defend their land often do so because they know that they have a historical claim to it. Ahab's wife was less scrupulous than Ahab, and she arranged to have Naboth condemned to death by stoning on trumped-up charges. That also has a contemporary ring to it. Those who want to hang on to power at all costs find ways to silence or do away with political opponents. The combination of Ahab's greed and Jezebel's unscrupulous nature meant Ahab got his vineyard and Naboth lost his life. When land or territory become more important than human life, terrible things happen. The teaching of Jesus in today's gospel reading could not be further from the behaviour of Ahab and his wife in the first reading. Great evil was done to Naboth. How is evil to be dealt with and addressed? Jesus declares in the gospel reading that evil is not to be responded to with more evil. The principle of 'an eye for an eye' leaves everyone blind. Jesus calls on us to overcome evil with goodness. It can be difficult to know what that means in practice, especially in a war situation. Yet the principle of overcoming evil with goodness is worth holding on to, especially when the temptation is very strong to keep returning evil with more evil.

18 June, Tuesday, Eleventh Week in Ordinary Time
Matthew 5:43–48

The Sermon on the Mount is probably the most challenging part of Jesus' teaching, and today's gospel reading is the most challenging part of the Sermon on the Mount. 'I say this to you: love your enemies and pray for those who persecute you.' It seems to go against every natural instinct to ask people to love those who are out to destroy them and to show their love for them by praying for them. How could a whole people who are suffering from an unprovoked invasion be expected to love those who invaded their land and have caused so much misery? The love that Jesus calls for here is not an emotion. No one could have any other emotion but extreme anger in the face of unprovoked aggression. The love Jesus asks for resides in the will. He asks us to want what is best, even for our enemies. We are to desire, to hope, to pray that our enemies would come to embrace the path that God wants for them and that will bring them happiness in this life and in the next. We are to hope and pray that they would be delivered from the evil to which they have succumbed, and we are to do whatever is in our power to help bring about such deliverance. In other words, we are to be instruments of God's saving purpose for their lives, in whatever small way we can. Jesus mentions praying for our enemies, and that may be as much as we can do at times. However, such prayer for the enemy surely falls within the ambit of Jesus' wider promise elsewhere in the Sermon on the Mount: 'Ask and you will receive, seek and you will find.'

19 June, Wednesday, Eleventh Week in Ordinary Time
Matthew 6:1–6, 16–18

In *Murder in the Cathedral* T. S. Eliot has Thomas à Becket say, 'The last temptation is the greatest treason / To do the right thing for the wrong reason.' In today's gospel reading, Jesus is concerned with the tendency of religious people to do the right thing for the wrong reason. Almsgiving, prayer and fasting were important Jewish practices, which Jesus valued. However, he warns against doing them for the wrong reason, in order to attract the notice of others, thereby receiving recognition and honour for oneself. Practices that seem God-centred and other-centred can be, in reality, self-serving. Writing to the church in Philippi from prison, Paul declares, 'These proclaim Christ out of love, knowing that I have been put here for the defence of the gospel; the others proclaim Christ out of selfish ambition, not sincerely but intending to increase my suffering in my imprisonment.' Even the preaching of the Gospel can become self-serving. Yet, Paul asks, 'What does it matter?' and answers, 'Just this, that Christ is proclaimed in every way, whether out of false motives or true.' Paul is suggesting that the preaching of Christ can touch the hearts of others, even if done out of selfish ambition. He seems to be implying that doing the right thing for the wrong reason is better than not doing the right thing. Yet he clearly favours doing the right thing for the right reason. It is always good to ask ourselves, 'Why am I doing what I am doing?' 'Who is being served here?' 'Is my giving ultimately with a view to getting?' In his first letter to the Corinthians, Paul declares that 'if I give away all my possessions ... but do not have love, I gain nothing.' It is the self-emptying love of Christ in our lives, the fruit of the Holy Spirit, that gives value to all we say and do.

20 June, Thursday, Eleventh Week in Ordinary Time
Matthew 6:7–15

Jesus contrasts the prayer that is to characterise his disciples with the prayer of the pagans, who 'think that by using many words they will make themselves heard'. They consider it necessary to use a multitude of words to get an indifferent deity's attention. If they use many words, sooner or later they will hit on the right formula to engage their god. However, Jesus declares that God his Father, and our Father, knows what we need before we even ask him. He is not a distant God who needs to be prodded into action by frantic prayers. The God whom Jesus reveals is unimaginably generous. What matters is to dispose our hearts to receive his generosity. The prayer that Jesus gives his disciples is with a view to opening up our hearts to all that God wants to give us. The opening petitions imply a surrender of ourselves to God's purpose for our lives, the prayer for the honouring of God's name, the coming of God's kingdom and the doing of God's will. The remaining petitions acknowledge our poverty before God and our need for all that God can and wants to give us, the satisfaction of our physical and spiritual hunger, forgiveness of our sins and the readiness to pass on God's forgiveness to others, and protection from the evil forces that seek to undermine our relationship with God. This surrender of ourselves to what God wants, and this recognition of our poverty and need before God disposes our heart to receive all that God wants to give us and to give our world through us.

21 June, Friday, Eleventh Week in Ordinary Time

Matthew 6:19–23

The words of Jesus in today's gospel reading from the Sermon on the Mount invite us to ask the question, 'Where does our treasure lie?' 'What is it that we truly treasure?' Jesus makes a contrast between treasures on earth and treasures in heaven, and he calls on us to store up treasures in heaven rather than treasures on earth. What does it mean to store up treasures in heaven? Elsewhere in the gospels, Jesus speaks about being rich in the sight of God, as distinct from being rich in worldly terms. We are rich in the sight of God when we use our possessions in the service of others, to promote their well-being. The Samaritan in the parable of the Good Samaritan is a good example of such a person. He had earthly resources; mention is made of oil, wine, a horse, money. That would suggest he was reasonably well-off in the culture of the time. Yet he used his earthly treasures to store up treasure in heaven, to become rich in the sight of God, by placing them at the disposal of someone from whom everything had been taken and who was literally at death's door. This is what Jesus had referred to a little earlier in this Sermon on the Mount as letting our light shine in the sight of all, so that, seeing our good works, they may give praise to God in heaven. In today's gospel reading, Jesus says, 'where your treasure is, there will your heart be also'. The Samaritan treasured the broken man lying by the roadside more than he treasured his possessions, so his heart was moved by this stranger's plight. He is very much the Jesus figure we are all called to grow up into.

22 June, Saturday, Eleventh Week in Ordinary Time

Matthew 6:24–34

We all worry about something or someone. We worry about those we care for and love. We worry over what matters to us. Jesus must have worried about his disciples, especially when they did not seem to be fully receptive to his message. There is, however, a certain kind of worry that can take over our lives and leave us with very little freedom to attend to others. This seems to be the kind of worry that Jesus warns against in today's gospel reading, a fretful preoccupation about what is not of ultimate importance. We can be overly preoccupied about food and clothing; we can fret about what we don't yet possess. Jesus calls on us to have the kind of trusting relationship with God that preserves us from being unnecessarily anxious and fretful. He wants us to trust that God will look after us, just as he looks after the flowers of the field and the birds of the air, and, we, of course, are even more precious in his sight than those. There is a healthy worry, but there is also an unhealthy worry that Jesus is warning against, a worry that shows a lack of trust in God as our loving and caring Father. At the end of the gospel reading, Jesus suggests what we need to be anxious about, namely, God's kingdom and his righteousness, the coming of God's kingdom and the way of life that helps to bring it about. Jesus says that if we give this the priority it deserves, then God will see to it that all our other needs will be met.

24 June, Monday, The Nativity of Saint John the Baptist
Luke 1:57–66, 80

Who gets to name a newborn child? Today we would presume it was the child's parents who made that decision. In the time and place of Jesus, the naming of a child was more of a decision of the wider family and community, rather than a decision just for the parents. In today's gospel reading, the neighbours and relations seem to have decided that Elizabeth's child would be called Zechariah after his father. However, the child's mother stood up against this consensus, declaring that he would be called John, after the name given to him by the angel Gabriel at the annunciation of the child's birth to

Zechariah. The wider family and community were stunned: 'No one in your family has that name.' Zechariah, who had been rendered dumb for doubting the promise made by Gabriel, confirmed in writing that his child would be called John. A new beginning in God's dealings with his people called for a new name, a name that conveyed the nature of this new beginning. Many Hebrew names have a religious meaning and the name 'John' means 'God is gracious'. The child of Elizabeth and Zechariah would announce the coming of someone who would reveal God's gracious love in a powerfully new way. According to the gospel reading, people were asking, 'What will this child turn out to be?' He turned out to be the adult that God wanted him to be, the one who witnessed to the arrival of God's special messenger to humanity and who prepared people to welcome this messenger by calling on them to be baptised. John would lead people to Jesus, God's gracious gift to all. On this feast of his birthday, we might give thanks for all those people in our lives who have led us to Jesus and have helped us to see him more clearly.

25 June, Tuesday, Twelfth Week in Ordinary Time
Matthew 7:6, 12–14

On two occasions in Matthew's Gospel, Jesus reduces everything in the Law and the Prophets to a simple formula. In today's gospel reading he declares that the Law and the Prophets can be summed up as 'Treat others as you would like them to treat you'. Later in this gospel Jesus declares that the Law and the Prophets can be reduced to two commandments, the commandment to love the Lord our God with all our heart, soul and mind, and the commandment to love our neighbour as ourselves. The first summary can be interpreted in the light of the second. How would we like others to treat us? We would like them to love us as they would love themselves; we would like their love for us to flow from their love of God, so that their love of us reflects something of God's love for them and for us. We would all wish to have an experience of God's love for us in and through those who relate to us. We would like to be treated by others in the same loving, merciful and compassionate way that God treats us. Jesus invites us to imagine what that would be like and then to treat others in a similar way. Jesus himself was the fullest revelation of God's love for others. In today's gospel reading, he is calling on us to be Jesus figures for others. There is something of the 'narrow gate' and the 'hard road' about this calling, in the language of today's gospel reading. Yet, in the power of the Holy Spirit, we can all be Jesus figures in our world today, to some degree.

26 June, Wednesday, Twelfth Week in Ordinary Time
Matthew 7:15–20
The expression 'wolves in sheep's clothing', based on today's gospel reading, has made its way into common speech. We instinctively understand what the image conveys. The sheep and the wolf are at opposite ends of the animal spectrum. The wolf is the enemy of the sheep and the sheep are helpless before the predatory instincts of the wolf, which is why the protection of a good shepherd was so important for sheep in the time of Jesus, and remains so today in many parts of the world. In John's Gospel, in contrast, Jesus speaks of the hired hand who 'sees the wolf coming and leaves the sheep and runs away, and the wolf snatches them and scatters them'. A wolf in sheep's clothing is someone who, in reality, is the opposite of his or her public persona. It is a case of what you see being the opposite of what you get. Such people can do untold damage to the unsuspecting in all spheres of life. Jesus goes on to say that it is the fruit of people's lives that allows us to judge their true reality. In his letter to the Galatians, Paul speaks of the fruit of the Spirit as 'love,

joy, peace, patience, kindness, generosity, faithfulness, gentleness and self-control'. In John's Gospel, Jesus declares that 'those who abide in me and I in them bear much fruit', and goes on to specify this fruit as loving one another as he has loved us. In Matthew's Gospel, from which we are reading at present, the 'good fruit' are the good works that flow from the values and attitudes articulated in the Beatitudes and the Sermon on the Mount as a whole. When we open our hearts fully to the Holy Spirit and allow the Lord to live in us, then the Lord will continue his good works through us and there will be harmony between how we appear to others and who we are in reality.

27 June, Thursday, Twelfth Week in Ordinary Time
Matthew 7:21–29
The image in Jesus' parable of a house built on rock and a house built on sand has certain resonances for us today. We are familiar with houses built in places where they should not have been built, such as on the natural flood plains of a river. As a result, when storms of heavy rain come, the excess water has nowhere to go and that can cause flooding further on down the river. The quality of a house relates as much to where the house is built, what it is built on, as to the actual fabric of the house. The most important part of a house is often what is not visible, the foundations. By means of this parable Jesus is inviting us to reflect on the foundations of our lives. Are our lives built on solid foundations, on rock, such that when the storms of life come, we will stand firm? As with the house, the most important feature of our lives is what is not most visible, the foundations our lives. We do that by listening to his word and putting it into practice. When our lives are shaped by the Lord and his word, when they are directed by the Lord's Spirit, they are solidly grounded and we will be able to withstand the worst that life can throw at us. In

one of his letters, Paul speaks about being 'rooted and grounded in love', in the love of Christ. When our lives are grounded in Christ's love for us and we allow that love to flow through us, then we walk and stand on solid ground.

28 June, Friday, Twelfth Week in Ordinary Time
Matthew 8:1–4

The leper in today's gospel reading did something very daring in approaching Jesus for healing. According to the Jewish Law he should have kept himself apart from everyone. There was a necessary social barrier erected between himself and everyone else. Yet, in his desperation and in his faith in Jesus, he broke through this barrier. Jesus, in turn, by stretching out his hand and touching the leper, did something very daring. It was against the Jewish Law to approach a leper, never mind to touch one. Yet Jesus was prepared to break through barriers of any kind to make contact with people in their brokenness and in their need. Jesus' gesture in touching the leper and declaring him cured shows us his entire ministry in miniature, God's outreach through him in compassion and healing to afflicted humanity. A meeting took place between Jesus and the leper that, according to the religious law at the time, should not have happened. It happened because the leper was desperate to meet Jesus and Jesus was even more desperate to meet him. The Lord is desperate to meet all of us and to touch our lives with his compassionate and healing presence, especially when we find ourselves shunned by others. What we need in response is something of the strong desire, the desperation, of the leper, who is prepared to stop at nothing to connect with Jesus. As the leper came up to Jesus and bowed down before him, we do the same whenever we pray. Our seeking the Lord in prayer opens us up to experience the Lord's even stronger seeking of us.

29 June, Saturday, Saints Peter and Paul, Apostles

Matthew 16:13–19

Peter and Paul were two very different people who, on at least one important issue in the early Church, were seriously at odds with one another. Peter wanted pagans who entered the Church to submit to the Jewish Law, whereas Paul insisted that this was an unnecessary imposition on them. Peter was a fisherman from Galilee, a predominately rural area. Paul was from the university city of Tarsus, in the south of modern-day Turkey. Peter was an Aramaic-speaking Jew; Paul was a Greek-speaking Jew. Peter probably just had the very basic education of his time and place; Paul was clearly a very well-educated and literate person. Peter, of course, knew Jesus personally and was with him throughout his public ministry. Paul only ever encountered the risen Lord. Peter's mission was primarily to preach the Gospel to the Jews. Paul's mission was to preach the Gospel primarily to pagans. According to Paul, in his letter to the Galatians, he met Peter for the first time in the city of Jerusalem, some three years after the risen Lord appeared to Paul: 'After three years, I did go up to Jerusalem to visit Cephas and stayed with him fifteen days.' No doubt, on that occasion, Peter had an opportunity to share with Paul his own experiences of Jesus during his public ministry. In spite of their many differences, they were both equally dedicated to serving the Lord. According to the first reading, Peter was imprisoned for his work of preaching the Gospel. In the second reading Paul speaks as one who is already 'being poured away as a libation', a drink offering in the Temple. They were each put to death because of their faith in Christ during the persecution of the church in Rome ordered by Nero, who blamed the Christians of Rome for the great fire in the city. The Lord worked very differently but very powerfully through each of them.

The Lord wishes to work through each of us and will do so in a way that is unique to each of us. The Lord needs diversity, not uniformity. Yet he needs us to work in harmony, like the different parts of one body. Sometimes our diversity can cause tension, as sometimes happened between Peter and Paul, but such tension can be healthy and can ultimately serve the Lord's purposes. Our tensions can be resolved if, like Peter and Paul, we keep our eyes fixed on the risen Lord whose servants we are.

1 July, Monday, Thirteenth Week in Ordinary Time
Matthew 8:18–22

The request of one of Jesus' disciples seems very understandable – 'let me go and bury my father first', before continuing on as Jesus' disciple. After all, the burial of the dead was considered a sacred duty in the Jewish tradition. However, the disciple's request does not necessarily mean that his father has just died and is in need of burial. More likely the man is asking to delay his departure to follow Jesus until after he has discharged his duty of caring for his aged parent until his death. His father's death could be some time away. Jesus was saying to this disciple, who had already decided to follow Jesus, that the call to follow is more urgent than that. It can't be put off until some indefinite time in the future. The call is for the present moment. The disciple had a strong desire to become a close follower of Jesus but he was putting off acting on it, for family reasons. The Lord often calls us to do something in the here and now and we can be tempted to put off responding to the call until some time in the indefinite future. When we put off acting in a way we feel called to act, the opportunity can pass us by. We may have had the experience of being prompted to do something worthwhile, without delaying, and, in spite of certain resistances in us, we responded to the prompt and then we discovered that it was well worth doing. Our calling is to be as open as possible to what the Lord is asking of us that particular day. In the words of a well-known hymn, 'This is the day the Lord has made, let us rejoice and be glad in it.'

2 July, Tuesday, Thirteenth Week in Ordinary Time
Matthew 8:23–27

The gospel reading suggests the suddenness of the storm on the Sea of Galilee: 'without warning a storm broke over the lake'. Most of us like to have some sense of what is coming our way, especially if it is unpleasant. Yet we know from experience that misfortune can strike us without warning. When we have no warning of some traumatic experience, and have not been able to prepare ourselves for it, we feel very vulnerable when it arrives. The disciples' sense of vulnerability is evident in their cry to the sleeping Jesus, 'Save us, Lord, we are going down.' The cry of the disciples in the corresponding scene in Mark's Gospel is, 'Teacher, do you not care that we are perishing?' Whereas this sounds like a rebuke of Jesus, in Matthew the cry of the disciples is more in the nature of a prayer. It almost has a liturgical ring to it. We are hearing here, perhaps, the prayer of Matthew's church in their time of great distress. It is a prayer that can be prayed by the Church in every era, and by individual believers, 'Save me, Lord, I am going down'. The sleep of Jesus suggests his sense that, in spite of the howling wind and breaking waves, all would be well. There was a calmness within Jesus that belied the outer disturbance that so frightened the disciples. Jesus' inner calmness was soon reflected in his calming of the storm. There are times in our lives when we need to enter the Lord's calmness by turning to him in prayer so that we too can remain calm, even as the storm is howling, trusting that the Lord is stronger than the storm and that the storm will eventually pass.

3 July, Wednesday, Saint Thomas, Apostle
John 20:24–29

In many ways, Thomas is the representative of us all. When the disciples were full of Easter joy on that Easter evening, declaring to Thomas, 'We have seen the Lord', he couldn't bring himself to believe their good news. He had been devastated once by the crucifixion of Jesus; he wasn't going to have his hopes dashed so cruelly again by wishful thinking. Unless very clear conditions were met, Thomas defiantly declares, 'I refuse to believe'. Thomas' doubts speak to our own doubts. There is always some element of doubt in our faith, because, as Saint Paul says in one of his letters, 'now we see as in a mirror dimly, then we will see face to face' (1 Corinthians 13:12). It is only in eternity that we will see the Lord face to face. In this life our seeing the Lord with the eyes of faith will always be a seeing dimly. Thomas was on a journey towards Easter faith, but he was travelling that journey at a slower pace than the other disciples. Everyone's journey towards a deeper, fuller faith is unique to them. When the risen Lord appeared to the disciples a week later, this time with Thomas present, there was no rebuke of Thomas for his refusal to believe the message of the other disciples. There was the same greeting from the Lord, 'Peace be with you', and an invitation to Thomas to doubt no longer but believe. The Lord always meets us where we are; he comes to us, as we are. Then, in response to the Lord's greeting, out of the mouth of the sceptic came one of the greatest confessions of faith in all four gospels, 'My Lord and my God.' Scepticism and deep faith can often be found in one and the same person. On this feast of Saint Thomas, we are invited to make Thomas's confession of faith our own, wherever we happen to find ourselves on our faith journey.

4 July, Thursday, Thirteenth Week in Ordinary Time
Matthew 9:1–8

When people bring a paralytic on a stretcher to Jesus, what they are hoping for is that Jesus would heal the man's paralysis. However, Jesus immediately goes to a deeper issue, assuring the paralytic that his sins are forgiven. There is no suggestion in the text that his physical paralysis was an outward expression of his sin. He is no greater a sinner than anyone else. All need assurance that God's forgiveness is abundantly available through Jesus, whose very name, according to Matthew, means 'he will save his people from their sins' (Matthew 1:21), and who, at the Last Supper, declares that 'this [cup of wine] is my blood of the covenant, which is poured out for many for the forgiveness of sins' (Matthew 26:28). Some scribes declare Jesus to be blaspheming for making a declaration that pertains to God alone. However, Matthew has already referred to Jesus as Emmanuel, 'God is with us' (Matthew 1:23). God's power of forgiveness is present on earth through Jesus. Jesus then heals the man of his paralysis to demonstrate this deeper truth. We may not all be physically paralysed but we are all equally in need of God's forgiveness. The gospel reading assures us that God's forgiveness is personally present to each one of us in a very complete way through Jesus, now risen Lord. Elsewhere in Matthew's Gospel, we hear that this free gift of God's abundant mercy requires us to forgive others as we have been forgiven (Matthew 18:21–35).

5 July, Friday, Thirteenth Week in Ordinary Time
Matthew 9:9–13

The call of Matthew, the tax collector, suggests that the Lord does not see someone's profession or former way of life as a block to their becoming his disciple and sharing in his mission. As Paul declares in his first letter to the Corinthians, 'God chose what is low and despised in the world, things that are not, to reduce to nothing things that are' (1 Corinthians 1:28). The Lord is like the fisherman who casts a very wide net that brings in all sorts of fish, or like the sower who scatters seed with abandon so that it falls on all sorts of ground. Matthew may have been an unlikely candidate to become a member of Jesus' inner circle, but according to the gospel reading, 'he got up and followed him'. The Pharisees were scandalised at the kind of people with whom Jesus shared table. Yet the gospels suggest that Jesus had a very broad table. He was ready to share table with the religious leaders and with those whom the religious leaders considered sinners. Jesus knew that all were sinners and in need of God's mercy. All were alike in that regard. What distinguished them was their awareness of their need of God's mercy and their openness to receive this gift from Jesus. Jesus also expected those who received God's mercy to be merciful in their dealings with others. Such a merciful attitude to others was lacking in the Pharisees, even though this was clearly revealed to be God's will in the scriptures they cherished. 'What I want is mercy, not sacrifice' (Hosea 6:6). In celebrating God's mercy, as Jesus did at table with tax collectors and sinners, we are called to share with others the mercy we celebrate.

6 July, Saturday, Thirteenth Week in Ordinary Time
Matthew 9:14–17
In today's first reading, the prophet Amos announces the coming of a time when 'the mountains will run with new wine', when people will again 'plant vineyards and drink their wine'. In the gospel reading, Jesus declares that the 'new wine' of his ministry requires new wineskins. The traditional regulations relating to fasting are not compatible with the new wine Jesus brings because they are more

suited to a time of mourning than to the period of his ministry which had more of the character of a wedding celebration. A wedding celebration often drew in the entire village. It was a rare opportunity for people to enjoy a feast with good food and wine. In every age the community of believers needs to find wineskins that can contain the new wine of Jesus' ministry. Is there a celebratory element to the way we preach the Gospel, to how we live out our faith, to how we worship together? On one occasion, Jesus associated children enacting a funeral with the ministry of John the Baptist and children pretending to play the flute (as at a wedding) with his own ministry: 'We played the flute for you, and you did not dance; we wailed and you did not weep' (Luke 7:32). In the past, certain expressions of the Christian faith, including within the Roman Catholic tradition, have seemed more funereal than celebratory. God's gift of Jesus to us is always good news, even when our own personal circumstances leave a lot to be desired. This is why Paul, while in prison, could say to the members of the church in Philippi, many of whom 'were suffering for him [Christ]' (Philippians 1:29), to 'Rejoice in the Lord always; again I will say, Rejoice' (Philippians 4:4).

8 July, Monday, Fourteenth Week in Ordinary Time
Matthew 9:18–26

In today's first reading, the Lord promises to lead Israel out into the wilderness. There he will speak to her heart and she will respond to him, as she once did. In the gospel reading, two members of God's people respond to Jesus. One, a synagogue official, approached Jesus in a public and confident way, as befits his status, and asked Jesus to lay hands on his daughter so that her life will be saved. The other, a woman with a flow of blood, approached Jesus in a very furtive, hidden way, in keeping with her non-status within the synagogue community. She only wanted to touch Jesus' cloak, without making herself known to anybody. However, Jesus refused to treat her as if she were invisible. As the synagogue official spoke directly to Jesus, Jesus wanted to speak directly to the woman. He saw no essential difference between the approach of the official and the woman. They were both in need, both had the faith to reach out to Jesus for help, and Jesus responded equally generously to them both. We all have our own way of approaching the Lord. We do so in a way that is unique to us and that reflects the circumstances of our lives. However, the Lord relates to all of us equally. In the words of the first reading, he wants to speak to the heart of each of us, drawing us to himself with tenderness and love. Regardless of how we are seen by others, the Lord looks upon us in a way that recognises our dignity. In the words of today's psalm, he is 'kind and full of compassion' towards all.

9 July, Tuesday, Fourteenth Week in Ordinary Time
Matthew 9:32–38

In today's first reading, the Lord bemoans the fact that the people of Samaria consider a human-made idol to be God. The opposite is the case in the gospel reading. The Pharisees identify what is of God as from the prince of devils, considering Jesus' healing ministry to be inspired by Satan. We can be prone to treating as divine what is merely human, while failing to recognise the ways that God is indeed actively working among us. According to the responsorial psalm, 'God ... is in the heavens; he does whatever he wills'. Yet God became flesh in Jesus and continues to work powerfully in and through the risen Jesus. We need to keep praying for eyes to recognise the various ways that God continues to work among us through his Son, while not assigning divine status to what is purely human. In the words of the alleluia verse for today, we need to pray that 'the Father of our Lord Jesus Christ' would 'enlighten the eyes of our mind'. Jesus had this clarity of vision. He often recognised that those who claimed to speak for God were not in fact speaking for God. He also recognised that certain human experiences could speak powerfully to us of God, such as the shepherd who leaves his flock to look for the one sheep who has strayed, and the father who welcomes back his renegade son with a feast. To begin to see with the eyes of the Lord, we need, in the words of today's psalm, to 'constantly seek his face'. In seeking the Lord's face in prayer we acquire something of his vision, and we need his vision if we are to become those labourers in the harvest he speaks of in the gospel reading.

10 July, Wednesday, Fourteenth Week in Ordinary Time
Matthew 10:1–7

In today's first reading, the Lord says of Israel, 'their heart is a divided heart'. They did not seek the Lord with a pure, undivided heart. Instead, they hedged their bets by building altars to other gods in the event of not being able to rely on the Lord. In the gospel reading, Jesus appoints the twelve as the initial labourers to work in God's harvest. In time, they too would show themselves to have a divided heart. They did not remain faithful to Jesus when it became costly to themselves, abandoning him in the hour of his passion and death, with Peter, the leader of the twelve, denying him publicly and Judas Iscariot betraying him to his enemies. Even though they were sent as shepherds to the lost sheep of the house of Israel, they themselves became lost sheep. As Jesus would say to them on the night of the Last Supper, 'You will all become deserters because of me this night; for it is written, "I will strike the shepherd, and the sheep of the flock will be scattered"' (Matthew 26:31). We can hardly sit in judgement on the people of Israel or on the disciples as we are all aware that our own hearts can easily be divided. In the Beatitudes, Jesus declares, 'Blessed are the pure in heart, for they will see God.' We are not always pure in heart, with an undivided focus on what God desires for us and our world. We need to keep hearing the call of the first reading, 'Break up your fallow ground: It is time to go seeking the Lord.' The good news is that the Lord is always seeking us, even when our heart is divided and we fail to seek him with all our heart. He came to seek out and save the lost and he never stops seeking even when we do.

11 July, Thursday, Saint Benedict, Abbot, Patron of Europe
Matthew 19:27–29

'The first monks in Italy and Gaul followed Eastern models and rules, which were usually marked by extreme austerity. It was Saint Benedict who adapted monasticism to European needs, and laid the foundations of the great monastic system that bears his name. Benedict was born in Norcia in Italy about the year 480, and as a youth studied in Rome. Disliking the licentiousness of the city, and feeling that he had a special call from God, he retired to a cave at Subiaco, about forty miles south of Rome. He lived there for three years. His manner of life attracted followers, and this led to the establishment of a monastery at Subiaco, which still exists. Later, probably in 528 or 529, he went further south and built the great abbey of Monte Cassino in the central Apennines. He remained there until his death in 547, and it is there that he drew up his famous "Rule for Monks"' (Website of Mount St Joseph's Abbey, Roscrea, Coounty Tipperary, Ireland). Saint Benedict taught his monks the value of the common life. They would often pray alone, but they would also pray and work together and show hospitality to visitors. Having left their families and home, the monks discovered a new family, the community of their brother monks and of the wider world. In response to Peter's question in the gospel reading, 'What about us? We have left everything to follow you. What are we to have then?' Jesus promises his disciples that everyone who has left home and family for his sake will be repaid a hundred times over. Most of us are not called to leave home and family for Jesus' sake, yet there is always something we have to leave or let go of if we are to remain the Lord's faithful followers. Jesus assures us that if we are prepared to take this path of letting go for his sake, we will always receive more from him than we have let go.

12 July, Friday, Fourteenth Week in Ordinary Time
Matthew 10:16–23

In today's first reading, the Lord not only calls on the people of Israel to turn back to him, but he provides them with words that will help them to turn back: 'Say to him, "Take all iniquity away so that we may have happiness again … "' In the gospel reading, Jesus promises his disciples that when they are handed over to governors and kings for his sake, they should not worry about how to speak or what to say, because 'what you are to say will be given to you when the time comes, because it is not you who will be speaking; the Spirit of your Father will be speaking in you'. There are times in the living out of our faith when we simply cannot find the right words for ourselves; we need them to come to us from the Lord. The readings assure us that the Lord stands ready to give us the words we need when the time comes, whether it is words that allow us to communicate with the Lord, as in the first reading, or words that allow us to communicate the Lord to others, as in the gospel reading. As Saint Paul declares in his letter to the Romans, 'the Spirit [of the risen Lord] helps us in our weakness'. Our awareness of our 'weakness' creates an opening for the Lord to help us, to give us the words we need, whether for prayer or for witnessing to his Gospel. In our hour of need, we can pray with confidence the prayer of today's responsorial psalm, 'Give me again the joy of your help; with a spirit of fervour sustain me'.

13 July, Saturday, Fourteenth Week in Ordinary Time
Matthew 10:24–38

The account of the call of Isaiah in today's gospel reading conveys a sense of the otherness and majesty of God. Isaiah saw the Lord seated on a high throne, with his train filling the sanctuary. The prophet had a profound sense of his own unworthiness to be in the presence of the all-holy one. In contrast, Jesus speaks of a God who is intimately involved with the details of his creation. Not one sparrow falls to the ground without God the Father knowing. The very hairs on the head of the disciples have been counted by God. If the humble sparrow, two of which can be bought for a penny in the marketplace, is precious in God's sight, Jesus' disciples are much more precious: 'You are worth more than hundreds of sparrows.' There is no conflict between the God of Isaiah and the God of Jesus. God is both infinitely beyond us and deeply involved in the details of our lives. It is because God the Father of Jesus cares so deeply about believers that we can be fearless in our witness to Jesus, declaring ourselves for him in the presence of others. The disciples are likely to suffer the same rejection as their master, but as God was faithful to his Son, bringing him through death to new life, so he will be faithful to his disciples, who are immensely precious to him. It is because of how much we mean to God that we are enabled to declare to others how much Jesus means to us.

15 July, Monday, Fifteenth Week in Ordinary Time
Matthew 10:34–11:1

In the gospel reading Jesus speaks of the value of giving a cup of cold water to one of his disciples. Giving a cup of cold water to someone who needs it is not going to make headlines. Most likely, only the giver and the receiver will be aware of it, yet Jesus holds up this small act of kindness as having immense value. Even the simplest acts in which we lose ourselves for others have eternal significance. The giving of a cup of cold water can stand for any number of small acts of kindness that give life to others. In a homily some years ago Pope Francis spoke of how love can find expression in simple ways. He refers to the encouragement of simple love, 'like a blessing before we go to bed, or a hug after we return from a hard day's work'. 'Love,' he says, 'is shown by little things, by attention to small daily signs which make us feel at home.' In the gospel reading Jesus is trying to teach us the value of what we might be inclined to dismiss as of very little significance. In all sorts of ways throughout this parish, this city, people are giving the equivalent of a cup of cold water to those who need it. Parents are doing it for their children every day of the week. Jesus also indicates in that reading that when we give the equivalent of the cup of cold water to someone, there is more going on than we might realise at the time. 'Anyone who welcomes you welcomes me; and those who welcome me welcome the one who sent me.' The way we relate to each other is an expression of how we are relating to Jesus and to God the Father, whether we are aware of that or not. In that sense, life is not divided into a secular area and a sacred area, the secular area being where we live, work and play, and the sacred where we pray and worship. The Word has become flesh. In our dealings with human flesh, with each other, we are dealing with the divine. We are standing on holy ground all the time.

16 July, Tuesday, Fifteenth Week in Ordinary Time
Matthew 11:20–24

According to today's first reading, at a time of national crisis, the Lord, speaking through the prophet Isaiah, says to the king of Judah, 'If you do not stand by me, you will not stand at all.' Faced with a coalition of enemy nations, Ahaz was tempted to seek refuge by relying on one of the great empires of the day, Assyria. Isaiah's message to him was that he needed to rely on the Lord, rather than on any human power, if he and the people were to remain secure. The preaching of Jesus to the towns of Galilee called on them to rely on God, present and active in the ministry of Jesus. According to the gospel reading, the towns of Chorazin, Bethsaida and Capernaum failed to do so. In spite of the ways God was powerfully at work through the ministry of Jesus, they didn't respond to him in a trusting, faithful way. Behind Jesus' oracle of judgement addressed to these towns lies a heart that is broken at their failure to respond to his life-giving message. In Luke's Gospel Jesus weeps over Jerusalem because of their failure to recognise the time of God's visitation through Jesus. Today's readings invite us to ask ourselves, 'To whom or what do we turn and on whom or on what do we rely?' In the words of today's responsorial psalm, 'God … has shown himself its stronghold'. Jesus as Emmanuel, God with us, offers himself to us as the stronghold of our lives, the rock on which we can build our lives, the one on whom we can rely when all else fails.

17 July, Wednesday, Fifteenth Week in Ordinary Time
Matthew 11:25–27
In the first reading, the Lord, speaking through the prophet Isaiah, critiques the arrogance of the ruler of the empire of Assyria. Failing to recognise his role in God's greater purpose, he puts his military successes down to his own strength and intelligence. It is as if the axe were to claim more credit than the one who uses it. In the gospel reading, Jesus refers to 'the learned and the clever', by which is meant those religious experts who are so sure of their interpretation of God's law as to reject Jesus' revelation of God through his words and deeds. However, although the learned and the clever may be rejecting Jesus' revelation of God, the 'little ones' are welcoming it. Those who are aware of their own poverty and need before God have come to

recognise the intimate relationship between the Father and the Son. They have welcomed God's coming to them through the words and deeds of Jesus. What is hidden to the learned and the clever is clear to the little ones. There is a sense in which we have to bend very low if we are to receive the revelation of God that Jesus came to give us. As Jesus says in the opening beatitude, 'Blessed are the poor in spirit, for theirs is the kingdom of heaven' (Matthew 5:3). As Paul says in his first letter to the Corinthians, God often chooses 'what is foolish in the world to shame the wise … what is weak in the world to shame the strong' (1 Corinthians 1:27). A self-emptying is needed on our part if God's purpose for our lives is to come to pass.

18 July, Thursday, Fifteenth Week in Ordinary Time
Matthew 11:28–30
The human longing for God is eloquently expressed in today's first reading from the prophet Isaiah, 'At night my soul longs for you and my spirit in me seeks for you … Distressed, we search for you, Lord.' It is often in times of distress that the deep longing in our hearts for God comes to the surface of our lives. In the gospel reading, Jesus responds to our longing for God, calling out to the distressed, to those who labour and are overburdened, to come to him, to learn from him. It is a very personal invitation: 'Come to me.' Jesus speaks here as Emmanuel, God with us. He alone can begin to satisfy our deep longing for God. In the setting of the ministry of Jesus, those who labour and are overburdened are the bulk of the people who have been burdened by the over-rigorous interpretation of the Jewish Law by the religious experts, the theologians of the day. 'They tie up heavy burdens, hard to bear, and lay them on the shoulders of others, but they themselves are unwilling to lift a finger to move them' (Matthew 23:9). The one who is 'gentle and humble in heart' is not in the business of burdening an already burdened people. Those who

respond to his invitation to come to him will experience the 'rest' for which our restless hearts are longing. Saint Augustine declared that our hearts are restless until they rest in God. We will only enter upon this rest to the full in the kingdom of heaven. However, here and now, in and through the Lord's personal relationship with each of us as members of the community of disciples, we will begin to taste something of this 'rest', this fullness of life, which alone can satisfy our human longing for God.

19 July, Friday, Fifteenth Week in Ordinary Time
Matthew 12:1–8

When Jesus quotes the Jewish Scriptures, it is often because he finds there a message or a word that corresponds to his own message and vision. At the end of today's gospel reading, he quotes from the prophet Hosea: 'What I want is mercy, not sacrifice.' For Hosea and for Jesus, what matters more to God than all the sacrifices that were offered in the Temple in Jerusalem was this attitude of mercy. How was mercy understood? In the parable of the good Samaritan, it was mercy that the Samaritan showed to the broken traveller on the roadside. Those who were broken in body and spirit often came up to Jesus with the prayer, 'Have mercy on me.' When Jesus brought life to the dying, healing to the sick, forgiveness to sinners, loving acceptance to the excluded, he was showing mercy. To show mercy is to recognise the need of others and to respond to it with a generous spirit. At the beginning of today's gospel reading, Jesus' disciples were in need of food; they were hungry. They picked ears of grain from a field to satisfy their hunger, which was perfectly legitimate at the time. When the Pharisees noticed this, they judged the disciples, saying that they were doing work on the sabbath, breaking the sabbath law of rest. The Pharisees lacked mercy, failing to understand the need of the disciples for food. They were judgemental rather than merciful. Jesus revealed the merciful love of God for all, and he called on us to show something of God's merciful love to others. As he says, quoting Hosea, this is what God wants. Jesus was closer to God than any human being; he was the Son of God. As a result, he knew better than anyone else what God wants. God wants to find among his people, among us all, a compassionate, understanding and merciful heart.

20 July, Saturday, Fifteenth Week in Ordinary Time
Matthew 12:14–21

Half of this morning's gospel reading is taken up with a quotation from the prophet Isaiah. It is a long quotation in comparison to other quotations from the Jewish scriptures in the gospels. Matthew clearly regarded this text from Isaiah as speaking powerfully about the person of Jesus and the nature of his mission. In the quotation from Isaiah, God addresses someone whom he describes as his chosen servant, whom he has endowed with his spirit. Jesus was certainly God's chosen servant, on whom the Holy Spirit had come down at the time of his baptism. It is said of this servant in the quotation that he will neither brawl nor shout. That reflects Jesus' reference to himself as 'gentle and humble in heart'. It is also said in that quotation from Isaiah that the servant will 'not break the crushed reed, nor put out the smouldering wick'. This reflects the portrayal of Jesus in the Gospel as one who is attentive and sensitive to the weakest and most vulnerable, who calls out to the burdened to come to him and find rest and refreshment. A reed that is crushed is easily broken; a wick that is smouldering is easily put out. Jesus had a special care for those who were frail and weak, all who were just hanging on by the skin of their teeth, as we often say. The risen Lord has the same loving concern for us when we are at our most vulnerable, when, in the imagery of Saint Paul, we are aware of ourselves as earthen vessels, prone to being broken. At such times, the Lord is present to us as strength in our weakness, as sustenance in our frailty. He not only comes to us as strength in our weakness, but, having done so, he wants to come through us as strength in the weakness of others. He looks to us to be as attentive to the crushed reeds and the smouldering wicks as he was.

22 July, Monday, Saint Mary Magdalene

John 20:1–2, 11–18

Saint Paul has a way of expressing very succinctly what is at the core of our faith. We find one such expression in today's alternative first reading where he declares that 'Christ died for all', so that those who live might 'live no longer for themselves, but for him who died and was raised to life for them'. In today's gospel reading, Mary Magdalene is aware only that Jesus has died; she does not yet know that he has been raised to life. Not only has Jesus been cruelly put to death, she assumes from the empty tomb that his body has been stolen. Immersed in grief, she is not yet capable of living for him who died and was raised to life. It was only when the risen Lord appeared to her that she could begin to live for him again, as she had done before he died. Like the two disciples on the road to Emmaus, however, Mary failed to recognise Jesus when she first saw him and entered into conversation with him. The two disciples' moment of recognition was when the stranger broke bread at their table. Mary's moment of recognition was when the stranger spoke her name, like the good shepherd who knows his own by name. She was now ready to live for Jesus crucified and risen. She would become a 'new creation', in the words of our first reading. Commissioned by the risen Lord, she became his messenger to the other disciples, declaring to them that she had seen the Lord. The risen Lord, our good shepherd, continues to call us by name. Having died and risen from the dead for us, he calls on us to live not for ourselves but for him, by witnessing to our faith in him as risen Lord. Living for the Lord gives value to all that we say and do. Like Mary Magdalene, we become a new creation.

23 July, Tuesday, Saint Bridget of Sweden, Patroness of Europe
John 15:1–8

Saint Bridget of Sweden was a mystic, a woman of deep prayer. She married when she was fourteen, and bore eight children, four daughters and four sons. Bridget's saintly and charitable life soon made her known far and wide. After her husband died, she became a member of the Third Order of Saint Francis and devoted herself wholly to a life of prayer and caring for the sick. She was inspired to form the religious community called the Order of the Most Holy Saviour, or the Brigittines. One distinctive feature of the houses of her order was that they were 'double' monasteries, with both men and women forming a joint community, though with separate cloisters. In 1350 she went to Rome, accompanied by her daughter and a small party of disciples. She wanted to obtain the Pope's authorisation for her new order. This was during the time of the Great Schism in the Church. Along with Catherine of Siena, Bridget worked hard to get Pope Clement VI to return from Avignon to Rome. While in Rome, she went on many pilgrimages in Italy and also made a pilgrimage to the Holy Land. She remained in Rome, becoming known for her kindness and good works, until her death on 23 July 1373. Her remains were returned to Sweden. She was canonised in 1391, eighteen years after she died. She exemplified what it is to be a contemplative in action. Through a deep prayer life, she made her home in the Lord and allowed the Lord to make his home in her, in the language of the gospel reading. As a result, her life bore rich fruit, the fruit of a love that reflected the Lord's love for us. As branches on the vine who is Jesus, we are all called to remain in him and to allow him to remain in us, so that our lives too can show forth the self-emptying servant love of the Lord in our own time and place.

24 July, Wednesday, Sixteenth Week in Ordinary Time
Matthew 13:1–9
Today's first reading is one of the great call stories in the Jewish Scriptures. When Jeremiah hears the call to be the Lord's prophet to the nations, he becomes aware of his own inadequacy, the many obstacles in his life that could hinder his response to the Lord's call, especially his youth. However, the Lord assures him that if his heart is open to the call, then he will be with Jeremiah to protect him, even placing his words in Jeremiah's mouth. In the parable in today's gospel reading, there are many obstacles to the growth of the seed that the sower sows with such abandon. Yet, in spite of those obstacles, some of the seed falls on soil that is receptive and the harvest from that soil is beyond all reasonable expectations, even a hundredfold. The Lord continues to scatter the seed of his word today. He does so with abandon, so that it reaches as many people as possible. There will be great obstacles in the lives of many that will prevent the word from taking root in their hearts and bearing fruit in their lives. Yet, if the Lord finds some hearts that are receptive to his word, as the heart of Jeremiah was, he will be able to work through them for the good of others in ways that go beyond all expectations.

25 July, Thursday, Saint James, Apostle
Matthew 20:20–28
It may seem strange that the gospel reading chosen for the feast of Saint James, brother of John and son of Zebedee, is one that doesn't reflect too well on him. He and John approach Jesus through their mother (in Mark's Gospel, they approach him directly), asking Jesus

for the most honourable seats in Jesus' kingdom, one on his right and the other on his left. The request reveals a failure to understand that the kingdom of God that Jesus came to proclaim bears no relationship to any earthly kingdom. As Jesus goes on to say to the other ten disciples, in earthly pagan kingdoms their rulers lord it over their subjects, making their authority felt. This is not how it is to be in the kingdom of God, nor in the community of Jesus' disciples, the Church, which is to be a beachhead for the kingdom. In God's kingdom and its earthly revelation, greatness consists not in honourable status expressing itself in oppressive rule but in self-giving service of God and God's people, after the example of Jesus, who came not to be served but to serve. Such self-giving service will often entail drinking the cup of suffering that Jesus had to drink. At this point in the gospel, Jesus is still struggling to convey his vision of leadership to the twelve, including James and John. Yet perhaps the reason this gospel reading is chosen for the feast of Saint James is because he did go on to drink the cup that Jesus drank, in the service of God and God's people. According to the Acts of the Apostles, 'King Herod laid violent hands upon some who belonged to the church. He had James, the brother of John, killed with the sword' (12:1–2). The story of James shows us that our past failings do not define our relationship with the Lord. With his help we can grow in our relationship with him. We can keep moving from living towards ourselves to living towards him, so that, eventually, in the words of today's first reading, 'the life of Jesus may always be seen in our body'.

26 July, Friday, Sixteenth Week in Ordinary Time
Matthew 13:18–23
The interpretation of the parable of the sower reveals some of the threats to our growing towards a mature faith. The first threat is a lack of understanding of the word that is proclaimed. We can grow

in our understanding of many areas of life as we get older, but our understanding of the faith can fail to develop beyond the understanding we had when we were children. This leaves our faith vulnerable to the critical questions of reason that we will inevitably encounter as we get older. Reason need not be an enemy of faith, but it can be experienced as such if our understanding of our faith does not grow with age. A second threat to a mature faith is a failure to allow our faith to take deeper roots in our lives. Our faith may be sustained by social compliance or the desire to please others, but it is not coming from a deep place in our hearts. As a result, when the living of our faith becomes costly, we can be tempted to turn away from it. In our present age, especially, our faith needs to be sustained by a personal conviction, a freely chosen decision to take the path it offers us because we recognise it to be the path of life. A third threat to a mature faith lies in the rival claims on our heart that life throws up, the worries and cares of the world and the lure of riches. We may have a deep conviction about the value of our faith, but somehow the demands and pleasures of life absorb us and our faith dies back for lack of attention. We neglect our faith and it becomes choked. The interpretation of the parable is a salutary reminder that, although faith is a gift from the Lord and the Lord remains faithful to us, there is work to be done by ourselves in keeping our relationship with the Lord alive and central to our lives.

27 July, Saturday, Sixteenth Week in Ordinary Time
Matthew 13:24–30
It has often been said that our weaknesses are the shadow side of our strengths. The line between the good and the not-so-good in our lives can be very subtle. If we are over-zealous in trying to root out that which is not so good in someone's life, or, indeed, in our own, we might also damage that which is good there. In the parable Jesus

speaks in today's gospel reading, the owner's servants wanted to root out the weeds that had appeared among the wheat. The owner had to restrain them. This was not the time for such separation. It is not always easy to distinguish wheat from weeds at an early stage of growth, and both can be closely intertwined. The separation would come at harvest time. In the meantime, patience is needed with the weeds. Jesus may have been warning against a kind of religious zeal that is too eager to identify weeds, what is considered worthless, and to separate it out from wheat, what is considered good. Saint Paul showed some of this kind of religious zeal before he encountered Christ on the road to Damascus. He saw the followers of Jesus as weeds in the field of Judaism; they had to be identified and rooted out. He was blind to the presence of God among them. Sometimes, there is no mistaking evil and evil people. However, we can also get it terribly wrong and misjudge others. There are times when we may need to live with the weaknesses of others for the sake of their great strengths. We are all a mixture of wheat and weed. The Lord's good work is ongoing in our lives, and yet it is always hindered by the presence of sin. Only beyond this earthly life will we be fully conformed to image of God's Son. In the meantime, we need a certain amount of patience with ourselves and others, while seeking to grow more fully into the person of Christ and helping each other to do so.

29 July, Monday, Saints Martha, Mary and Lazarus

John 11:19–27

We don't often have the feast of two sisters and a brother. John's Gospel suggests that Jesus had a warm and friendly relationship with this family. Earlier in the chapter from which our gospel reading is taken, the evangelist tells us that 'Jesus loved Martha and her sister and Lazarus'. When the sisters sent word to Jesus that Lazarus was ill, their message was, 'Lord, he whom you love is ill.' Later on in this same chapter, when Jesus saw Mary weeping because her brother Lazarus had died, it is said that, 'Jesus began to weep', and those present said, 'See how he loved him'. Martha, Mary and Lazarus are beloved disciples of Jesus. To that extent they represent us all. What Jesus said to his disciples at the Last Supper in John's Gospel is said to us all: 'As the Father has loved me, so I have loved you; abide in my love.' Beloved disciples, like Martha, Mary and Lazarus, are not spared the trauma of profound loss in the face of death. Jesus himself, the beloved Son of God, experienced the cruellest of deaths on a Roman cross. Yet Jesus' words to Martha in today's gospel reading assure her, and all beloved disciples, that the bond that his love for us and our faith in him creates will not be broken by death. Rather, that bond will be deepened as we come to share in his own risen life. 'If anyone believes in me, even though they die they will live, and whoever lives and believes in me will never die.' Yes, the Lord's beloved disciples will die, as he did, but beyond death they will live, and, therefore, they will never die in the ultimate sense. According to our first reading, the essence of God is love, and God's love for us was revealed when 'God sent into the world his only Son so that we could have life through him'. This is the hope that the feast of this beloved family gives us.

30 July, Tuesday, Seventeenth Week in Ordinary Time
Matthew 13:36–43
Today's gospel reading of the interpretation of the parable of the wheat and the darnel acknowledges that all is not well with the world. We don't need reminding that there is much evil in our world. However, it is not the case that the Church is a field of goodness and all beyond it is a field of evil. This Gospel of Matthew readily acknowledges that sin is to be found in the community of believers. Peter's question, unique to Matthew, was a very relevant one for Matthew's

community: 'Lord, if another member of the church sins against me, how often should I forgive? As many as seven times?' (Matthew 18:21). In recent times, we have been made only too well aware of how the sins of some of the Church's most trusted members have been a source of enormous scandal for believers. As a community of faith we can easily make our own the words of Jeremiah in today's first reading, 'Lord, we do confess our wickedness … we have indeed sinned against you.' Yet we can also make our own the words Jeremiah goes on to speak, 'O our God, you are our hope'. The existence of evil, even in the holiest of places, is not a cause for disillusionment or despair. The Lord remains faithful to his flawed Church and to his broken world. He continues to work among us to recreate us in his image through the power of the Holy Spirit. As Paul expresses it so succinctly in his letter to the Romans, 'where sin increased, grace abounded all the more' (Romans 5:20). There is a great onus on us all to cooperate with the Lord, who is always striving to bring the good work he has begun in us to completion.

31 July, Wednesday, Seventeenth Week in Ordinary Time
Matthew 13:44–46

Farmers working away on their land or in a local bog have often stumbled upon some great treasure. Looking for treasure was the furthest thing from their mind. They were just going about their daily work. However, out of the blue, they hit upon something that turned out to be a very precious object. Many of the treasures in our national museum were found in that way. This is the kind of situation we find in the first parable that Jesus speaks. Probably a day labourer working in someone's field finds an unexpected treasure and in his joy he sells everything he owns to buy the field with its treasure. Jesus is saying that we can sometimes stumble upon the treasure of the kingdom of heaven in this way. We are going about our daily lives, without thinking of the Lord at all, and, suddenly, we have a sense of the Lord's presence. The Lord touches our lives out of the blue in a way that leaves us feeling we have been blessed with a great treasure. The Lord can break through to us even when we are not looking for him. The second parable is a little different. The rich merchant was looking for a particular treasure, a pearl of great value. Eventually, after much searching he found it and he sold all he owned to buy it. The one who searched eventually found. Through this parable the Lord is saying to us that if we keep seeking him we will find him. As Jesus says elsewhere in the gospels, 'Seek and you will find'. We need to keep seeking the Lord, but the first parable reminds us that the Lord is always seeking us and sometimes he will find us and touch our lives, at a time when he is far from our mind and heart. There is always a greater search going on than our search for the Lord, and that is the Lord's search for us.

1 August, Thursday, Seventeenth Week in Ordinary Time
Matthew 13:47–53

The parable in today's gospel reading presupposes the practice of the fishermen on the Sea of Galilee dragging a large net between two boats or drawing it towards the land after it has been dropped in the sea. Such a way of fishing would have drawn in a very large variety of fish, some of which could have been sold at the market-place and others that could only be thrown away. Jesus is suggesting that his ministry casts a very wide net. He had earlier said in this gospel, in the setting of the Sermon on the Mount, that 'your Father in heaven … makes his sun rise on the evil and on the good, and sends his rain on the righteous and the unrighteous' (Matthew 5:45). The indiscriminate nature of God's generous, providing love is reflected in the broad, inclusive ministry of Jesus. Like the sower, Jesus casts the seed of his word with abandon. Jesus reveals a God who seeks to embrace all sorts, without exception. Like the potter in the first reading, Jesus did not reject what was far from perfect, what 'came out wrong'. He was at home with tax collectors and sinners, with the weaknesses and frailties of others, knowing that God's love at work through him could recreate all who came to him so that they could become all that God was calling them to be. Yet, having been embraced by the Lord's love, conversion is required of us, a daily turning towards the one who is always turned towards us.

2 August, Friday, Seventeenth Week in Ordinary Time
Matthew 13:54–58
Asking questions is an important expression of our faith journey. When we are trying to respond to the Lord's presence and call in our lives, there will always be room for questions. The Lord is infinitely mysterious; he is always beyond us as well as being present among us and within us. We are always searching for him, as well as responding to his daily presence to us. As we search for him, we will ask questions, and our questions can lead us closer to him. However, in today's gospel reading, the questions asked by the people of Nazareth did not lead them closer to Jesus. Rather, their questions led them away from him. When Jesus taught in his home synagogue, the people of Nazareth asked very good and valid questions: 'Where did the man get this wisdom and these miraculous powers? So where did the man get it all?' They recognised the wisdom of his preaching and teaching, the healing and life-giving power of his ministry, and they wondered where it all came from. These were questions that could have led the people of Nazareth to recognise Jesus as someone who had come to them from God. Instead, their questions led them to reject Jesus. After all, he was one of their own; they knew him as the son of a carpenter; they were very familiar with his mother and the other members of his family. How could someone so like them

come from God? How could one of their own be God's special messenger to them? They had asked good questions, but, in the end, they rejected him. The people of Nazareth could not come to terms with God powerfully present in one like themselves. Yet this is the mystery that is at the heart of our faith. God became human in Jesus. When we look upon the human life of Jesus, his words and deeds, his ministry, his death, we are looking upon the face of God. Here is a mystery to be delighted in, rather than rejected. Just as God came to us through one like us in all things but sin, so God continues to come to us in and through the ordinary circumstances of our day-to-day lives. The risen Lord who is beyond us, with God the Father, is also present with us to the end of time.

3 August, Saturday, Seventeenth Week in Ordinary Time
Matthew 14:1–12
The story in today's gospel reading is one of the darker stories in the gospels. The story of the passion and death of John the Baptist anticipates, in many ways, the story of the passion and death of Jesus. Both John and Jesus were executed by agents of Rome because they proclaimed God's word to powerful people. John proclaimed God's word as found in the Jewish Law. Jesus proclaimed God's word in a new way, which was in continuity with the Jewish Law but went beyond it. Powerful people found God's word as proclaimed by John and Jesus so disturbing that they wanted the preachers of that word put to death. Jeremiah's proclamation of God's word in today's first reading met with a similarly negative response. Some of the worst instincts of human nature are to be found in the story in today's gospel reading. Herod, his wife, Herodias, and their daughter, traditionally named as Salome, have been described as a kind of unholy trinity. Between them they conspired to put a holy man of God to death. Even in situations where the worst instincts of human nature

are to the fore, there is often to be found some redeeming feature. The redeeming feature in today's story is the person of John the Baptist himself. He is the light that shines in this very dark scene. His faithfulness to the Lord's calling shines brightly against the dark backdrop of the worst instincts of human nature displayed by Herod Antipas, his wife and her daughter. John did not allow his goodness to be overcome by evil. The same is true, to an even greater extent, of Jesus. John and Jesus did not allow the light of God's loving presence in their lives to be dimmed by the darkness in the lives of others. That is our calling too, as followers of the risen Lord. We are to allow the light of God's loving presence to shine through us, regardless of the situation in which we find ourselves.

5 August, Monday, Eighteenth Week in Ordinary Time
Matthew 14:22–36

We can easily get upset when our plans don't work out. We might plan for a time of rest and something comes along unexpectedly that we have to deal with. We feel ourselves getting annoyed. In the gospel reading, Jesus planned to go away with his disciples to a lonely place where they could be by themselves. However, a crowd of people got there ahead of them, wanting to be in the presence of Jesus. The gospel reading says that, far from getting upset or annoyed, Jesus had compassion on the crowd and began to heal their sick. The needs of others always come first for Jesus; his own plans will always come second to their needs. The Lord is always there for each one of us. When we come before him, we are never disturbing him. He lives to serve us just as much today as during his public ministry. As the day wore on, Jesus' disciples recognised that people were getting hungry. The obvious solution to this problem for the disciples was to send the crowds away to buy food in the neighbouring villages. However, Jesus saw a different solution to their need for food; he would feed them himself, with the help of the disciples. The disciples brought the little food the crowd had to Jesus and in some mysterious way we don't understand, Jesus fed the crowd so that everyone was satisfied. Having served the crowd by healing their sick, he now served them by feeding them, satisfying their hunger. The actions of Jesus over the bread – taking, blessing, breaking, giving – remind us of what Jesus would go on to do at the Last Supper and of what happens at every Mass. At every Mass, Jesus in his compassion continues to feed us, not with bread and fish, but with himself, the Bread of Life. If the Lord is always there for us, he is there for us in a very special way at every Eucharist. He then sends us out from Mass to feed others with his presence, as the disciples fed the crowd with the food Jesus provided.

6 August, Tuesday, The Transfiguration of the Lord
Mark 9:2–10

The second reading for today's feast speaks of a 'lamp for lighting a way through the dark until the dawn comes'. That seems like a good description of the disciples' experience of Jesus being transfigured on the mountain. Jesus had just spoken of himself to his disciples as the Son of Man who would be rejected and put to death; he was just about to set out with them on the road to Jerusalem, where he would be crucified. There were heading into a valley of darkness. The experience of Jesus transfigured on the mountain was like a lamp for lighting a way through the dark that lay ahead. It would help to sustain Jesus and his disciples, until the dawn came, the dawn of Easter Sunday, which would proclaim the triumph of light over darkness and of life over death. We are all familiar with the experience of darkness in one shape or form. We have all spent time in some valley of darkness or other, because of suffering and loss. Within our darkness, the Lord will always be a lamp for lighting our way through the darkness until the dawn comes. The Lord is always coming to us as light in our darkness. If we can open ourselves to his presence, even in our valleys of darkness, we might find ourselves saying with Peter, 'it is wonderful for us to be here'. As we pray in the psalm, 'The Lord is my Shepherd', 'you are there with your crook and your staff'. At those moments, when the Lord makes himself present to us as light in our darkness, God the Father is saying to us what he said to his disciples in the gospel reading, 'This is my Son, the Beloved. Listen to him.' The Lord speaks to us in the darkness if we open our ears, our hearts, to him at such times. Such experiences of the light of the Lord's presence in our dark times are an anticipation of the dawning of eternal light beyond this earthly life.

7 August, Wednesday, Eighteenth Week in Ordinary Time
Matthew 15:21–28

There is no stronger bond than that between a mother and her child. In today's gospel reading, a pagan woman approaches Jesus on behalf of her seriously ill child. It is striking that she says to Jesus, 'Take pity on me', and 'Help me', rather than 'Take pity on my child', and 'Help my child'. She identifies fully with her child's condition. The suffering of her child is her own suffering. In the gospels, Jesus is generally very well disposed to children and he always responds to parents who approach him on behalf of their children, such as Jairus, the synagogue official, whose daughter was on the point of death. Yet, on this occasion, Jesus seems detached from this pleading mother. His initial response is one of silence. He explains to his disciples that, for now, his primary mission is to the lost sheep of the house of Israel, rather than to the equally lost pagans. When he finally speaks to the woman, his words seem harsh. In a mini parable, he declares that children cannot be deprived of food to feed the house dogs. In other words, the children of Israel have to be fed first, before pagans, whom many Jews referred to as 'dogs'. The woman cleverly turns Jesus' image around, declaring that the untidy eating habits of children often allow the dogs to feed off their scraps and crumbs. She identifies with the house dogs and declares that she would be happy with scraps from Jesus' table for the sake of her daughter. Jesus recognises what he calls her 'great faith'. In the Gospel of Matthew, Jesus often addresses his own disciples as people of little faith, but here is a woman of great faith. Jesus cannot but respond to such great faith. This woman inspires us all to keep knocking on the Lord's door, to keep seeking, to keep asking. This is how great faith expresses itself and the Lord will eventually work powerfully through the opening that such great faith creates.

8 August, Thursday, Eighteenth Week in Ordinary Time
Matthew 16:13–23

According to today's gospel reading, just at the very moment when Jesus gave Peter a very special role, as the rock on which he would build the Church, Peter became not a rock but a stumbling stone, an obstacle, to Jesus. Jesus knew that if he was to remain faithful to the mission God had given him, it would lead down the path of suffering and death. However, Peter tried to tempt Jesus to take an easier path: 'This must not happen to you.' This was a very powerful temptation, so Jesus had to confront it in a very uncompromising way. He turned to Peter and said, 'Get behind me, Satan.' Peter, who had just expressed a wonderful insight into Jesus, a God-given insight, 'You are the Christ, the Son of the living God', is now addressed by Jesus as Satan. Peter, who was inspired by God at one moment, was being inspired by Satan in the next moment. Peter was a mixture of the good and the not so good. He was both a man of deep faith who could be entrusted by Jesus with great responsibility and a man who could become a block to the work that Jesus wanted to do. We are all a little like Peter, a mixture of wheat and weed, to use the imagery of one of Jesus' parables. After addressing Peter as Satan, Jesus did not go back on Peter's calling to be the rock on which the Church would be built. Jesus continued to invest in Peter, to trust that he would turn out well in the end. Indeed, Peter went on to become a good shepherd who laid down his life for his flock, like Jesus. The Lord never gives up on us either. Even after we fail him, he continues to invest in us. He keeps calling us to become the person he wants us to be and knows we can be with his help, the help of the Holy Spirit.

9 August, Friday, Saint Teresa Benedicta of the Cross, Virgin and Martyr

Matthew 25:1–13

Edith Stein was born on 12 October 1891 to a Jewish family in Breslau, Germany. Though she became agnostic in her teens, through her passionate study of philosophy as an adult she searched for truth and found it in reading the autobiography of Saint Teresa of Avila. In 1922, she was baptised a Catholic, and in 1933 entered the Discalaced Carmel of Cologne where she took the name of Teresa Benedicta of the Cross. When the Nazis came to power she was sent to the Carmel in Echt, Netherlands. When the Nazis occupied the Netherlands all Jews and Jewish converts were arrested. Sister Teresa Benedicta, along with her sister Rosa, was arrested at this time. She was gassed and cremated at Auschwitz on 9 August 1942. A woman of great intelligence and learning, she left behind a body of writing notable for its doctrinal richness and profound spirituality. She was beatified by Pope John Paul II at Cologne, Germany, on 1 May 1987 and was canonised on 11 October 1998. The gospel reading chosen for her feast day is the parable of the ten bridesmaids from Matthew's Gospel. The lamp of Teresa's faith burnt brightly from the moment she gave her life over to the Lord, having read the autobiography of Saint Teresa of Avila. Her faith in the Lord was a light in the awful darkness of Auschwitz. When the Lord came to her at the hour of her death in that inhuman place, she was there ready to meet him with the lamp of her faith burning brightly. That same light was lit in our own lives at our baptism. Our calling is to keep that light of our faith, the light of the Lord, alive in our hearts, no matter how great the darkness that bears down upon us. If we are to be faithful to that calling we need to keep turning in prayer towards the one who spoke of himself as the light of the world and promised that whoever follows him will never walk in darkness.

10 August, Saturday, Saint Laurence, Deacon and Martyr
John 12:24–26

I have always liked that saying in today's first reading, 'God loves a cheerful giver.' There are various ways of giving. We can give grudgingly, in the words of Saint Paul in that reading. My mother had a habit of saying, when we did something she asked us to do but moaned and groaned about it, 'Don't take the good out of it.' We can take the good out of our giving by doing it with a face on us, as they say. People sense that we are going through the motions of giving but our heart is not in it. A cheerful giver is someone who gives willingly, gladly. This is the way Jesus gave. He gave with the joyful freedom of the Holy Spirit. Saint Paul in today's reading assures us that when we give in this way, there is no limit to the blessings that God can send us. Giving cheerfully and willingly opens us up to receive God's blessings. In giving in this way, in the Spirit of the Lord, we discover that we end up receiving far more than we gave. This is reflected in the image Jesus uses in the gospel reading of the grain that dies but in dying yields a rich harvest. There is a certain dying to ourselves when we give cheerfully. We are not

looking for anything for ourselves, such as sympathy or appreciation. When we die to ourselves in this way, our life yields a rich
harvest, both for ourselves and for others. When there is no selfish
concern in our giving, the Lord can enrich us with his blessings and
greatly bless others through our giving. Saint Laurence, the deacon,
exemplifies the cheerful giver who gave without looking for anything in return.

12 August, Monday, Nineteenth Week in Ordinary Time
Matthew 17:22–27

In today's first reading, the prophet Ezekiel has a vision of God. He
found it very difficult to describe this experience. He uses the
phrase, 'something that looked like' and 'what looked like'. It
looked like a sapphire, a throne, fire. It looked like all of these elements but it wasn't any of them. It is very tentative language. Ezekiel is aware that his description doesn't do justice to what he saw.
God is always beyond our words. Human words fail us when it
comes to speaking of God. Yet God has spoken a powerful word to
us to help us to see who God is, and that word is Jesus. To see Jesus
is to see God. How Jesus relates to us shows us how God relates to
us. In today's gospel reading, Jesus shows great sensitivity in the
way he relates to those who put a hostile question to Peter: 'Does
your master not pay the half shekel?' This was a tax paid to the
Temple in Jerusalem for its upkeep. It is clear from the gospel reading that Jesus felt no obligation to pay this tax, yet he told Peter to
pay it, 'so as not to offend these people'. Even though Jesus felt
totally free in regard to this tax, he paid it because he didn't want to
offend those for whom the tax was very important. There was a
great sensitivity there to the feelings of others. Sensitivity to others,
to what is important to them, to what they hold dear, is one of the
expressions of love. There are different ways of expressing our

relationship with God. Some people's way of relating to God, their way of praying, for example, may not appeal to us, but we are respectful of it and sensitive to their feelings around it. Jesus revealed God's love, a love that was full of sensitivity towards others. Through the Holy Spirit he empowers us to give expression to this sensitive love in our own lives.

13 August, Tuesday, Nineteenth Week in Ordinary Time
Matthew 18:1–5, 10, 12–14

In the gospel reading Jesus' disciples ask him, 'Who is the greatest in the kingdom of heaven?' In response to their question, Jesus does not say the greatest are the most successful, the strongest, those who outdo others in skill and power. Rather, he took a child, one of the least significant in the culture of the time, and declared that children are the greatest in the kingdom of heaven. Those who, in Jesus' time, had no status or power or influence or expertise or skill are the greatest in the kingdom of God. What makes them great in God's kingdom is their openness to receive God's presence in Jesus. Today we can still recognise that openness to the Lord in children. Jesus then goes on to call on his disciples and on all of us to become like little children, and he declares that unless we do so we will not enter the kingdom of God. Children can be our teachers. As adults we need to be as open to the Lord's presence as children are. Then we will be great in the kingdom of God. From speaking of children, Jesus goes on to speak of 'little ones'. This phrase may refer to those people whose faith is not yet fully mature and therefore are vulnerable … vulnerable to being scandalised. The parable of the lost sheep or, better, the 'Devoted Shepherd', suggests that God has a special concern for this group within the Church. We are called to share God's concern that their faith is not weakened further by attitudes and actions that are contrary to the mind of Christ.

14 August, Wednesday, Nineteenth Week in Ordinary Time
Matthew 18:15–20

Jewish rabbis claimed that when two pious Jews sat together to discuss the words of the Jewish Law, the divine presence was with them. In today's gospel reading, Jesus declares that where two or three of his followers meet in his name, he will be there with them. The meeting in his name that Jesus refers to is a meeting for worship, for prayer. As a church we gather not around the words of the Jewish Law but around the words of Jesus, and when we do that Jesus will be among us, and he will be among us as Emmanuel, God-with-us. The first reading portrayed the 'glory of the Lord', the presence of God, leaving the Jewish Temple; the gospel reading speaks of the presence of God, the presence of Jesus, God-with-us, among the disciples of Jesus. For the Lord to be with us whenever we gather to worship is a great privilege, a great grace. Yet we are called to live in a way that is worthy of such a grace. The Lord, who is present among us when we gather for prayer, calls on us to reveal his presence to others when we rise from prayer and go about our daily tasks.

15 August, Thursday, The Assumption of the Blessed Virgin Mary
Luke 1:39–56

Mary's assumption reminds us of our own heavenly destiny. Her earthly life reminds us of our own baptismal calling. In today's gospel reading, Mary physically carries Jesus in her womb to Elizabeth, her older cousin. As disciples of the Lord, we are all called to carry Jesus to others. Our baptismal calling is to become bearers of the Lord's presence to all. Mary gives expression to our own baptismal calling. As the first disciple of her son, she shows what it means to follow in the Lord's way. Mary could bring the Lord to Elizabeth because, at the moment of the annunciation, she had given herself over to God's purpose for her life and she had consented to allow the Holy Spirit to overshadow her, to take hold of her. To the extent that we give ourselves over to God's purpose for our lives and allow the Holy Spirit to overshadow us, we too will become people who bring the Lord to others.

When Mary reached her destination and greeted Elizabeth, Elizabeth was filled with the Holy Spirit. Mary's way of relating to Elizabeth resulted in Elizabeth being filled with the Holy Spirit. We too are called to relate to others in ways that help them to become filled with the Holy Spirit, that open them up more fully to the working of the Holy Spirit in their lives. In response to Mary's greeting, Elizabeth declares Mary blessed because of her faith: 'Blessed is she who believed'. Mary's faith showed itself in love, in a journey of loving concern to her older, more vulnerable, pregnant cousin. She shows us that genuine faith always expresses itself in loving service of others. Just as Mary's presence filled Elizabeth with the Holy Spirit, Elizabeth's way of relating to Mary filled Mary with a spirit of prayer. Because of the way Elizabeth welcomed Mary, Mary prayed her great prayer, the Magnificat. Mary's prayer shows her to be a woman who hungers for a new justice on earth, where the lowly are exalted, the hungry are filled, and oppressive powers are overcome. Mary shows us that genuine faith expresses itself not only in love but in hunger for justice.

If Mary's life shows us the shape of our own faith journey, her assumption shows us our final destiny, beyond this earthly life. The feast of her assumption celebrates her full sharing in the risen life of Christ. She gives us hope that, in the words of today's second reading, 'all will be brought to life in Christ'. As those who now share fully in the Lord's risen life, we can confidently turn to her, asking her to pray for us now so that we can each be the complete disciple of the Lord that she was and to pray for us at the hour of our death so that we too can come to share in the Lord's risen life to the full.

16 August, Friday, Nineteenth Week in Ordinary Time
Matthew 19:3–12

In today's gospel reading, when Jesus is put on the spot by some Pharisees regarding the question of divorce, he turns to the opening chapters of the first book of the Bible, the Book of Genesis. The Jewish law made provision for divorce. The only issue of debate among the religious leaders was the grounds for divorce. One school of thought favoured very lenient grounds; another school insisted on much stricter grounds. However, both schools followed the Jewish Law in asserting that it was only the man who could initiate divorce proceedings, whatever the grounds. The woman was not free to do the same. The divorce laws gave a freedom to men that it did not give to women, and it left women very vulnerable to being cut adrift by their husbands, for the flimsiest of reasons. In that context, Jesus' teaching on marriage was intended to protect women. It reminded men of their obligation to love and honour their wives as they would their own body. Jesus went back beyond what the Jewish Law allowed to God's original intention as expressed in the Book of Genesis, according to which husband and wife are to become one in love, faithful to each other all the days of their lives. It is a wonderful vision for married life, yet we all know from experience that people's marriages don't always reflect this vision of Jesus. Jesus has a desire for all our lives, whether we are married or single; it is that we would love one another as he loves us. We don't always live out of that vision of Jesus, but it is always worth striving towards, and if we open ourselves to the help of the Holy Spirit, the Spirit of the Lord's love, we will manage to give expression to this vision, at least from time to time.

17 August, Saturday, Nineteenth Week in Ordinary Time
Matthew 19:13–15

I always read this gospel reading on the occasion of a baptism because it seems so appropriate for baptism. When children are baptised, the Lord is welcoming them into his family, the community of believers we call the Church. They are being greatly blessed and graced by the Lord. In today's gospel reading Jesus wanted to welcome the children whom the parents brought to him for a blessing, but the disciples were turning the children away. Perhaps they thought that Jesus only had time for adults. However, they completely misread Jesus, who said to them, 'Let the little children alone, and do not stop them coming to me.' Jesus wanted children to be central to the life of the community he was gathering about himself. He would want them to be central to the life and worship of the Church. Jesus goes on to declare in the gospel reading that the kingdom of God belongs to them as much as to anyone else. They have the same right as adults do to receive the gift of the kingdom of God. Jesus wants them to be blessed by God who is working powerfully through him. The risen Lord wants us all to open up the riches of the Gospel to children. Unlike the disciples in the gospel reading, he wants us, his disciples today, to bring children to himself for prayer and worship. He wants us to help children to come to know him as a friend, so that they can draw strength from his loving presence to them all through their lives.

19 August, Monday, Twentieth Week in Ordinary Time
Matthew 19:16–22

The question the young man asked Jesus in today's gospel reading, 'What good deed must I do to possess eternal life?' was a question of great importance to him. Here was a serious young man who wanted to live as well as he could, in a way that was in accordance with God's will. It is clear from his conversation with Jesus that he was already living a very good life. Jesus put before him the commandments that have to do with how we relate to others, and he could confidently say that he had kept all these commandments. Yet he felt there was something more he could be doing. 'What more do I need to do?' It is admirable when people who are living good lives want to live even better lives. We sense that desire within ourselves. We may be living well, in ways that are in keeping with God's desire for our lives, but we sense there is another step we could take. We could launch further into the deep. We could be more generous in our response to the Lord's call. That realisation can leave us a little unsettled, just as the young man was unsettled, in spite of all his good qualities. This sense of feeling unsettled is ultimately something good. It brings home to us that the Lord is always calling us beyond where we are in some way. In the gospel reading, the young man couldn't respond to the Lord's call to him to go beyond where he was. In his case, it would have involved letting go of his great wealth, giving it to the poor and following Jesus in a very radical way. As a result, he went away sad. The Lord's call to us to go beyond where we are, to grow in our relationship with him, will take a different form for each one of us. The 'more' the Lord is calling us into will always take account of our own unique circumstances and situation in life. If we can discern what that call of the Lord means for us personally and respond to it, then we will find life, both in the here and now and in eternity.

20 August, Tuesday, Twentieth Week in Ordinary Time
Matthew 19:23–30
Jesus' image of a camel passing through the eye of a needle has been spoken of as an example of comic exaggeration. The person with the plank in their eye would be another example. Jesus often used such comic exaggeration to get people's attention and perhaps to shock them out of a sense of complacency. When Jesus said it would

be easier for a camel to pass through the eye of a needle than for a rich person to enter the kingdom of heaven, the astonished disciples ask, 'Who can be saved, then?' Jesus' reply, 'For people, this is impossible; for God everything is possible', suggests that the attaining of salvation is primarily God's doing rather than our doing. It is a divine attainment rather than a human one. We can only enter into the life of God with the help that God alone can give us. We need to depend fully on God to enter the kingdom of heaven, opening ourselves up in our poverty to his gracious working on our behalf. This is where Jesus sees the problem with excessive attachment to wealth or possessions. If we seek our security in wealth or possessions, we will cease to rely on God, who alone gives access to salvation, to life in abundance. They might even lead us to say, in the words of today's first reading, 'I am a god.' If, acknowledging our poverty, we place our security in God, in the Lord, then, according to Jesus in today's gospel reading, we will be abundantly repaid in this earthly life, and also inherit eternal life.

21 August, Wednesday, Twentieth Week in Ordinary Time
Matthew 20:1–16
Most of us react instinctively against any form of behaviour that we consider to be unfair or unjust. If we think we are being treated unfairly or unjustly we can feel especially irate. It is probably that instinct in us that leaves us feeling a bit uneasy about the story that Jesus tells in today's gospel reading. We can easily sympathise with the complaint of the workers who bemoan the fact that those who worked for only an hour got the same wages as those who worked all day. Yet, whereas those workers were operating out of the category of justice, the employer was operating out of the category of generosity. He wasn't unjust to those who worked all day; he paid them what he agreed with them. He was simply extremely generous

to those who worked for only an hour. Perhaps Jesus was saying to us through this parable that God's generosity cannot be contained within the categories of human justice; it explodes those categories. God does not deal with us according to our efforts, on the basis of what we deserve. There is nothing calculating about God's generosity. Perhaps we are all encouraged to identify with those who worked for only an hour; we are all, in a sense, latecomers. The parable assures us that God's generosity will surprise us and leave us humbled.

22 August, Thursday, The Queenship of Mary
Luke 1:26–28

This feast is a relatively recent one in the Church. For centuries Mary had been venerated as queen of the angels and the saints. She is depicted thus, for example, in some very early mosaic works in the apses of the great basilicas. Jesus is portrayed as king of heaven and earth, and, alongside him, Mary is portrayed as queen. In 1955, at the end of the Marian Year, Pope Pius XII gave formal expression to this popular belief of the faithful, by promulgating this feast of the Queenship of Mary. He placed it on this date, 22 August, to stress the connection with the feast of the Assumption. Like that feast, this feast of the Queenship of Mary proclaims the very special union between Mary and her Son in heaven. The Church understands this special relationship between Jesus and Mary in heaven as the continuation and deepening of their special relationship on earth. In the gospel reading, Mary consents to be the mother of Jesus, God's Son. She carried Jesus in her womb for nine months and, having given birth to him, she nursed him as only a mother could. No other human being had such a deeply personal relationship with Jesus from the first moment of his existence. Before she conceived Jesus in her womb, she conceived him in her heart, through her faith, by surrendering herself to God's purpose and desire for her life: 'I am the handmaid of the Lord, let what you have said be done to me.' When Mary visited her cousin Elizabeth, according to Luke's Gospel, Elizabeth declared Mary blessed because of the child she was carrying in her womb, but then went on to declare Mary blessed because of her faith: 'Blessed is she who believed that there would be a fulfilment of what was said to her by the Lord.' Mary inspires us to keep growing in our faith, to keep giving ourselves over to God's purpose, God's desire, for our lives, so that Christ can live in us, as he lived in Mary, and so that we become people who bring the Lord to others as she brought the Lord to us. Christ, who lives in us in this earthly life, will then draw us into a deeper relationship with himself in the life beyond this earthly life.

23 August, Friday, Twentieth Week in Ordinary Time
Matthew 22:34–40

Life can be very complex and we often feel the need to cut through all the complexities to what is essential and truly valuable. In the time of Jesus, the Jewish religion had become a little complex. There were many laws and regulations governing all sorts of areas of life. The question that was put to Jesus at the beginning of today's gospel reading was looking for what was essential and valuable in the midst of all this complexity: 'Which is the greatest commandment of the Law?' In other words, 'What does it all boil down to in the end?' In answering that question, Jesus found it necessary to give not just the one greatest commandment of the Law, but the greatest and the next greatest commandment of the Law. He couldn't really boil the Jewish Law down to one commandment, but he could boil it down to two commandments. However, the two commandments have something essential in common. They are both commandments to love. In a way, Jesus was saying that all the laws and regulations of the Jewish religion can be boiled down to the commandment to love. Yet, for Jesus, there is a primary love and a secondary love. Our primary love is due to God. Only God is to be loved with our whole being, all our heart, all our soul and all our mind. God is deserving of such love because that is how God loves us. God loves us with all God's being, and we are to love God with all our being. However, for Jesus, this total love of God is inseparable from the love of our neighbour and our neighbour is every human being, regardless of their race, religion, background or way of life. We are to love others in the way God loves them. It is our loving relationship with God that empowers us to love others in this Godlike way.

24 August, Saturday, Saint Bartholomew, Apostle
John 1:45–51

Bartholomew is listed as one of the twelve apostles. He has tended to be identified with Nathanael, who features in today's gospel reading. Nathanael starts off being very sceptical about Jesus: 'Can anything good come from that place – Nazareth?' However, he finishes by making a great confession of faith: 'Rabbi, you are the Son of God, you are the King of Israel.' Yet Jesus goes on to tell him that although he has journeyed from scepticism to faith he is still only at the beginning of his journey of faith. Jesus promises him, 'You will see greater things … You will see heaven laid open and, above the Son of Man, the angels of God ascending and descending.' Nathanael will eventually come to see Jesus as the meeting point of heaven and earth, the one in whom God has taken flesh. Nathanael had made great progress on the journey of faith but he will make even further progress. His initial movement beyond scepticism was inspired by the witness of one of the disciples of Jesus, Philip, who shared his faith with Nathanael and encouraged him to meet Jesus in spite of his scepticism. We are all on a journey of faith. On that journey there may be a moment or many moments of scepticism. Yet the Lord keeps calling out to us, very often through others, and promises us that we will see greater things. If that is to come to pass, we need people like Philip to support us on every step of our faith journey and we, in turn, need to be a Philip to others on their faith journey.

26 August, Monday, Twenty-first Week in Ordinary Time
Matthew 23:13–22

One of the ways we connect with each other is by praying for each other. If we were to look at our prayer, we would probably find that a lot of it is prayer for others, intercessory prayer. We pray for each other all the time, especially when we go to places of pilgrimage, like Lourdes. At the end of today's first reading, Paul declares that he prays for the church in Thessalonica. I am struck by the content of that prayer: 'We pray continually that our God will fulfil all your desires for goodness and complete all that you have been doing through faith.' We all have what Paul refers to in that prayer, 'desires for goodness'. We desire to be good; we want to become all that God is calling us to be. That desire is crucial; it is something God can work with. As Paul says in that prayer, 'God will fulfil all your desires for goodness'. God needs our desire. Our desire gives God an opening to work in our lives. No matter how many times we fall short, as long as we retain our desire for goodness, our desire to walk in the way of God's Son, God can work powerfully within us, and, in the words of that first reading, will be able to complete all that we have been doing through faith. A good prayer to make for ourselves is to pray that our desire for goodness would never weaken. If we remain true to our desire for goodness, we will be 'found worthy of the kingdom of God', in the words of Paul in the first reading. In contrast, those to whom Jesus refers in the gospel reading as shutting up 'the kingdom of heaven in people's faces' will not be found worthy of that kingdom. Jesus was always very critical of those who are an obstacle to others reaching all that God desires for them.

27 August, Tuesday, Twenty-first Week in Ordinary Time
Matthew 23:23–26

Jesus often uses humorous images to illustrate his teaching, such as his reference to those who try to take a splinter out of someone's eye while not noticing the plank in their own eye. We have another such humorous image in today's gospel reading. Jesus addresses the scribes and Pharisees as blind guides, 'straining out gnats and swallowing camels'. They pay excessive attention to what Jesus considers to be minor matters of the Jewish Law, such as tithes to be paid on various herbs, while, at the same time, neglecting the weightier matters of the Law, 'justice, mercy and faith', or 'faithfulness'. Justice consists in rendering to others what is their due, as human beings made in God's image. Mercy goes beyond justice in graciously bestowing on others even more than their due. The father in the parable of the prodigal son was merciful in that sense. Faith could refer to either dealing faithfully with others or entrusting oneself in faith to God. Faith in that second sense, a faithful relationship with God, is the source and inspiration of the more social virtues of justice and mercy. In that way, the three qualities of justice, mercy and faith would be closely aligned to the inseparable twin commandments to love God with all our being and our neighbour as ourselves. In the gospel reading, Jesus was calling on his critics to keep going back to the essential core of their religious tradition. It is a call we all need to keep hearing. We can get so preoccupied with what is relatively peripheral to our faith that we undermine what is essential there. We need always to keep in view the essential trinity to which Jesus refers in the gospel reading, justice, mercy and faithfulness.

28 August, Wednesday, Twenty-first Week in Ordinary Time
Matthew 23:27–32

It is clear from today's first reading that Paul was anxious not to be a financial burden on the young church in Thessalonica. 'We worked night and day, slaving and straining, so as not to be a burden on any of you.' It was Paul's policy to earn his keep by working at his trade as a tentmaker, so as to be able to preach the Gospel free of charge. Paul was also concerned about some members of the church becoming an unnecessary financial burden on the community, when, in reality, they were well capable of working to support themselves. Elsewhere in his letters Paul says to the members of the church to 'bear one another's burdens, and in this way you will fulfil the law of Christ' (Galatians 6:2), which is the law of love. We are called to help to carry the burden of others, while not becoming an unnecessary burden on other people. In the gospel reading, Jesus highlights one way that people can become a burden on others, namely, when they give the appearance of 'good honest people' but, in reality, are full of 'hypocrisy and lawlessness'. Elsewhere, Jesus uses the image of wolves in sheep's clothing. We would all find such people burdensome, as we try to discern whether or not to rely on them and believe what they tell us. At the end of the first reading, Paul writes his name in his own handwriting as a 'mark of genuineness'. The genuine person is never a burden. Their honesty and truthfulness, their transparency and lack of deceit, is burden lifting rather than burden imposing. Jesus was the supremely genuine person; he revealed God's truth to the full. He offered himself as the one who can lift our burdens: 'Come to me all you who are weary and are carrying heavy burdens.' He wishes to continue this burden-lifting work as risen Lord in and through each one of us.

29 August, Thursday, The Passion of Saint John the Baptist
Mark 6:17–29

We know from our own experience that anger can be a difficult emotion to manage. It can lead us to say and do things we might subsequently regret. According to today's gospel reading, the anger of Herodias, the wife of Herod Antipas, would have led her to kill John the Baptist. He was momentarily saved from her deadly anger by Herod, who, instead, had John imprisoned, knowing John to be a good and holy man. Yet it was Herod's rash promise to Herodias's daughter at his birthday banquet that allowed Herodias to give full expression to her anger. Herod's promise to her, 'I will give you anything you ask', was enough of an opening for Herodias to ask for the head of John the Baptist. Rather than lose face and honour by going back on a promise he had made on oath, Herod now submitted to Herodias's request, made through her daughter. Because of Herod, Herodias and her daughter, a 'good and holy man' was brutally put to death, without even the semblance of a trial. Every generation before and since has witnessed similar callous abuses of power. Yet this is the world in which we are asked to live out our faith in the Lord, who himself was a victim of such abuse of power. The greater the darkness, the more the light of our faith needs to shine. In the Gospel of John, Jesus refers to John the Baptist as a 'burning and shining lamp' (John 5:35). His light shone at its brightest in the hour of his execution. Similarly, the light of God's love shone most brightly through Jesus when he was lifted up on the cross. As people of faith, we don't get discouraged when evil seems to triumph. Instead, we turn trustingly towards the Lord and ask that the light of his loving presence would shine all the more brightly through our lives.

30 August, Friday, Twenty-first Week in Ordinary Time
Matthew 25:1–13

It seems that in the time of Jesus young unmarried women waited with the bride at her family home for the arrival of the bridegroom. Then, when he arrived, they would escort the couple with lighted lamps to the house of the bridegroom, where the marriage feast had been prepared and the guests were waiting for the couple's grand entry. It was an important task for these bridesmaids to accompany the couple and to guide them through the darkness with lamps burning brightly. It would have been very embarrassing if they didn't have enough oil to keep their lamps lighting for the length of the procession to the house of the bridegroom. In the parable, five of the ten bridesmaids discovered at the last moment that they didn't have enough oil for their role of accompanying the married couple. 'Our lamps are going out,' they cried. Jesus may be saying to us that we need to keep the lamp, the flame, of our faith burning brightly to the very end, and not allow it to go out. At the baptism of a child, when the godfather lights the baptismal candle from the Paschal candle, the priest says to the parents of the child, 'Keep the flame of faith alive in his/her heart.' That is our baptismal calling, to keep the flame of faith alive in our hearts and to allow our faith to show itself in the loving service of others. Elsewhere in the Gospel of Matthew, Jesus says to his disciples, to us all, 'You are the light of the world ... let your light shine before others, so that they may see your good works and give glory to your Father in heaven.' We are called to let the light of the Gospel shine through us, for the long haul, and to do that we will always need the help of the Holy Spirit, who kindles in us the fire, the flame, of loving faith.

31 August, Saturday, Twenty-first Week in Ordinary Time
Matthew 25:14–30

What distinguished the third servant in today's parable from the other two servants was fear: 'I was afraid, and I went off and hid your talent in the ground.' Fear disabled him and prevented him from responding to the trust that his master had placed in him by giving him a significant sum of money as a gift. In the gospels, fear is often portrayed as the opposite of faith or trust. In the storm at sea, Jesus asked his disciples, 'Why are you afraid, you of little faith?' (Matthew 8:26). The first letter of John declares, 'There is no fear in love, but perfect love casts out fear; for fear has to do with punishment, and whoever fears has not reached perfection in love. We love because he first loved us' (1 John 4:19). God has revealed his perfect love for us through the life, death and resurrection of Jesus. Because we know ourselves to be perfectly loved by God, we can entrust ourselves to God, taking risks on behalf of God, knowing that if we fail God continues to love us. The Lord's love frees us to live fearlessly and generously. When Peter started walking towards Jesus across the water from the boat, 'he noticed the strong wind … and became frightened and began to sink', and Jesus asked him, 'You of little faith, why did you doubt?' (Matthew 14:30–31). When we forget how much the Lord loves us and focus instead on what seems threatening, we easily find ourselves sinking out of fear. If, however, we keep looking to Jesus, 'the pioneer and perfecter of our faith', then we will fearlessly 'run the race that is set before us' (Hebrews 12:1–2). The Spirit of God's unconditional love has been poured into our hearts and, as Saint Paul says, 'you did not receive a spirit of slavery to fall back into fear, but you have received a spirit of adoption. When we cry out, "Abba! Father!" it is that very Spirit bearing witness with our spirit that we are children of God' (Romans 8:15–16). This Spirit allows us to use our gifts in the service of the Lord without fear.

2 September, Monday, Twenty-second Week in Ordinary Time
Luke 4:16–30

Today's gospel reading begins with an account of the liturgy of the word in the synagogue of Jesus' home town in Nazareth. Jesus stands up to read from the prophet Isaiah and then sits down to comment on what he read. Jesus identifies himself with the prophet who was sent to bring good news to the poor, to proclaim liberty to captives, new sight to the blind, to set the downtrodden free. Jesus goes on to identify himself with two other prophets, Elijah and Elisha, who ministered to people outside Israel, a hungry widow from Sidon and a leper from Syria. Jesus was saying to the people of Nazareth that he had come for those in greatest need, regardless of who they were or where they were from. The generous vision Jesus had of his mission made the people of Nazareth very angry. Jesus was one of their own and they expected special treatment. However, the good news is that Jesus has come for us all. If he has favourites it is those who are broken in body, in mind and in spirit. The Lord is constantly reaching out to us in our brokenness, in our pain and suffering. All he asks is that we receive him as he is, on his own terms, which the people of Nazareth could not do. The Lord is always close to all of us; it is our need, our suffering, whatever form it takes, that can bring us close to him.

3 September, Tuesday, Twenty-second Week in Ordinary Time
Luke 4:31–37

There are times in all our lives when our spirit is disturbed. We are not ourselves. We find ourselves distressed and it can cause us to respond to people in ways that we normally would not. There can be a sharpness in our tone or an anger in our voice. We might look back on those moments and wonder what got into us. We have an extreme case of this phenomenon in today's gospel reading. In the synagogue of Capernaum, Jesus encounters a very disturbed person, who shouted at Jesus in a very aggressive way, 'What do you want with us, Jesus of Nazareth?' Luke the evangelist tells us that this man was possessed by an unclean spirit. The spirit that had taken hold of him was not the Spirit of God; it was a spirit that was opposed to God. It was not the Spirit that Paul speaks about in the first reading, the Spirit that comes from God who alone knows the depths of God. Jesus released this man of this spirit that was destructive of him and of others. He restored him to God and to himself. There are times when we too need to be released from some spirit that holds us back from becoming the person God is calling us to be. The same Lord, who was in the synagogue on that sabbath, stands among us today to deliver us from the spirits that diminish us and, sometimes, others. He continues to offer us the Holy Spirit, so that our lives can bear God's fruit more fully. We need to stand ready to keep receiving this gift of the Spirit that comes from God.

4 September, Wednesday, Twenty-second Week in Ordinary Time
Luke 4:38–44

In today's gospel reading, Jesus brings healing to many people in Capernaum. Understandably, the people of Capernaum wanted to hold on to him. When Jesus went off to a lonely place just outside Capernaum to pray they caught up with him and tried to prevent him leaving them. However, Jesus was very clear that he had to move on: 'I must proclaim the kingdom of God in the other towns too.' The people of Capernaum had to let him go; Jesus was at the disposal of God's purpose and that took priority over what the people of Capernaum wanted. We began reading from the Gospel of Luke last Monday; Luke consistently portrays Jesus as someone who was totally at the service of God's purpose. That often brought him into conflict with human purposes that were opposed to God's purpose. We are all called to live our lives in accordance with God's purpose. We try to do what we think God wants of us. That will often bring us into conflict with what other people want of us and want from us. In our struggle to do what God wants, however, we have the risen Lord to help us to walk that way. He can empower us to take the path he took, through his presence to us in his word, in the Eucharist and in each other.

5 September, Thursday, Twenty-second Week in Ordinary Time
Luke 5:1–11

Today's gospel reading suggests that just when a situation seems hopeless, without promise, there is often an abundance of life just below the surface, if only we could see it. Simon Peter and his companions had worked hard all night long, fishing on the Sea of Galilee, and had caught nothing. Night-time was the best time to catch fish. There was no reason to think that it was worth their while to go out again in full daylight. However, Jesus could see that there was life below the surface of the sea and he told them to put out into deep water and let down their nets for a catch. When they did so, they were overwhelmed by the abundance of the catch. They had to call on other boats to come and help them. Very often the Lord can see signs of life that we miss. Our past failures, the size of the task before us, our sense of our own limitations, can immobilise us and leave us feeling despondent and even hopeless. It is at such times that we need to turn to the Lord and ask him to help us to see as he sees, with eyes that are sensitive to the promise and hope that even the most difficult situations can hold. We might think in our wisdom that some situation, or even some person, is a lost cause, but as Saint Paul says in the first reading, 'the wisdom of the world is foolishness to God'. God brought new life out of the most unpromising situation imaginable, the crucifixion of his own Son, who was the embodiment of his love for the world. The God whom Jesus revealed is a God who sees abundance in the most unpromising of situations. With the help of the Holy Spirit we can begin to see life as the Lord does, with eyes that are attentive to the signs of life beneath the surface.

6 September, Friday, Twenty-second Week in Ordinary Time
Luke 5:33–39

There is a wisdom in what Paul says in today's first reading, 'There must be no passing of premature judgement'. He made that statement in response to people who were judging his ministry as not powerful enough. He goes on to say that judgement should be left until the Lord comes. He alone can reveal the secret intentions of people's hearts. Interestingly, Paul says, 'I will not even pass judgement on myself'. We know ourselves better than we know others, yet Paul is saying that we don't know ourselves well enough to make a judgement about ourselves. It is only the Lord who can light up what is hidden in the dark, whether in ourselves or in others. We can obviously make a judgement that certain ways of behaving are better than others, but Paul is saying that we cannot really judge what is in another's heart because we don't have access to it. In the gospel reading, we find the Pharisees judging the behaviour of Jesus' disciples and getting it wrong. They judged that the behaviour of Jesus' disciples fell short of what God wanted because they didn't pray in the way other religious people prayed, and they didn't fast in ways other religious people did, such as the disciples of John the Baptist and the disciples of the Pharisees. Jesus went on to say that he came to bring new wine that needed new wineskins, new ways of expressing faith in God, new forms of prayer, new ways of understanding fasting. Jesus acknowledges that the response he often got from people to the new wine he was offering was 'the old is good'. Jesus would have acknowledged that there was much good in the past, but he also knew that we cannot remain there. The risen Lord is always doing something new, in our own lives, in our parishes, in the wider Church. Our calling is to be ready with the new wineskins that can better contain, better express, the new initiative the Lord is always taking.

7 September, Saturday, Twenty-second Week in Ordinary Time
Luke 6:1–5

In today's first reading, Saint Paul asks a question that is worth reflecting upon: 'What do you have that was not given to you?' Paul is reminding the members of the church in Corinth that so much in life is gift. We might work for something, but even the ability to work is itself a gift. The people who matter most to us in life are a gift. We probably didn't go looking for them; they came to us. We have just begun the Season of Creation in the Church, which goes from 1 September to 4 October, the feast of Saint Francis of Assisi. It is a good time to recall how the natural world is a gift that has been given to us. Nature is a wonderful gift that can bring us healing and can help to renew our spirits. In the gospel reading, Jesus' disciples were treating the ears of corn in the cornfield through which they walked as a gift. The Pharisees accused them of breaking God's law, but Jesus defended their actions. They were hungry, and the taking of a few ears of corn to satisfy their hunger was perfectly acceptable. It might be the equivalent of us picking and eating the blackberries that are appearing in various hedgerows at the moment. Jesus would want us to appreciate the ways in which God is always gracing us and bestowing gifts on us. The appropriate response to the experience of being gifted is gratitude. A spirit of thanksgiving to God is to characterise the Lord's followers. As Saint Paul says in another of his letters, 'Give thanks in all circumstances'. He doesn't say '*for* all circumstances' but '*in* all circumstances'. No matter how difficult life may be for us, there is always something for which we can give thanks.

9 September, Monday, Twenty-third Week in Ordinary Time
Luke 6:6–11

In today's gospel reading we are told that when Jesus went into the synagogue on the sabbath the Pharisees were watching him to see if he would cure a partly paralysed man, hoping to find something to use against Jesus. In other words, even though Jesus was clearly doing good, the Pharisees were on the lookout for the negative in him; they were suspicious of him. Because they were predisposed to seeing the negative, they couldn't see the good that God was doing through Jesus on that particular sabbath day in the synagogue. Sometimes how we see someone or some situation determines what we see. If we look at people through suspicious lens, negative lens, we will see the negative and miss the good. We always have to be cleaning our lens, as it were, so that we can see clearly, so that we can see not just the problems that may be there, but the much greater good that is often there as well. On this occasion, the problem for the Pharisees of the sabbath law being broken should have been far outweighed by the greater good of a broken man being healed. The gospels are always calling us to see the good work that God is doing, even when things are not happening quite as we might expect or want them to happen.

10 September, Tuesday, Twenty-third Week in Ordinary Time
Luke 6:12–19

I was struck by the last line in today's gospel reading, 'everyone in the crowd was trying to touch him because power came out of him that cured them all'. People wanted to touch this man through whom God was working so powerfully. It wasn't enough just to hear him or to see him; they needed to touch him. Touching the Lord is a more intimate, more personal form of communication with him than hearing or seeing. The sense of touch remains important in the faith life of us all. We too want to touch the Lord, and to be touched by him. It is above all in and through the sacraments that we touch the Lord and allow him to touch our lives. In the Eucharist, for example, we take the bread in our hands or on our tongue and eat it; we take the chalice in our hands and drink from it. The sense of touch is very real there. As we take the bread and take the cup, as we touch the Lord in this way, the Lord takes us; he touches our lives. Like the people in the gospel reading, we too can experience the healing and renewing power that comes from him. The Lord who touches us in the Eucharist sends us forth to touch the lives of others in life-giving ways.

11 September, Wednesday, Twenty-third Week in Ordinary Time
Luke 6:20–26

In the gospel reading, Jesus speaks a word of consolation to those who are struggling the most, the poor, the hungry, all who weep, those experiencing rejection because of their loyalty to him. He declares that God is working to transform their situation for the better. The day will come when they will be satisfied, when they will laugh, when the kingdom of God will be theirs. Jesus is revealing God to be one who is not only present to us in our most vulnerable situations but who is actively working on our behalf to bring a change for the better to our lives. This is the God whom Jesus revealed by his deeds and his words. He invited the poor to his table, he fed the hungry in the wilderness, the brought the joy of God's kingdom to those who were weeping, such as the widow at Nain. Jesus wants his disciples, all of us, to reveal this same God by our deeds and our words. The risen Lord wants to work through us to bring something of that fullness of life that characterises the kingdom of God to those who are poor, hungry and weeping today. We are aware of some people who are bringing hunger, poverty and sadness to others by their actions or even complacent indifference. It is this group that Jesus addresses in the second half of the gospel, declaring that God will hold them to account for the suffering they are inflicting on others, very often growing rich in the process. There are forces around that are death dealing, and in the face of such forces the Lord needs us all the more to be instruments of his life-giving work in the world.

12 September, Thursday, Twenty-third Week in Ordinary Time
Luke 6:27–38

We live in an information age. We have access to information today to a degree that wasn't conceivable even a generation ago. We are more knowledgeable about so many things, compared to our parents or grandparents. We place a high value on knowledge and on those who have it, people who are experts in their field. It is clear from the beginning of today's first reading that some members of the church in Corinth also placed a high value on knowledge, declaring proudly, 'We all have knowledge'. However, in Paul's view, this claim to know has made some of them very arrogant and somewhat indifferent to the impact of their knowledge on others in the community. They may have knowledge but they lack love, the fruit of the Spirit which, according to Paul in that reading, 'makes the building grow', builds up the Church. Paul was convinced that knowledge without love can be destructive of others or, as he puts it, 'could become the ruin of someone weak'. In the gospel reading, Jesus elaborates on this love which the Spirit inspires. It embraces those who have done nothing to deserve it, our enemy. It is given to those from whom no return of love can be expected. It is a love that is compassionate, that is ready to suffer with others, no matter who they are, and that refuses to condemn others, leaving judgement to God. This quality of love, which is a reflection of God's love for us, has a much higher value in God's eyes than any form of knowledge. If knowledge is to serve others well, it needs to be infused with such love. Jesus concludes by declaring that those who love in his way and who allow this love to shape all their other qualities will be opening themselves up to receiving the 'full measure' of God's generous love.

13 September, Friday, Twenty-third Week in Ordinary Time
Luke 6:39–42

We often use the expression 'the blind leading the blind', which is inspired by today's gospel reading. Jesus uses the humorous image of someone with a plank in their eye trying to take out a splinter from someone else's eye. We all know the difference between a plank and a splinter, one is large and heavy and the other is tiny and light. Jesus is suggesting that someone with a significant failing can end up trying to correct someone with a very small failing. It is a case of a completely blind person trying to heal or lead someone who is only partially blind. We are all flawed in some way and, as a result, we do not see clearly. We don't see others clearly, and we don't even see ourselves clearly. Given our blindness, Jesus declares that we should be slow to start trying to put others right. Rather, he says, we need to attend to putting ourselves right first. 'Take the plank out of your own eye first.' He is suggesting that we have enough to be getting on with there. We are all a work in progress. The Lord has begun a good work in all our lives, but he has yet to bring that work to completion. Putting ourselves right is really about allowing the Lord to work on us, giving him the space to complete his good work in our lives. It is only the Lord who can make us the person God is calling us to become. As the gospel reading suggests, we can be blind to our failings, but we can also be blind to the good work that the Lord is doing within us and through us. Our daily calling is to allow the Lord to get on with his good work in our lives.

14 September, Saturday, The Exaltation of the Holy Cross
John 3:13–17

Today's feast is not like Good Friday. Our focus is not so much on the sufferings of Jesus. Rather, we celebrate what the gospel reading refers to as the lifting up of the Son of Man. The term 'lifting up' suggests not just his being lifted up physically on the cross but also his being lifted up in glory. There are some depictions of the cross that highlight this double sense of Jesus being lifted up, where the body of Jesus on the cross is almost glorified. You may be familiar with the cross of San Damiano in Assisi. When Saint Francis was praying before it, he heard the Lord call on him to rebuild the Church. The image of Jesus that is painted on that cross has a glorious, luminous quality. It is that kind of depiction of the cross that reflects the meaning of today's feast, which celebrates the triumph or exaltation of the cross. In what sense was the crucifixion of Jesus a triumph? It was firstly the triumph of love over hatred, the triumph of God's love over human sin. All authentic love is life-giving and God's love is supremely life-giving. That is why the crucifixion of Jesus was a triumph in another sense, the triumph of life over death, of God's life over human death, a triumph in which we can all share. That verse in today's gospel reading, which has spoken to believers down the centuries, really sums up the meaning of today's feast: 'God loved the world so much that he gave his only Son, so that everyone who believes may have eternal life in him.' Today we are invited to look upon the cross as the explosion of God's life-giving love for us all and then to allow ourselves to be drawn into that love so that we can reflect it to others through our lives.

16 September, Monday, Twenty-fourth Week in Ordinary Time
Luke 7:1–10

I have always been drawn to that first reading from Paul's first letter to the Corinthians. It is a brief account of the Last Supper that Paul claims to have received 'from the Lord', perhaps meaning from those who were present at the Last Supper with the Lord. This letter was written about fifteen years before the first gospel (Mark) was written, so it is the earliest account of the Last Supper that has come down to us. We are in touch here with the very earliest tradition about the Eucharist in the Church. There is also a link between the gospel reading and the Eucharist. The words of the response we say together before receiving Holy Communion, 'Lord, I am not worthy to receive you …', are, more or less, the words spoken by the Roman centurion to Jesus as Jesus approached his house. Isn't it strange that the words of a pagan have become part of the text of our Mass? According to the gospel reading, Jesus was astonished at the words of this pagan, declaring, 'Not even in Israel have I found faith like this'. Here was a pagan who didn't feel worthy enough to have this Jewish man of God come to his house. Yet Jesus does not ask us to be worthy before coming to us in Holy Communion. He asks only that we be open and receptive to his coming. In the first reading, Paul says, 'Every time you eat this bread and drink this cup, you are proclaiming his [the Lord's] death.' The Lord's death, according to Paul, was the demonstration of his love for us, of God's love for us. 'God demonstrates his love for us in that while we were still sinners Christ died for us' (Romans 5:8). When we celebrate the Eucharist, we are proclaiming the Lord's unconditional love for all and that love becomes present to us in a special way. At every Eucharist, we are invited to receive that love into our lives and then to share it with all whom we meet, so that our lives can proclaim the Lord's love.

17 September, Tuesday, Twenty-fourth Week in Ordinary Time
Luke 7:11–17
In today's gospel reading, Jesus ministers to a grieving widow. He restores her son to life and then he gives the restored young man to

his mother. Jesus regularly ministered to those who were broken in body, mind and spirit. In this instance, he is moved with compassion by the broken heart of a grieving widow. Jesus was close to people in their grief. In John's Gospel he stands alongside Mary and Martha whose brother Lazarus had just died, and brings life out of their experience of death. We can all find ourselves with an opportunity from time to time of ministering to the bereaved, to someone whose heart is broken because they have lost a loved one. We may not be able to do what Jesus did for the widow at Nain, but our compassionate presence can be truly life-giving for a person who is grieving. We may not have much to say to them, but our presence, our desire to be with them in their grief, can itself be a very consoling message. It is striking that no reference is made to the faith of the widow in the gospel, or to the faith of her son. She didn't approach Jesus trusting in him for help, as so many others did. Jesus simply took an initiative towards her because he was deeply moved by her brokenness of heart and spirit. Our own ministry to the bereaved needs to be just as spontaneous. Without raising any question regarding their faith, we are there with those who grieve simply because they need us. Compassion does not ask questions; it is happy to walk alongside those whose brokenness is calling out for companionship.

18 September, Wednesday, Twenty-fourth Week in Ordinary Time
Luke 7:31–35

In today's first reading, Paul declares, 'When I was a child, I used to talk like a child, and think like a child, and argue like a child, but now I am a man, all childish ways are put behind me.' In the gospel reading, Jesus gives us a portrait of children talking and behaving as children. They are playing children's games in the marketplace, imagining themselves to be playing the pipes at a celebratory event, like a wedding, and to be singing dirges, as at a funeral. Yet some children simply don't want to play; they are equally unmoved by the imaginary pipe playing and by the dirge singing. Jesus is reminded of how unmoved the people of his generation have been by the some- what sombre ministry of John the Baptist and his own much more joyful ministry. They labelled John as 'possessed' and Jesus as a 'glutton and a drunkard, a friend of tax collectors and sinners'. In the first reading, Paul declared that love 'does not take offence, and is not resentful'. Many of Jesus' contemporaries took offence at both John and Jesus and resented their ministries. They lacked the qual- ity of love towards John and Jesus that Paul describes in the first reading. This quality of love is more than a human love. It is what Paul calls elsewhere the fruit of the Spirit. It is the outward expres- sion of God's love that has been poured into our hearts through the Holy Spirit. If we open our hearts to the Spirit, we will see others with the eyes of love, recognising their inalienable worth, rather than dismissing them with the kind of cheap labels that Jesus' contempo- raries used for himself and John the Baptist.

19 September, Thursday, Twenty-fourth Week in Ordinary Time
Luke 7:36–50

In many ways today's gospel describes one of the most striking scenes in all of the gospels. A woman breaks uninvited into a meal at which Jesus is a guest. She weeps unrestrainedly, her tears falling on the feet of Jesus. She proceeds to wipe her tears away from Jesus' feet with her hair. She then covers his feet with kisses and anoints them with an alabaster jar of ointment she had brought with her. To the Pharisee who had invited Jesus to his house, the behaviour of this woman was unseemly, unbecoming and scandalous, especially as she had a reputation as a sinner. Yet Jesus understood what lay behind the woman's extravagant and unconventional behaviour. It was loving gratitude for the experience of God's merciful love conveyed earlier to her through Jesus. It was love in return for love. She had received the gift of God's unconditional love from Jesus and now she was responding in kind. The Pharisee had not experienced God's loving forgiveness in the way the woman had, so he could not understand her gestures. The portrayal of the woman reminds us that we give to the Lord in response to the experience of being gifted by the Lord. The experience of receiving the Lord's unconditional love is the wellspring of a life of loving service of the Lord. There is the Lord's commandment to love, but prior to the commandment is the invitation to receive the gift of the Lord's love. Receiving from the Lord is the inspiration for our giving to him.

20 September, Friday, Twenty-fourth Week in Ordinary Time
Luke 8:1–3
Today's gospel reading presents us with a picture of Jesus and the twelve disciples travelling in the company of certain women who provided for Jesus and the twelve out of their own resources. They were clearly women of means, who had resources that they could place at the disposal of Jesus and his closest associates. He, in turn, must have been grateful to have been supported and provided for in this way. In his life of service of others he had no opportunity to provide for himself in a material way and he was dependent on the generosity and hospitality of others. This group of women played a key role in giving Jesus the freedom to do God's work by supporting him materially and financially. The gospel reading calls on us to imitate the women by using our material resources to further the work of God and the coming of God's kingdom. These women can inspire us to use what we have been given to serve the Lord and his people. The Lord needed the service of these women and he needs the service of women and men of faith today.

21 September, Saturday, Saint Matthew, Apostle and Evangelist
Matthew 9:9–13

According to Saint Paul in today's first reading, 'each of us ... has been given their own share of grace, given as Christ allotted it'. We have each been gifted in some way by the Lord for his service and the service of his people. Each one of us has been gifted by the Lord, not just some of us. We all have a role to play in the Lord's work of making present the kingdom of heaven in the here and now. Jesus saw that Matthew had been gifted by God in a way that could serve all of God's people. Because Matthew was a tax collector, collecting taxes from his own people on behalf of the Romans, many would have dismissed him as a traitor, and those who thought of themselves as religious would have considered him a sinner, someone who did not do God's will. Yet Jesus saw something much more in Matthew, and he called him to become one of his closest followers, one of the twelve. He saw in Matthew what others failed to see, refused to see. Jesus looked upon people with generous and merciful eyes. The risen Lord looks on all of us in the same way. He doesn't just see our failings; he sees all we can become with his help. Sometimes it can be a struggle to see ourselves with the same generous and merciful eyes as the Lord sees us. Jesus reminds his critics in today's gospel reading what it is that God really wills, quoting from the prophet Hosea: 'What I want is mercy, not sacrifice.' More important to God than all the sacrifices in the Temple at the time is that merciful perspective on others, and on ourselves, that Jesus gives expression to in his whole way of life.

23 September, Monday, Twenty-fifth Week in Ordinary Time
Luke 8:16–18

The sayings of Jesus in today's gospel reading begin, 'No one lights a lamp to cover it with a bowl or to put it under a bed.' What did it mean to 'light a lamp' in the time of Jesus? The reference is to a small lamp, usually made of clay, filled with oil and with a wick. It could be set on a stand or hung from it. It is obvious that no one would hide a burning lamp by putting a bowl over it or putting it under a bed. It is lit to give light to those who are in the house or to guests who may come into the house. Jesus is referring to the light of the Gospel, which is not to be hidden but should be allowed to stream forth into the darkness in the world. We have been given the light of the Gospel. Our calling is to allow that light to shine through our lives. On one occasion, Jesus addressed his disciples as the light of the world and called on them to let their light shine by their good deeds, deeds inspired by the message of the Gospel. The Gospel is not a secret message intended to be kept hidden or revealed only to a select few. It is the Lord's light, which is to shine for all to see. We each have a role to play in allowing the light of the Lord's Gospel to shine in our world. First, however, we need to allow ourselves to be illumined by the light of the Lord's word by listening carefully to it. Only then can we be channels of that light to others, thereby sharing in the Lord's mission of being a light to the world.

24 September, Tuesday, Twenty-fifth Week in Ordinary Time
Luke 8:19–21
Family means a great deal to all of us; we treasure our parents, our spouses, our brothers and sisters, our sons and daughters. We can have mixed feelings from time to time about the members of our family, but, at the end of the day, we tend to rally around and stick by our own flesh and blood. The gospels suggest that whereas Jesus valued his natural family greatly, his real focus was elsewhere. He looked beyond his flesh-and-blood family to a different kind of family that he was engaged in forming, the family of his disciples.

That is clear from today's gospel reading. Without disowning in any way his mother, his brothers and sisters, he says that his real mother and brothers and sisters are those who hear God's word and do it. Jesus, more than any human being, heard God's word and did it; his life was thoroughly shaped by God's word and God's will. He called on people to surrender to God's word, to God's purpose, as he did, and he recognised those who did so as members of his new family. This new family is what we call the Church. The earliest Christian documents we possess are the letters of Paul, and in those letters Paul refers to the members of the Church as brothers and sisters in Christ, and speaks of himself as father and, indeed, mother of his communities. The gospel reading reminds us that we are all part of the great spiritual family of the Church; we are brothers and sisters of Jesus, sons and daughters of God, and we look to Mary as our mother. We might pray today for a deeper appreciation of the special bond that unites us all as members of the Church, as people who have been baptised into Christ and who, however imperfectly, share in his relationship with God the Father.

25 September, Wednesday, Twenty-fifth Week in Ordinary Time
Luke 9:1–6

There is a striking contrast in today's gospel reading. Jesus gave the twelve a share in his own power to heal and cure as he sent them out on mission. Yet he also sent them out in weakness, telling them to take very little for the journey, no staff or haversack or bread or money or spare tunic. It is as if Jesus wanted his power to be revealed in human weakness and vulnerability. It is often the case that the Lord works most powerfully through our experiences of weakness and frailty. Many of us feel weak and frail from time to time. Just as Jesus in the gospel reading asks his disciples to forego much of what most people rely on, we all find ourselves having to forego something or someone. Yet in such times of loss and weakness the Lord continues to work powerfully within us and among us. Such times can throw us back more fully on the Lord, who is present to us in difficult times as well as in good times. The first reading declares that God is the shield of those who take refuge in him. When Jesus sent out the twelve in such a vulnerable state, it was because he wanted them to rely on God as their shield, rather than relying on themselves too much. When we experience our weakness and frailty in a more pronounced way, it is an opportunity to rely more fully on the Lord as our shield. As Saint Paul reminds us in one of his letters, the Lord's power can be made perfect in weakness (2 Corinthians 12:9).

26 September, Thursday, Twenty-fifth Week in Ordinary Time
Luke 9:7–9

At the end of today's gospel reading it is said of Herod Antipas, the tetrarch of Galilee, that 'he was anxious to see Jesus'. Why would a powerful ruler like Herod Antipas want to see a preacher and healer from a small village in Galilee? The gospel reading says that he was puzzled because of the various reports he was hearing about Jesus. He was asking himself, 'Who is this?' This is the same Herod who had John the Baptist beheaded in prison. According to Luke's Gospel, from which we are reading, Herod did get to see Jesus on the eve of Jesus' death by crucifixion. Pilate sent Jesus to Herod to get his view on this troublesome prophet. According to Luke, Herod questioned him at some length but Jesus gave him no answer. So Herod and his soldiers treated Jesus with contempt, putting an elegant robe on him in mockery, and sent him back to Pilate. Herod's curiosity about Jesus did not bring him to faith in Jesus. Yet sometimes people's curiosity about Jesus does bring them to faith.

According to the Gospel of John, Nicodemus's curiosity about Jesus brought him to faith eventually. Even people of faith can be curious about Jesus and their curiosity can help to deepen their faith. There is much to be curious about when it comes to Jesus. There is such a depth to him that there is no limit to the questions we could ask about him. To believe is to see dimly, as Saint Paul says, and, as people of faith, we will always be trying to see more clearly. It is good to notice the questions that our faith gives rise to, questions about God, about Jesus, about the world. Exploring those questions can lead to a deepening of our faith, to a growth in our relationship with the Lord.

27 September, Friday, Twenty-fifth Week in Ordinary Time
Luke 9:18–22

Some questions are easier to answer than others. In the gospel reading, Jesus asks the disciples two questions. The first question would have been much easier for them to answer: 'Who do the crowds say I am?' They had their answers immediately – John the Baptist, Elijah, one of the ancient prophets come back to life. However, they would have found Jesus' second question more difficult to answer: 'But you, who do you say I am?' This question required them to look into their own hearts and be open and honest about who they understood Jesus to be. We sense a hesitation on the part of the disciples. It was Peter who eventually spoke up on behalf of the others: 'The Christ of God'. Peter confesses Jesus to be the long-awaited Jewish Messiah. He thereby showed great insight into Jesus, yet it was only a limited insight. His answer left open the question as to which kind of Messiah Jesus would turn out to be. Jesus immediately began to indicate the kind of Messiah he would be by speaking of himself as the Son of Man who was destined to suffer, to be rejected by the religious authorities and to be put to death, all in the service of his loving mission to humankind. It was probably not the kind of Messiah Peter had in mind. There was more to Jesus than even Peter understood. There is always more to the Lord than we can grasp or understand. He is more loving, more merciful, than we could ever grasp. In one of his letters, Saint Paul spoke of 'the love of Christ that surpasses knowledge' (Ephesians 4:19). We spend our lives growing in our appreciation of the Lord's love for us, until we reach that eternal moment when we will see him as he really is.

28 September, Saturday, Twenty-fifth Week in Ordinary Time
Luke 9:43–45

Jesus, it seems, did not allow other people's admiration of him to go to his head. According to today's gospel reading, just at the time when everyone was full of admiration for all he did, he began to speak of himself in a way that would not have endeared him to many. 'The Son of Man is going to be handed over into the power of men.' Jesus was looking ahead to his passion and death. No one would admire him when he hung from a Roman cross. At that moment, it was mockery and scorn that he mostly received. Yet God would have been full of admiration for Jesus in that dark hour, not because he wanted his Son to suffer, but because Jesus on the cross was revealing God's love for the world to the full. It was Jesus' message of God's merciful love for all that put him on the cross. He remained faithful to preaching and living that message, even though he knew it would result in his being handed over to death. No one has greater love than to lay down one's life for one's friends. It was this greater love, this divine love, that shone through Jesus on the cross. It was only in the light of Jesus' resurrection that people of faith would become full of admiration, not only for the way he lived but for the way he died. Until that Easter moment, all Jesus' talk about his coming passion and death made no sense to his disciples. In the words of the gospel reading, 'it was hidden from them'. We who live in the light of Easter can be full of admiration, not only for all Jesus did during his earthly life, but especially for his passion and death and for the tremendous love that it revealed.

30 September, Monday, Twenty-sixth Week in Ordinary Time
Luke 9:46–50

It is often the way in the gospels that the disciples are on a very different wavelength from Jesus. We find an example of that clash of mindsets in today's gospel reading. The disciples were having an argument among themselves as to which of them was the greatest. Jesus had been gathering a group of disciples about himself. He wanted them to regard one another as equals. Jesus once referred to his disciples as his brothers and sisters. Yet some of them at least were trying to get ahead of others, perhaps claiming that they were closer to Jesus than others were and, therefore, would have a more prominent role in the coming kingdom of God. This seeking after status, position and influence is a very human phenomenon. We are being reminded that Jesus' first disciples were as flawed as the rest of us. Jesus responded to this argument among his disciples by doing something and saying something. He took a child and set the child by his side, and he said, 'Anyone who welcomes this little child in my name, welcomes me.' A child had no power or rank or influence. Children were considered among the least, at the other end of the spectrum to the high and mighty of the world. Jesus was saying to his disciples that the truly great in his community are those who welcome the least in the world as if they were Jesus himself. He wants his disciples, all of us, to stand alongside the least, those who have least influence, least power, least prestige and least honour. The community he was forming was to befriend and welcome those whom the world tends to consider unimportant. That is the kind of church we are all called to help create in our own place and time.

1 October, Tuesday, Twenty-sixth Week in Ordinary Time
Luke 9:51–56

In today's gospel reading we find Jesus setting out on what will be a difficult journey, his journey to Jerusalem, where he is aware that rejection and death await him. That is why Luke says at the beginning of the gospel reading that Jesus resolutely took the road for Jerusalem. We all face difficult journeys in life. We find ourselves heading into some situation that we know is going to make demands on us. The supportive presence of others can mean a lot to us at such times. As Jesus set out on his difficult journey, he would have welcomed support too. Yet, according to today's gospel reading, his first experience, having set out on his journey, was one of rejection. A Samaritan village refused him hospitality because he was a Jew heading for Jerusalem. His journey began as it would end, in rejection. Like Jesus, we too don't always receive the support we need at those vulnerable moments in our lives. How do we respond when that happens? We can learn from Jesus' response in today's gospel reading. He did not react angrily towards the Samaritan village, which is what his disciples wanted. He just continued on his journey and preached the Gospel elsewhere. He remained true to God's purpose for his life. His way is to be our way. In the power of his Spirit, we too keep journeying on, always remaining true to God's purpose for our lives and to our baptismal identity, which is our deepest and best self.

2 October, Wednesday, The Guardian Angels

Matthew 18:1–5, 10

There is a verse in the letter to the Hebrews that states, 'Do not neglect to show hospitality to strangers for by so doing some have entertained angels without knowing it.' The author seems to be saying that there can be more to those who cross our path in life than we realise. Jesus makes the same point in today's gospel reading when he says, 'anyone who welcomes a little child like this in my name welcomes me'. In the world of Jesus, the child had no social status or position. Yet Jesus declares to his disciples that in welcoming the least, like little children, they are welcoming him. He comes to them in and through the least. This is a sobering lesson for the disciples, who have just been arguing over which of them was the greatest. Not only do we welcome Jesus when we welcome a child, Jesus declares that unless we become like children we will never enter the kingdom of God. Instead of the grasping attitude the disciples had just shown in arguing over which of them was the greatest, if we are to enter the kingdom of heaven we need something of the open, receptive attitude of children who depend totally on others. Jesus is saying that only those who admit their littleness and put their trust in God will enter the kingdom of heaven.

3 October, Thursday, Twenty-sixth Week in Ordinary Time

Luke 10:1–12

When Jesus sends out the seventy-two in the gospel reading, he makes clear to them that, whereas they will be well received by some towns, they will most certainly not be made welcome by other towns. However, regardless of how they are received, their message is to be the same, 'the kingdom of God is very near to you'. The reign of God in Jesus is equally present to those who reject it as it is to those who welcome it. We are being reminded that we do not make God present, nor, indeed, can we drive God away. God is present to us, through his Son, now risen Lord, whether we want God's presence or not, whether we are aware of God's presence or not. God is change-less in that God cannot but be present to us, even though as human beings we can change; we can be more or less present to God. Because the kingdom of God is always very near to us, because God's loving and just rule is powerfully present to us at all times, our calling is to keep opening ourselves to God's presence, to allow God to be Emmanuel, God with us. God has done and is doing all God can do for us; it falls to us to keep opening ourselves more fully to what God is doing for us. It has pleased God to give us the gift of the king-dom, the gift of his loving presence; God wants us to receive this gift and then to live out of its fullness and richness. God has drawn near to us through his Son, and desires us to draw near to him, to be in communion with him, and then, in the strength of that commu-nion to go forth and become his labourers in his harvest, like the seventy-two in today's gospel reading.

4 October, Friday, Twenty-sixth Week in Ordinary Time
Luke 10:13–16
Sometimes we can all get frustrated at what we see as a lack of response to our efforts to reach out to people. We try to do our best for someone and we seem to get nowhere. The energy, the love and the concern we extend to someone we care about doesn't appear to bear any fruit. This was the experience of Jesus in today's gospel reading. He invested time and energy in proclaiming the good news of the presence of God's kingdom to the towns on the shore of the Sea of Galilee, places like Chorazin, Bethsaida and Capernaum, but his words fell on deaf ears and his deeds left people unmoved. We have a sense that this lack of response to his deeds and his words

had a deep impact on Jesus. The gospels tells us that on another occasion, Jesus wept over the city of Jerusalem because they had not welcomed him and had not recognised him as God's special visitor to them. God was powerfully at work through the ministry of Jesus, but Jesus was powerless before people's refusal to recognise and receive him for who he was. God continues to work through the risen Lord today, but the risen Lord can be equally powerless before people's refusal to welcome his presence, his message, his values, his Spirit. The Lord is always drawing us to himself; he is always knocking on the door of our lives, but he needs us to allow ourselves to be drawn; he waits for us to open our lives to his presence. The smallest opening is all the Lord needs, what he referred to once in the gospels as faith the size of a mustard seed. He is prepared to wait on us to offer him that smallest of openings. If we do so, our lives will never be the same again. In the words of the response to today's psalm, the Lord will lead us in the path of life eternal.

5 October, Saturday, Twenty-sixth Week in Ordinary Time
Luke 10:17–24
In the gospel reading, Jesus praises God his Father in prayer because it is 'mere children' who are receiving the gospel message he is proclaiming, whereas the learned and the clever are not. 'Mere children' are primarily those adults who have the openness of the child to all that Jesus is saying and doing. Whereas those who claim to know God, the learned and the clever, are rejecting Jesus, those who are searching for God and who recognise that they have a long way to go to find God are welcoming the message and ministry of Jesus with open arms. They are the ones who are seeing what the learned and clever are failing to see and are hearing what the learned and clever are failing to hear. Jesus turns to this group at the end of the gospel reading and declares them blessed: 'Happy the eyes that see what

you see.' Children are full of questions. I once went into a classroom in one of the primary schools and I was bombarded with questions about God, Jesus, heaven and earth. Children have an openness to learning about God. We all need to retain something of that child-like quality of the searcher and the questioner. It is an attitude that leaves us open to the new ways in which the Lord can touch our lives. In the first reading, Job declares that he thought he knew God, but it was his experience of great suffering that made him realise that he knew God 'only by hearsay'. Having come through that painful experience he can now claim to have seen God 'with my own eyes'. When it comes to God and to Jesus, his Son, we are all on a journey of discovery. The Lord always has so much more to reveal to us of himself and of God, which is why we need to retain the openness and humility of the child.

7 October, Monday, Our Lady of the Rosary

Luke 1:26–38

The great Marian prayer of the Rosary is sometimes traced back to Saint Dominic and his companions who preached against the Albigensian heresy in the thirteenth century. However, it seems more likely to have taken its present familiar form some centuries later. The structure of the Rosary evolved between the twelfth and fifteenth centuries. During the sixteenth century, the structure of the five-decade Rosary based on the three sets of mysteries prevailed. Since then it has become a much-loved prayer of believers in every generation. The Rosary has been described as the Gospel on its knees. The fifteen decades, or twenty decades if we include the Mysteries of Light introduced by Pope John Paul II, are an invitation to reflect on the great mysteries of the Lord's life, passion, death, resurrection and glorification, and on the role of Mary within those great mysteries. Two of these mysteries feature in the two readings for this memorial, the coming of the Holy Spirit on the disciples and Mary in the first reading and the annunciation to Mary in the gospel reading. Both readings feature the Holy Spirit, the first reading implicitly. It was through the coming of the Holy Spirit upon Mary that she brought her son, who is also God's Son, into the world. It was through the coming of the Holy Spirit upon the first disciples, including Mary, that they were empowered to proclaim the Gospel of Christ crucified and risen, beginning in Jerusalem and extending to the ends of the earth. In the first reading the disciples and Mary were in continuous prayer before the coming of the Spirit. Prayer opens us up to receive the Spirit afresh into our lives. In praying the Rosary, we are opening our hearts to the coming of the Holy Spirit, through whose power we can continue to bring the Lord to others. In that sense, the praying of the Rosary can be our own Annunciation and Pentecost moments.

8 October, Tuesday, Twenty-seventh Week in Ordinary Time
Luke 10:38–42

There are different forms of hospitality; there is the hospitality of activity and the hospitality of presence. In today's gospel reading, Martha exemplifies the hospitality of activity and Mary the hospitality of presence. It seems that on this occasion, it was the hospitality of presence rather than of activity that Jesus was really looking for. In that sense, Mary read the situation better than Martha did. In the words of Jesus, she chose the better part. Jesus was not looking for an elaborate meal; he had a word to speak and what he wanted above all was a listening ear. It was Mary who noticed this and who sat at his feet to listen to his word. Mary was more hospitable on this occasion because she was more attentive to the needs of the guest than Martha was. In our own relationship with the Lord there is a time for both sitting at his feet to listen to whatever

word he may wish to speak to us and there is a time for rolling up
our sleeves and serving in a very active way, as the Samaritan did
in the parable that comes before this passage. We need to be attentive both to the Lord of the work and the work of the Lord, and we
need the wisdom to discern what is being called for at any particular moment.

9 October, Wednesday, Twenty-seventh Week in Ordinary Time
Luke 11:1–4

According to our first reading, it had been the custom of Peter 'to
eat with the pagans'. The reference to 'pagans' there is to members
of the Church whose background was pagan and who would have
had no familiarity with Jewish food laws. It seems that Peter was
initially prepared to forgo Jewish food laws so that he could share
table fully with these believers in the Lord who came from a pagan
background. However, according to Paul, under pressure from James,
the leader of the church in Jerusalem, Peter stopped doing this, for
fear of offending those Jewish Christians who held that all believers
should submit to the Jewish Law. Paul clearly felt that Peter should
have stood up to James, resisting his pressure, and Paul tells us that
he opposed Peter to his face. We have only Paul's side of the story
here. Perhaps Peter would have told it a little differently. There is no
doubt that both Peter and Paul, and James, were absolutely committed to doing the Lord's will and working for the coming of God's
kingdom. They could easily have prayed together the words of the
prayer Jesus gave to his disciples in the gospel reading, 'Father, may
your name be held holy, your kingdom come'. Although both Paul
and Peter wanted to create spaces for the coming of God's kingdom,
they seemed to have different views on what that meant in practice.
They had at least one strong disagreement. Perhaps, subsequent to
this heated exchange, another petition of the Lord's Prayer would

have become very relevant, 'Forgive us our sins, for we ourselves forgive each one who is in debt to us'. We can have strong disagreements about what the Lord is asking of us as a community of believers and still remain in communion with one another. Discerning what the Lord is asking of us in complex situations is not always easy. Tensions and disagreements among committed believers are inevitable. Yet we all need to be able to pray the prayer that Jesus gave us, recognising that we are all brothers and sisters under God our Father, who stand in need of forgiveness as we work for the coming of God's kingdom on earth.

10 October, Thursday, Twenty-seventh Week in Ordinary Time
Luke 11:5–13

There are various forms of prayer, such as the prayer of petition, the prayer of thanksgiving, the prayer of praise, the prayer of contrition, the prayer of surrender. It is probably true to say that the prayer that comes most naturally to us is the prayer of petition. If we reflect on our prayer life, we will likely find that the prayer of petition, the prayer of asking God for help of some kind, is very much to the fore. There is a prayerbook in the Bible, the Book of Psalms, composed long before the coming of Jesus, and the dominant prayer in that collection of prayers is the prayer of petition. Jesus was aware of the significance of the prayer of petition in the life of believers and today's gospel reading suggests that he encouraged his disciples to pray that form of prayer, 'Ask [keep on asking] … search [keep on searching] … knock [keep on knocking] … '. He promises that our prayer of petition will always be answered, 'It will be given to you … you will find … the door will be opened to you.' It often seems as if our prayers of petition are not answered. We ask for healing for someone, and they don't get better. Yet the Lord assures us in the gospel reading that no prayer of petition goes unanswered. Our prayer may not be answered in the way that we had hoped, but Jesus assures us that God is never deaf to our cries for help. At the end of the gospel reading, Jesus says, 'How much more will the heavenly Father give the Holy Spirit to those who ask him?' Our prayer of petition will always create a space for the Holy Spirit to work more powerfully in our lives. Saint Paul wrote in his letter to the Romans, 'the Spirit helps us in our weakness'. In response to our prayer of petition we can be assured of receiving the help of the Spirit to strengthen us in our need.

11 October, Friday, Twenty-seventh Week in Ordinary Time
Luke 11:15–26

According to today's gospel reading, when some people looked at the healing ministry of Jesus, instead of seeing the finger of God, the reign of God at work, they saw the activity of Satan. The gospels suggest that Jesus was completely misunderstood by some. It is hard to imagine a greater misunderstanding than what we find in today's gospel reading, yet he continued to reach out to those who misunderstood him; he worked to get them to see that it was the Holy Spirit and not some evil spirit that was at work in his ministry. Even on the cross, according to Luke, Jesus prayed for those who were executing him as a common criminal or rebel. We can all experience misunderstanding, even if not on the scale that Jesus experienced it. It can sometimes be the price we pay for doing something worthwhile. Jesus remained faithful to his calling and his mission, in spite of the kind of misunderstanding of him shown by many. In similar circumstances, we too need to remain faithful and not lose our nerve. In doing this, the Lord's Spirit will help us.

12 October, Saturday, Twenty-seventh Week in Ordinary Time
Luke 11:27–28

In the gospel reading, a woman in the crowd singles out Jesus' mother as worthy of special praise, distinguishing her from all others. In response, Jesus seems to relativise this distinction, declaring that those who hear the word of God and keep it are worthy of even greater praise. If Mary is worthy of praise, it is not because Jesus is her son but because she heard God's word and kept it in her life. Yet, in this regard, she is no different from other disciples who have done the same. Mary is blessed because she is a faithful disciple, and all faithful disciples are equally blessed. In the first reading, Paul also makes little of distinctions within the community of believers, declaring that 'All baptised in Christ, you have all clothed yourselves in Christ, and there are no more distinctions between Jew and Greek, slave and free, male and female, but all of you are one in Christ Jesus.' If, for Jesus, faith is the great leveller, for Paul, faith resulting in baptism is the great leveller. We are all indispensable members of Christ's body, as he states elsewhere. No one should feel that they do not belong: 'If the foot would say, "Because I am not a hand, I do not belong to the body", that would not make it any less a part of the body' (1 Corinthians 12:15). Equally, no member of the Church should make any member feel as if they have nothing to offer: 'The eye cannot say to the hand, "I have no need of you", nor again the head to the feet, "I have no need of you"' (1 Corinthians 12:21). The Lord needs each member of his body to make the unique contribution that only they can make, if he is to be present in the world today in the way he desires to be.

14 October, Monday, Twenty-eighth Week in Ordinary Time
Luke 11:29–32

In today's gospel reading, people come to Jesus looking for a sign. He replies that the signs they are looking for are actually there in front of their eyes if only they could see them. The people of Nineveh took Jonah more seriously than some of the people of Jesus' generation were taking him, yet there were far more powerful signs of God's presence in the life of Jesus than in the life of Jonah: 'There is something greater than Jonah here.' The Queen of Sheba took Solomon more seriously than some of the people of Jesus' generation were taking him, yet there were far more powerful signs of God's presence in the life of Jesus than in the life of Solomon: 'There is something greater than Solomon here.' In looking for some striking and spectacular signs from Jesus, many of his contemporaries were missing the signs that were staring them in the face. In looking for the extraordinary, we too can miss the richness in the ordinary. In many ways Jesus was very ordinary. 'Is not this the son of the carpenter?' the people of Nazareth asked. When Jesus spoke about God's kingdom, the ways of God, he did so in very ordinary terms, the sower going out to sow, the man robbed on the road from Jerusalem to Jericho, the father whose son left home in a very selfish fashion, the weeds that grow among the field of wheat. These were scenes from ordinary life. Jesus was saying that the signs of God's presence are to be found there in the ordinary stuff of life, for those who have eyes to see. Today we pray for eyes to see the many signs of the Lord's presence in our day-to-day lives.

15 October, Tuesday, Twenty-eighth Week in Ordinary Time
Luke 11:37–41

We all find ourselves asking at some time in our lives, 'What is it that matters in life?' 'What is more important than anything else?' For people of faith, that becomes, 'What is it that matters to the Lord?' 'What is most important in his eyes?' Both of today's readings give us a sense of what matters most to the Lord. In the gospel reading, Jesus is the guest of a Pharisee, someone who tried to live

by God's law. The Pharisee was concerned that Jesus had not followed the Jewish laws about handwashing before he sat down to eat.
For Jesus, however, such regulations were not all that important. He
goes on to say that what is really important, what really matters, is
what is to be found in a person's heart. Is there something of God's
own love in our hearts? Jesus had a heart that was full of God's love,
and he looks for a loving heart in us, a heart that expresses itself in
almsgiving, the service of those in greatest need. As Jesus says to
his host, 'Give alms from what you have'. In the first reading Paul
is upset that some members of the church are giving so much
importance to the demands of the Jewish Law. What is it that matters,
according to Paul? He states it very clearly at the end of the reading:
'What matters is faith that makes its power felt through love.' What
matters to the Lord, according to Paul, is faith, a loving relationship
with the Lord, that then flows over into the loving service of others.
It is worth holding on to that statement of Paul as we try to find our
way in life: 'What matters is faith that makes its power felt through
love.'

16 October, Wednesday, Twenty-eighth Week in Ordinary Time
Luke 11:47–54
In the first reading, Saint Paul lists what the Holy Spirit brings, or
in a more literal translation, 'the fruit of the Spirit'. We tend to speak
about the 'fruits' of the Spirit, but the singular 'fruit' suggests that
all the qualities Paul lists are not to be separated out but are interconnected. It is as if this fruit of the Spirit is so rich that it needs to
be spoken of in a variety of ways, as love, joy, peace, patience, kindness, goodness, trustfulness, gentleness and self-control. Paul is por-
traying the richly human life that the Holy Spirit creates in us when
we give ourselves over to the Spirit. At the head of the list of these

interconnected qualities is 'love', perhaps suggesting that all the other qualities are expressions of love. The Holy Spirit is the Spirit of God's love, and a life shaped by the Holy Spirit will be a life that reflects God's love, which was fully revealed in Jesus. Our calling from baptism is to open ourselves in faith to God's gift of the Holy Spirit and to allow the Spirit to bear the fruit of love in our lives. This comes before all else. In the gospel reading, Jesus says to the Pharisees and the experts in the Jewish Law that what comes before all else is justice and the love of God, a loving relationship with God that overflows into a just and loving relationship with all of God's people. We need to be reminded every so often what is at the heart of our faith, and both of today's readings put before us what matters most to God.

17 October, Thursday, Twenty-eighth Week in Ordinary Time
Luke 11:47–54

There is a very striking statement at the end of today's first reading. According to Saint Paul, God's purpose is to bring everything together under Christ, as head, everything in the heavens and everything in the earth. There is a wonderful sweep to this vision of God's purpose. It can excite our imagination, move our heart and intrigue our mind. Yet we know that everything has not yet been brought together under Christ, as head. Many have yet to hear of Christ and many who have heard of him seem indifferent to him. Indeed, in today's gospel reading, those who heard Jesus 'began a furious attack on him'. Such a hostile response to Christ and his message, and the community he formed about himself, has been there all through history, up to and including our own time. We might wonder if God's purpose will ever come to pass. Will everything ever be brought together under Christ as head? The risen Lord wants to work through each one of us to bring this wonderful purpose of God to pass. We can only help to bring everything under Christ as head if we ourselves in our own personal lives are allowing God to bring us under Christ as head. Only if Christ is head or Lord of our own lives can we have a role in God's work of bringing everything under Christ as head. If, however, we can proclaim 'Jesus is Lord', not just with our lips but with our lives, we can never underestimate the ways that God can work through us to bring his purpose for our world to pass.

18 October, Friday, Saint Luke, Evangelist

Luke 10:1–9

It is appropriate that on this feast of the evangelist Luke we read from a passage of his gospel that is unique to him. He alone has the passage of Jesus sending out seventy-two ahead of him, in pairs, to all the towns and places he himself was to visit. Jesus had previously sent out the twelve on mission, but, because the harvest is so rich, many more labourers are required, including this group of seventy-two. In Luke's second volume, the Acts of the Apostles, a variety of labourers enter the Lord's rich harvest, proclaiming the Gospel of Christ crucified and risen. Perhaps the greatest of the labourers in this second volume is Paul, the apostle to the pagans. Paul himself had many co-workers, including a man called, Luke, whom tradition has identified as the author of this two-volume work. In today's first reading, from Paul's second letter to Timothy, Paul conveys a sense of having been abandoned by many of his co-workers in his hour of need: 'every one of them deserted me'. However, he identifies Luke as the exception: 'only Luke is with me'. When Paul goes on to say that, although everyone has deserted him, 'the Lord stood by me and gave me power', we are led to believe that one of the ways the Lord stood by him was through the person of Luke. Luke revealed the Lord's faithful presence to Paul in his hour of need. One of the ways we can become a labourer in the Lord's harvest is by being a Luke to those who feel abandoned. Our faithful presence to those who are at their most vulnerable can be a powerful revelation of the Lord's enduring love for them.

19 October, Saturday, Twenty-eighth Week in Ordinary Time
Luke 12:8–12

In today's gospel reading Jesus calls on his disciples to be courageous in bearing witness to him, in declaring themselves for him in the presence of others. He also promises them that in bearing witness to him they won't be left to their own resources. Rather, as Jesus says, when the time comes the Holy Spirit will teach them what they must say. Declaring ourselves for the Lord today can be difficult because of the climate in which we live, which is so often hostile to faith and religion, and to our Catholic faith in particular. It is easy to become discouraged when there is so much hostile and negative press around. We can easily be cowed into silence and invisibility. The gospel reading today suggests that we must work to resist that temptation. It calls on us to declare ourselves for the Lord publicly and it promises help in doing that, the help of the Holy Spirit. As Paul says, the Holy Spirit helps us in our weakness. We need to keep on praying for a daily Pentecost in our lives, as individuals and as a community of faith, so that we have the courage to declare for the Lord who himself had the courage to declare for God his Father even though it meant having to submit to death on a cross.

21 October, Monday, Twenty-ninth Week in Ordinary Time
Luke 12:13–21

The rich man in the parable in today's gospel reading asked the right question: 'What am I to do?' He had more crops than he had barns to hold them. However, from God's perspective he gave the wrong answer to his question. He decided to build more barns to store his bumper crop. Holding on to what he had was his priority. The option of sharing his surplus with those who were struggling to live never crossed his mind. He was completely focused on himself. His speech to himself was full of the little words 'I' and 'my' – 'my crops, my barns, my grain', my goods and, even, 'my soul'. Yet his soul belonged to God, just as his crops belonged to all of God's people. When God called back his soul, the inner poverty of this rich man was revealed. He had done nothing with the good fortune that came his way as a gift from God to be shared with others. He stored up treasure for himself, but did not make himself rich in the sight of God. In the first reading, Paul speaks of God's goodness towards us in Christ and how infinitely rich God is in grace. We have all been richly graced and gifted by God in Christ, which has made us, in the words of that reading, 'God's work of art'. God has worked richly in all of our lives, and we are called to allow God's work to overflow through us to enrich the lives of others. As one of the contemporary hymns puts it, 'freely you have received, freely give'. When we ask the question, 'What am I to do?', our answer will be inspired by the message and the life of Jesus, who, in the words of Saint Paul, made himself poor for our sakes, so that by his poverty we might become rich (2 Corinthians 8:9).

22 October, Tuesday, Twenty-ninth Week in Ordinary Time
Luke 12:35–38
There is a striking image in today's gospel reading of a person of authority putting on an apron, inviting his servants to sit at table and then serving them. Such a reversal of roles would have been unthinkable in the culture of Jesus. For a person of authority to take on the task of a servant would have been considered shameful.

It represented an enormous loss of face and prestige. Yet Jesus' highly unconventional image here reminds us of the Last Supper scene in the Gospel of John, where Jesus wraps a towel around his waist and gets down on his knees to wash the feet of his disciples. We are now reading from the Gospel of Luke, and later in that gospel, in the setting of the Last Supper, Jesus says of himself, 'I am among you as one who serves' (Luke 22:27), rather than as one who sits at table. Jesus, now risen Lord, wants to serve us today. However, today's gospel reading suggests that we need to have a certain attitude of heart if we are to experience the Lord as our servant. We are to be 'dressed for action', with our lamps lit, waiting for the Lord to come and knock. We are to be attentive to the Lord, to his daily coming and his daily call. We are to be faithful in our attentiveness to the Lord, through all the watches of the night. Such a faithful alertness to the Lord's presence and call will open us up to receive the Lord's self-emptying service.

23 October, Wednesday, Twenty-ninth Week in Ordinary Time
Luke 12:39–48

A section of today's gospel reading seems to be addressed to those who have positions of leadership in the Church. They are stewards whose responsibility it is to give those in God's household 'their allowance of food at the proper time'. This could be understood as both material and spiritual food. If they abuse their authority, there will be serious consequences for them. In one of his letters, Saint Paul declares, 'Think of us in this way, as servants of Christ and stewards of God's mysteries. Moreover, it is required of stewards that they be found trustworthy' (1 Corinthians 4:1–2). In today's first reading we find Paul exercising his stewardship of God's mysteries. He refers to 'the depths that I see in the mystery of God'. He succinctly expresses this 'mystery' as 'the infinite treasure of Christ'. Paul is reminding us that there are depths to the Gospel that we will never fully explore in this earthly life. There is a treasure here which is infinite and can never be fully exhausted on this side of eternity. In his first letter to the Corinthians Paul refers to Christ as the 'wisdom of God' (1 Corinthians 1:24). In our reading he wonders at 'how comprehensive God's wisdom really is'. There is a wonderful treasure here and, to some extent, every member of the Church is a steward of this treasure. We are asked to value the 'infinite treasure of Christ' above all earthly treasure, by being attentive and alert to the presence of Christ in our lives, our Church and our world. In the words of the gospel reading, we are to stand ready for his coming, not just his coming at the end of time or at the end of our lives, but his daily coming throughout our lives.

24 October, Thursday, Twenty-ninth Week in Ordinary Time
Luke 12:49–53

In today's first reading, we find that wonderful phrase of Saint Paul, 'knowing the love of Christ, which is beyond all knowledge'. On the one hand, Paul prays that we would come to know the breadth and the length, the height and the depth of the love of Christ. On the other hand, he declares that the love of Christ is beyond all knowledge. Paul seems to be saying that in this earthly life we will never know the immensity of Christ's love fully. In his first letter to the Corinthians, he states, 'Now I know only in part; then I will know fully, even as I have been fully known' (1 Corinthians 13:12). In eternity we will know the love of Christ as fully as the Lord now knows us. The more we come to know the breadth, length, height and depth of Christ's love in this life, the more our hidden self will grow strong, in the words of our first reading. When Jesus says in the gospel reading that he has come to bring fire to the earth and expresses a desire that this fire is burning already, we can understand him to mean the fire of his love, the fire of the Holy Spirit, the Spirit of God's love. We have a prayer to the Holy Spirit, inviting him to kindle in us the fire of his love. Yet Jesus is aware that the fire of his love will be experienced as threatening by many, who will seek to extinguish it. It will lead him to the cross, which is why he goes on to say, 'There is a baptism I must still receive, and how great is my distress until it is over.' At the beginning of his ministry, he was plunged into the waters of the Jordan to be baptised by John the Baptist. At the end of his ministry, he will be plunged into suffering and death. His death on the cross will become the fullest revelation of his love for all humankind. The risen Lord wants us to know the depth of his love for us, so that he can ignite the fire of his love in our own lives and, through us, reveal his love to others.

25 October, Friday, Twenty-ninth Week in Ordinary Time
Luke 12:54–59

There is a wonderful call for unity in today's first reading, what Saint Paul calls the unity of the Spirit. As followers of the Lord, we can have disagreements over many things, but we are always united on the fundamentals. We all acknowledge one Body, one Spirit, one hope, one Lord, one faith, one baptism and one God who is Father of all. The unity is already there; it has been given to us by God. Paul calls upon us not so much to create unity, but to preserve the unity we already have, and to do so by attitudes of selflessness, gentleness and patience. In this way, we will be living lives worthy of our baptismal vocation. In the gospel reading, Jesus remarks on how well his contemporaries can interpret the sky to forecast the weather and yet how poor they are at interpreting the times in which they live. They fail to recognise God powerfully at work in the ministry of Jesus and they fail to respond to Jesus as God's powerful presence among us. A question believers always live with is, 'What is God saying to us through the times in which we live?' One of the characteristics of the times in which we live, one of the signs of the times, is disharmony, division, divisiveness, conflict. In and through that worrying sign of our times, the call of God to us may be the call of today's first reading, the call to live in such a way that the unity that God is always creating becomes more and more of a reality. God is always at work to gather all humanity around his Son, to create the unity of the Spirit. Anything we do to allow that unity of the Spirit to become more visible among us is an important sharing in God's own work.

26 October, Saturday, Twenty-ninth Week in Ordinary Time
Luke 13:1–9

We live in an age when people expect results and if results are not forthcoming then there are certain consequences. The television series *The Apprentice* comes to mind, with its famous line, 'You're fired'. The poor unfortunates who don't deliver the goods are unceremoniously given their walking papers. Yet some people need time to deliver, even a lot of time. We can write off someone far too quickly; most people have abilities they are not fully aware of, and what they need is a mentor who is prepared to give them time and patience. The fig tree in the parable that failed to bear fruit after three years would be lucky, in today's world, to get one year, never mind three. Yet, in the parable, we find the man who looks after the tree persuading the owner of the vineyard that the fig tree should be given a fourth year. He was all on for giving it every possible chance, not just time, but tender loving care in the form of fertiliser. The parable is an image of how the Lord relates to us. He is slow to give up on us even when the signs are not promising. He will continue to pour his grace into our lives; he will do all he can to ensure that our lives bear fruit, the rich fruit of the Holy Spirit. We have a part to play; the Lord cannot work in our lives despite us. Yet the parable assures us that the Lord's efforts on our behalf will always far exceed whatever efforts we might make. As Paul says, grace abounds, and even when sin abounds, grace abounds all the more.

28 October, Monday, Saints Simon and Jude, Apostles

Luke 6:12–19

Two of the twelve whom Jesus called to himself were called Simon and two were called Jude or Judas: Simon Peter and Simon the Zealot, and Judas son of James and Judas Iscariot. Simon Peter and Judas Iscariot are the better known, for opposite reasons. Today's feast celebrates the other Simon and Jude. Simon's other name, 'the Zealot', suggests that he was zealous to keep God's law. If so, he came to recognise Jesus as a fuller revelation than the Jewish Law of God's will for our lives. There is an ancient tradition that both Simon and Jude were martyred on the same day. They remained faithful to the Lord's call, even at the cost of their lives. In the first reading, Paul reminds us that we are part of a spiritual building that has the apostles, like Simon and Jude, for its foundations, and Christ Jesus himself for its main cornerstone. We call this spiritual building the Church. The physical buildings we call 'churches' are there to help us to be true to our calling as members of a spiritual building, what Paul calls in our reading, a holy temple in the Lord, where God lives in the Spirit. As Simon and Jude were faithful to their calling, each day we seek to be faithful to our calling to allow God's Spirit, the Spirit of the risen Lord, to shape our lives. We never fully answer this calling in the course of our earthly lives. We are always growing into this calling. If we are to grow into our calling to allow God's

Spirit to shape our lives, we need to do what the members of the crowd are depicted as doing in the gospel reading. We need to keep on reaching out towards the Lord, to touch his presence, and allowing him to touch us. One of the primary ways we do this is through prayer. At the beginning of the gospel reading, Jesus went out into the hills to pray. We need to find our own version of those hills, where we can be prayerfully present to the Lord.

29 October, Tuesday, Thirtieth Week in Ordinary Time
Luke 13:18–21

In today's gospel Jesus takes an image from the world of men and the world of women in that culture, a man who takes a mustard seed and throws it in his garden and a woman who takes some yeast and mixes it in with three measures of flour. In each case the small gesture produces significant results. The mustard seed becomes a tree where the birds find shelter; the yeast mixed with the flour produces bread that satisfies human hunger. These are images, Jesus declares, of the kingdom of God. Jesus seems to be saying that the coming of God's kingdom is not always about grand gestures. The coming of God's kingdom, the doing of God's will on earth as in heaven, is often to be found in what to an outside observer seems small and insignificant. Jesus is suggesting that God can work powerfully through the smallest gestures, when they reflect something of God's Spirit. God is present in our world in and through our small acts of kindness, through our largely unnoticed actions of caring for one another. Jesus would say that even the giving of a cup of cold water has significance beyond our imagining. The eternal can be present in the simplest of gestures. Our daily efforts to be faithful to the Gospel in small ways can have consequences that would surprise us. The miraculous is all around us, working through our smallest efforts at goodness, if we have eyes to see.

30 October, Wednesday, Thirtieth Week in Ordinary Time
Luke 13:22–30

There are some very hopeful and encouraging statements in the letters of Paul. In his letter to the Romans he assures us that 'the Spirit comes to help us in our weakness'. As an example of our 'weakness', he cites our struggle to pray, to find the words that give expression to our desire to pray. At such times, Paul tells us that 'the Spirit himself' expresses our prayer in a way that could never be put into words. The Spirit does our praying for us. This suggests that our prayer consists more in entering into the prayer of the Spirit that is going on within us. Prayer is more God's work within us than our work. A couple of verses later Paul makes another reassuring statement, declaring, 'we know that by turning everything to their good God cooperates with all those who love him'. Paul is saying that God can work for our ultimate good through everything that happens to us, if we open our hearts to him in love. God can bring new life even out of tragedy. The Spirit of God helps us not only when we struggle to pray, but also when we struggle to come to terms with the darker experiences of life. The same hopeful, encouraging note is struck by Jesus in the gospel reading, when he presents a very broad and generous vision of life in the kingdom of heaven: 'People from east and west, from north and south, will come to take their places at the feast in the kingdom of God.' Jesus portrays a God who wants people from every corner of the earth at the banquet of life in his kingdom, a God who will work to turn everything in our lives to that ultimate goal. Yet the gospel reading also strikes another note. We have a part to play if this desire of God is to come to pass. We have to try and enter by the narrow door, the door that is Jesus himself. However, if we keep the Lord in view, striving to walk in his way, we won't find God wanting. As we strive to enter by the narrow door, the Lord will be on the opposite side drawing us through the door.

31 October, Thursday, Thirtieth Week in Ordinary Time
Luke 13:31–35

There is mention of two animals in today's gospel reading from Luke. Jesus refers to Herod Antipas, the ruler of Galilee, as a fox: 'You may go and give that fox this message'. Jesus then compares himself to a hen who 'gathers her brood under her wings'. In rural Galilee, as much as in rural Ireland today, foxes threaten hens and chickens. Herod Antipas, as a vassal ruler of Rome, was a threat to Jesus. In Luke's account of the passion and death of Jesus, Herod would play a minor role alongside Pilate in condemning Jesus to death. Jesus was working to gather people to himself, at the same time as others, like Herod and the Pharisees, were conspiring against him. The risen Lord continues to gather us to himself, to gather us around himself, today, even as there are forces at work in our culture that seek to prevent that from happening. We can look out at the various 'foxes' on the horizon and get discouraged, perhaps even allowing ourselves to be reduced to fearful inertia. Or we can look upon the Lord who works to gather us all to himself out of love for humanity. The letter to the Hebrews calls on us to keep looking to Jesus, 'the pioneer and perfecter of our faith'. If we focus on the Lord and his efforts to gather us all we will be inspired rather than discouraged. The Lord doesn't get discouraged by the foxes of this world, and neither should we. As Jesus says in the gospel reading, 'today and tomorrow and the next day, I must go on'. That is the spirit we need today.

1 November, Friday, All Saints
Matthew 5:1–12

The feast of All Saints begins the month of November. It is a month when we remember in a special way our loved ones who have died. Whenever we have a brush with death, either because of some seriousness illness in ourselves or because of the death of a loved one, important questions are often raised for us. We may find ourselves asking, 'What is beyond this earthly life?' 'What is our ultimate destination?' 'What is the path that leads to this final goal of our journey?' 'In what way should our ultimate destination impact on the way I live my life here and now?' This feast of All Saints invites us to engage with these questions.

The 'saints' referred to in the title of today's feast are all those women and men who have reached that ultimate goal of eternal life for which God has created us. They are those who have lived in a way that was in keeping with that final destiny. These 'saints' are also those who are still with us in this earthly life and who are now living in the way that leads to life eternal. In that sense, the group we call 'all saints' embraces both those who are with God in heaven, the 'huge number' spoken of in the first reading, and people who are all around us. All three of the readings for this feast speak of our ultimate destiny in different ways. In the second reading Saint John declares, 'what we are to be in the future has not yet been revealed'. In other words, there is a necessary 'not knowing' when it comes to life beyond this earthly life. Saint Paul is of this same view. In his first letter to the Corinthians, he writes, 'no eye has seen, nor ear heard, nor the human heart conceived, what God has prepared for those who love him' (1 Corinthians 2:9). Yet this healthy agnosticism about life beyond this earthly life does not stop the writers of the New Testament from speaking about it.

In that second reading, having declared what we *don't* know about this life beyond earthly life, Saint John states what we *do* know, 'all we know is, that … we shall be like God, for we shall see him as he really is'. Elsewhere in his letter, Saint John tells us who God really is. In one of the most profound statements about God, he declares, 'God is Love'. Beyond this earthly life, according to Saint John, we shall see God as Love. The verb 'to see' is obviously being used in a different way than when it describes how see in our earthly, physical body. When the writers of the New Testament speak about what eye has not seen, nor ear heard, nor the human heart conceived, they have to use language drawn from this earthly life, as it is the only language they have. Saint John is expressing his conviction that beyond this earthly life, we will come to experience God as Love. It will be an encounter with Love at its most complete. Furthermore, John declares, this encounter with God as Love will have a transforming effect on us. 'We shall be like God, because we shall see him as he is'. There is a sense in which, even in this earthly life, we become what we observe. Saint John is suggesting that in seeing God as Love beyond this earthly life, we will become loving in the way God is loving. It could be said that our ultimate destiny is to become fully alive with the life of God, which is a life of Love.

If that is our ultimate destiny, then the path to that destiny is to grow more and more into the loving person we are destined to become. Such growth in love is not just our work. It is ultimately God's work in our lives, the work of the Holy Spirit, with which we cooperate. At the beginning of that second reading, Saint John calls on us to 'think of the love that the Father has lavished on us, by letting us be called God's children'. As we think of God the Father's lavish love for us, as we open our hearts to that love, we are empowered to become more loving, more alive with God's life of love, the life of the Spirit. The Beatitudes in the gospel reading are Jesus' portrait of this loving person, the disciple who is on the way to becoming as loving as God. Such a person will have something of the gentleness of Christ, will reflect his merciful love to others, will mourn over our broken world and will work to bring God's justice and peace to that world, even if it means being persecuted in the process. Such a person will do all this out of a poverty of spirit and a purity of heart, recognising their dependence on God for everything, and seeking God's glory in all things rather than their own glory. This is Jesus' portrait of the living saint. We might recognise such saints among us; we might even occasionally catch a glimpse of such a one when we look into the mirror!

2 November, Saturday, Commemoration of All the Faithful Departed
Mark 15:33–39; 16:1–6

The opening prayer of today's Mass sets the tone for this commemoration. 'God … may all your people who have gone before us in faith share Christ's victory and enjoy the vision of your glory for ever.' The Prayer after Communion likewise prays for 'our brothers and sisters who have died', asking, 'Bring the new life given to them in baptism to the fullness of eternal joy.' Enjoying the vision of God's glory for ever and attaining the fullness of eternal joy is what we are praying for as we remember our deceased loved ones on this day. The suggested gospel reading for this year of Mark is a combination of the account of the crucifixion of Jesus and the finding of the empty tomb. It is said of Jesus in the gospel reading that he 'gave a loud cry and breathed his last'. Many of us will have been present when a loved one breathed their last breath. No matter how much we have been expecting it, that moment remains a traumatic one. There is a sense of finality about it for which no amount of anticipation can fully prepare us. The dark sadness of death engulfs us, just as it must have engulfed the disciples of Jesus, including the women who stood at a distance watching Jesus die, Mary Magdalene, Mary the mother of James, and Salome. On the third day, these women went to the tomb of Jesus to dignify his body with aromatic oils. Yet, to their amazement, where death was to be expected, life reigned: 'You are looking for Jesus of Nazareth, who was crucified: he is risen, he is not here.' It is as if the young man was saying to the women, 'If you want to meet Jesus, don't come to his tomb.' God had brought Jesus

through death into a new and more powerful life over which death
has no power. The risen Jesus would meet his disciples in Galilee,
where he first called them, and, thereafter, 'the Lord worked with
them and confirmed the message by the signs that accompanied it'
(Mark 16:20). The life that Jesus now enjoys is the ultimate destiny
of all who believe in him. Earlier in Mark's Gospel, Jesus declared
that those who follow him 'will receive a hundredfold now in this
age ... and in the age to come eternal life' (Mark 10:30). This is the
hope that the Gospel gives us and, as Saint Paul says in our second
reading, 'Hope is not deceptive, because the love of God has been
poured into our hearts by the Holy Spirit which has been given to
us.' The Holy Spirit gives us the assurance of God's love, a love
that, in the words of Paul's first letter to the Corinthians, 'never
ends', remaining faithful to us beyond death. Although 'now we
see in a mirror dimly ... then we will see face to face' (1 Corinthians 13:8, 12).

4 November, Monday, Thirty-first Week in Ordinary Time
Luke 14:12–14
Jesus was very aware that, in the culture of his time, especially among
the elite sections of society, giving was generally with a view to receiving something in return. People like the leading Pharisee in today's
gospel reading, the host at a meal at which Jesus is a guest, would tend
to invite the members of his own social class to a meal, so that they
would invite him in return. As a result, people of a certain social standing tended to form something of a closed circle. Jesus has a different
vision for humanity, where there is genuine communion between
people of different social classes and different backgrounds. That is
why he challenges his host to broaden his guest list when hosting
meals in future, inviting not only his friends and social peers, but those
with whom he would not normally associate, those whom he would

consider his inferiors, the poor, the crippled, the lame and the blind. They will not be able to give anything back to the host for his generosity but he will receive repayment from God in the fullness of time. The call of Jesus in the gospel reading is reflected in Paul's call to the church of Philippi in the first reading: 'Always consider the other person to be better than yourself, so that nobody thinks of his own interests first, but everybody thinks of other people's interests instead.' Each of us in our own way, in our own sphere of influence, is called to help create, with the Lord's help, this new kind of diverse community that Jesus began to form during his ministry and continues to inspire as risen Lord. The Lord inspires us to build communion, not just with our own kind but with those who are very different from us.

5 November, Tuesday, Thirty-first Week in Ordinary Time
Luke 14:15–24

The beatitude spoken by one of the guests at the meal where Jesus is present looks ahead to the banquet of eternal life, 'Happy the one who will be at the feast in the kingdom of God!' However, the parable Jesus speaks in response to this beatitude shows that, whereas the banquet in the heavenly kingdom is in the future, the invitation to that banquet is a present reality. God is inviting people to that future banquet of life through Jesus. The parable suggests that God is a very persistent host. When those originally invited did not come, a new invitation went out at short notice to people in the town who rarely got an invitation to anything. Then when they responded and there was still room another invitation at short notice went out to another group beyond the streets and alleys of the town, until the banquet was full. Jesus is suggesting that God's call to the banquet of life is not in doubt; it is persistent. What is in doubt is our response. We can get so attached to the things of this world that God's call gets drowned out. We are to live our lives before the Lord in all we do; we are to be present to his presence to us. Then we are more likely to notice his call, when it comes.

6 November, Wednesday, All Saints of Ireland
Luke 6:20–26

The gospel reading for this feast of all the saints of Ireland is the Beatitudes as found in the Gospel of Luke. They are less familiar to us than the Beatitudes as found in Matthew, and, perhaps, more difficult to come to terms with. In what sense are the poor, the hungry, the weeping and the persecuted happy or blessed? They are happy because, according to Jesus, God is close to them and is working to reverse their miserable situation: 'yours is the kingdom of God … you shall be satisfied … you shall laugh … your reward will be great in heaven.' Is it the case then that they should accept their plight in the hope that all will be well in the next life? Jesus' words and actions in the Gospel of Luke as a whole would not suggest so. In the parable of the rich man and Lazarus, Lazarus is certainly poor, hungry and weeping. He had no one who tried to improve his situation, even though the rich man on the other side of the gate could have transformed his miserable state with just a little effort. Beyond death, God not only improved his situation, but completely reversed it. At the banquet of Abraham, he enjoyed the hospitality of the kingdom of God; he was satisfied and joyful. Yet the clear message of the parable is that Lazarus should not have had to wait until after his death for his situation to be reversed. God wanted and expected the rich man to begin to do for Lazarus what God did for him in the kingdom of God. Luke's Gospel as a whole is clear that God wants the work of reversing the situation of the most vulnerable to begin in the here and now. Throughout his ministry, Jesus powerfully revealed this hospitable, transformative love of God to those who found themselves living on the margins. He looks to his disciples to do the same. The saints were those through whom God's hospitable, welcoming love began to transform the lives of those in greatest need. Because of their lives, the kingdom of God was not just a future hope but was also something of a present reality for those who longed for its coming.

7 November, Thursday, Thirty-first Week in Ordinary Time
Luke 15:1–10

When Jesus wanted to communicate who God is like, he often pointed to some human experience. He recognised that sometimes the way humans behave can give us an insight into God. There is something to be learned about God, Jesus suggests, by looking at how ordinary people live their lives. Even those who would not see themselves as especially religious can reveal God to us. In today's gospel reading, Jesus invites his critics, who thought of themselves as religious, to look at how a shepherd and a woman might behave when they lose something precious. The shepherd who loses one of a hundred sheep will go looking for that one sheep until he finds it. He will passionately search for it, and then, when he has found it, he will gather his friends and neighbours in his home to share his joy. When one went missing, he didn't say, 'Well, I have another ninety-nine, so let him go.' Similarly, a woman who loses one of her ten precious coins will sweep every nook and cranny in her house until she finds it, and so great is her joy upon finding it that she invites her neighbours to share her joy. Jesus is saying, 'God is like this shepherd and this woman.' God is always searching for the lost, those who have not come to know his tremendous love for them. He wants everyone to know that they are God's beloved sons and daughters. That is why he sent Jesus into the world, to show to the world God's passionate, searching love for all. Each one of us is invited to allow ourselves to be found by this loving God whom Jesus reveals and continues to make present to us today.

8 November, Friday, Thirty-first Week in Ordinary Time

Luke 16:1–8

Sometimes the principal characters in the stories that Jesus tells leave a lot to be desired, such as the younger son who left home in the parable of the prodigal son. Very often those characters who leave a lot to be desired have some redeeming feature. That younger son did make the journey home again, even if it was out of desperation. Today's gospel reading gives us another example of a story in which the principal character is anything but a paragon of virtue. He is described as a dishonest steward who was wasteful with his master's property. Yet he too had a redeeming feature. Perhaps Jesus is reminding us that everyone has some redeeming feature. The redeeming feature of the dishonest steward was his shrewd ability to take decisive action when his back was to the wall, so as to ensure that after he lost his job there would be people who would be well disposed towards him. Jesus' comments on the story suggest that we have something to learn, not from the steward's dishonesty, but from his shrewdness, from his ability to take decisive action when required. Very often our following of the Lord requires us to take decisive action to ensure that we continue to take the path the Lord is calling us to take. There can be something we need to do or to stop doing if, in the words of today's first reading, we are to remain faithful to the Lord.

9 November, Saturday, The Dedication of the Lateran Basilica

John 2:13–22

The Basilica of Saint John Lateran in Rome is the cathedral church of the Pope in his role as Bishop of the Diocese of Rome. It is called

'Saint John' after the two monasteries once attached, dedicated to Saint John the apostle and Saint John the Baptist. As the cathedral church of the Pope it has the title 'Mother and Head of all the Churches of the City and of the World'. It is sometimes called the Lateran Basilica or the Basilica of Saint John Lateran. The 'Laterani' were an old Roman family who probably once owned the land on which Emperor Constantine, the first Christian emperor, built this basilica in the early decades of the fourth century. The present basilica retains the plan given to it by Constantine, but it has been rebuilt and restored over the centuries. It is one of the most important religious buildings in the Catholic Church. The most important religious building in the time of Jesus and the early Church was the Jewish Temple in Jerusalem. In the words of today's responsorial psalm, it was 'the holy place where the Most High dwells. God is within, it cannot be shaken'. At a time when this Temple was still standing in all its glory, Paul, writing to the church in Corinth, makes the extraordinary statement in today's second reading, 'Don't you realise that you are God's Temple and that the Spirit of God is living among you?' Paul is declaring that the Most High now dwells in the community of believers who gather around the risen Lord. The focal point of God's presence is no longer a building, no matter how magnificent, but the community of those who have responded in faith to the preaching of the Gospel of Christ crucified and risen. Paul declares that the foundation of this building is the one he has laid, namely, Jesus Christ. If someone came along and tried to replace that foundation with another, the Church would no longer be the focal point of God's presence in the world. In today's gospel reading from John, which was written perhaps thirty years after the Jewish Temple was destroyed by the Romans, Jesus speaks of himself as the temple of God, the focal point of God's presence. The Word who was God became flesh in Jesus; to see Jesus is to see God the Father. The risen

Lord is the primary temple of God and the Church can only be God's temple if the risen Lord remains its foundation. As individual believers, we can only mediate God's presence to our world to the extent that we allow his Son, our risen Lord, to live out his life in and through us.

11 November, Monday, Thirty-second Week in Ordinary Time
Luke 17:1–6

The prayer of the disciples in today's gospel reading is probably one we could all make our own: 'Increase our faith.' Jesus had just issued a very challenging call to his disciples, not to do anything that would lead a member of the Church astray and to keep forgiving without reservation those who do them wrong repeatedly and who ask pardon repeatedly. On hearing this, the disciples may have felt that their faith was not strong enough to live up to these ideals. We can all feel from time to time that the call of the Gospel is beyond us. It is too demanding for our fragile faith. We pray to the Lord out of our need, asking him to increase our faith so that we can rise to the call of the Gospel. Yet, in the gospel reading, Jesus wanted the disciples to recognise the potential of the faith they already had. He was suggesting that God can work powerfully through faith as small as a mustard seed. God needs only the tiniest of openings to enter our lives and work through us. We may think that our faith is weak, but, as Saint Paul says in one of his letters, God's power is often made perfect in weakness. The humble acknowledgement that our faith is not as deep or as strong as it could be gives the Lord space to work in and through us in ways that can surprise us. The gospel reading invites us to value the faith that we have, even though it may seem weak and fragile to us at times. All the Lord asks is that we keep seeking him, out of whatever faith we have, and if we do that he will see to it that our faith grows and deepens.

12 November, Tuesday, Thirty-second Week in Ordinary Time
Luke 17:7–10

The short parable Jesus speaks in today's gospel reading reminds us that we never have a claim on God. After we have done all that God asks of us, we cannot then say to God, 'I am due some recompense for all that I have done'. That would be usual in the world of human affairs. People expect to be recompensed in proportion to the work they have done. However, that is not how we are to relate to God. God is never in debt to us no matter how generous we have been towards God. This is because our good work on God's behalf is itself due to God's good working within us. All the good we do is of God. Without God's loving initiative towards us, we could do nothing that is pleasing to God. Saint Paul speaks in today's first reading of how God's grace was revealed towards us in the life, death and resurrection of Jesus. We have been greatly graced by God and all that is good in our lives is the fruit of that gracious initiative of God towards us. In faithfully serving God we are giving back to God what God has already given to us. Yet, elsewhere, the Gospel makes clear that our efforts to serve the Lord well will always be met by further loving initiatives of the Lord towards us. The Lord's love for us is a given; it doesn't have to be earned. Our lives of loving service in response to the Lord's love for us opens us up more fully to the Lord's love for us. As Jesus says elsewhere, if we give to God, it will be given to us by God; a full measure, running over, will be poured into our lap.

13 November, Wednesday, Thirty-second Week in Ordinary Time
Luke 17:11–19

Normally Jews and Samaritans did not associate with each other; they lived apart from one another. However, leprosy was a great leveller. Jewish and Samaritan lepers occupied the same space, ostracised by the community for fear of contagion. If a leper approached a healthy Jewish man, he had no interest in whether the leper was Jewish or Samaritan. Both were equally to be shunned. In today's gospel reading, a group of lepers, one of whom was a Samaritan, 'stood some way off and called on' Jesus, 'Jesus! Master! Take pity on us.' The Jews and Samaritan were united in their desperate plea to one whom they believed could heal them. It is only after their healing, while on their way to the priests, that the distinction between Jew and Samaritan shows itself. However, contrary to the expectation of the time, it is the Samaritan who emerges as the one who is closer to God. In the words of today's first reading, 'the kindness and love of God our saviour for humankind were revealed' to all ten lepers, through the ministry of Jesus. However, whereas nine no doubt rejoiced in the gift of new health they had received from Jesus, only the Samaritan looked beyond the gift to the ultimate giver, God. The Samaritan alone 'turned back praising God at the top of his voice'. In praising God, he fell at the feet of Jesus and thanked him, because he recognised that it was through Jesus that God had worked in such a life-giving way. In the language of the first reading, God has renewed us 'with the Holy Spirit which he so generously poured over us through Jesus Christ our saviour'. Like 'the other nine', we can be so absorbed by the gifts that God has given us that we fail to go beyond the gifts to the giver and to the one through whom God has given us these gifts, Jesus our Lord. The Samaritan prompts us to keep 'turning back' to the Lord, recognising that 'every generous act of giving, with every perfect gift, is from above, coming down from the Father of lights' (James 1:17).

14 November, Thursday, Thirty-second Week in Ordinary Time
Luke 17:20–25
Sometimes we can miss something of great significance. It is there before us but we do not see it. In today's gospel reading the

Pharisees ask Jesus when the kingdom of God was to come. In reply Jesus says to them, 'You must know, the kingdom of God is among you.' They failed to see that the kingdom of God was present to them in and through the person of Jesus. They were not alert to the signs of God's kingdom in the ministry of Jesus. The kingdom of God was there but in a less dramatic form than they expected. The gospel reading reminds us that the Lord is present in our lives in more ways than we realise. His presence does not always admit of observation, in the words of today's gospel reading. It will often be undramatic, without fanfare. Yet the Lord is really present, especially in the words and deeds of people that build up and heal and bring life. The Lord has assured us that we will never be without his presence. What we need are eyes to see and ears to hear, the eyes and ears of faith. Like the disciples earlier in Luke's Gospel we need to pray, 'Increase our faith'.

15 November, Friday, Thirty-second Week in Ordinary Time
Luke 17:26–37
The gospel describes a situation in which the normal business of life is suddenly cut short by some unexpected event. The eating, drinking, buying, selling, planting, building, marrying wives and husbands that went on in the days of Noah and the days of Lot were suddenly brought to a stop by catastrophic events, the great flood and the destruction of a city. In our own lives we can have a similar experience. We are caught up in the ordinary day-to-day business of living, and suddenly something happens that renders all of that of secondary importance. What is it that keeps us going when those familiar routines no longer sustain us? For us as Christians, it can only be our faith in the Lord. We know that when all else changes, when everything else collapses around us, the Lord endures. In the words of yesterday's gospel reading, 'the kingdom of God is among

you'. God's reign, God's power, is among us, in and through his Son, our risen Lord. When all else fails, we can rely on that good news. Like Saint Paul, we can discover that God's power is made perfect in weakness. In our times of greatest weakness we can experience the Lord's power most fully.

16 November, Saturday, Thirty-second Week in Ordinary Time
Luke 18:1–8

According to today's gospel reading, Jesus spoke the parable of the judge and the widow to encourage his disciples not to lose heart but to keep on praying, to pray continuously, even in times of great darkness. By means of this parable Jesus is encouraging us to have a persistent faith. The widow is an example of such persistent faith. When an injustice was done to her, she did not lose heart. She kept hammering away at the judge who alone could grant her justice until he caved in to her demands, fearful perhaps that she would resort to violence if he didn't respond to her. Jesus is encouraging us to have something of the gutsy determination of the widow. Our persistent prayer is not to an unjust judge who couldn't care less about God or his fellow human beings. We pray to a God who is passionately concerned about us, which is all the more reason why we should have a persistent faith that finds expression in continual prayer. Having spoken the parable, Jesus asks the question, 'When the Son of Man comes will he find any faith on earth?' When he comes at the end of time, will he find people of the kind of persistent faith displayed by the widow, or will his disciples have lost heart by then, worn down by the trials of life? It is a question that puts it up to us, in the words of the letter to the Hebrews, 'to run with perseverance the race that is set before us, looking to Jesus the pioneer and perfecter of our faith' (Hebrews 12:1–2).

18 November, Monday, Thirty-third Week in Ordinary Time

Luke 18:35–43

The figure of the blind man in today's gospel reading is one of those gospel characters who can cast light on our own faith journey. Although he couldn't see, there was clearly no problem with his hearing or his speech. When he heard a crowd going past, he asked what it was all about. The question, 'What is it all about?' is one of those fundamental questions of meaning that remains with us throughout the course of our faith journey. It is a question we live with and struggle with, rather than one that lends itself to an easy answer. The answer people gave to the blind man's question was that Jesus of Nazareth was passing by. The Lord continues to pass us by today. Even if we don't see him clearly and don't have a strong sense of his presence, he is continually passing us by. We don't have to do anything to make Jesus pass us by, to make him present. He is present to us, and it only falls to us to respond to his presence. In that regard, the blind man can be our teacher. He called out to Jesus in prayer, even though the people around Jesus insisted in no uncertain terms that he be quiet. Sometimes, we too need to show our faith in the Lord, in the face of pressure to keep quiet, to keep our faith to ourselves. Just as the man was not put off by the crowd's insistence that he be quiet, neither was Jesus put off. He insisted that the man's desire for a real communion with him be respected. As Saint Paul reminds us, nothing need come between us and the love of God made visible in Jesus. The personal question Jesus asks the man is addressed to us all, 'What do you want me to do for you?' We each have to answer that question for ourselves, but, again, the blind man has something to teach us about how to answer it. Aware of his blindness, he asked Jesus to let him see again, and with his restored sight he followed Jesus on the way. We are always in need of healing for our own blindness, our spiritual blindness, so that we can follow in the way of Jesus more fully.

19 November, Tuesday, Thirty-third Week in Ordinary Time
Luke 19:1–10

In today's first reading, the risen Lord criticises the church of Laodicea because, even though the church declares itself to be materially well off – 'I am rich, I have made a fortune, and I have everything I want' – the people do not realise that, at a deeper, spiritual, level, they are wretchedly and pitiably poor. The same could not be said of Zacchaeus in today's gospel reading. He too could say of himself, 'I am rich, I have made a fortune, and I have everything I want', yet he was also aware of a deeper poverty in his life. That is why he desired to see Jesus. Such was his desire that he was prepared to climb a tree to see Jesus above the crowd. All he wanted was to see Jesus. He discovered that Jesus wanted much more. Jesus wanted to meet him. He called Zacchaeus by his name and declared that he wanted to share Zacchaeus's table. In seeking the Lord, Zacchaeus found more than he could possibly have hoped for, what Jesus goes on to call 'salvation'. The figure of Zacchaeus reminds us that there is a poverty deep within us to which only the Lord can respond. This story also assures us that if we keep seeking the Lord, in spite of the obstacles that may be put in our way, we will discover much more than we were seeking. The Lord is always seeking us with a greater passion than we are seeking him, and he is always offering us more than we can conceive or imagine.

20 November, Wednesday, Thirty-third Week in Ordinary Time
Luke 19:11–28

In the time when the Book of Revelation was written, towards the end of the first century, the Emperor Domitian was on the throne in Rome. Historical sources suggest that he was happy to be addressed as 'Lord and God'. According to our first reading, there is a throne that is higher than the throne of the Roman emperor, and the one seated on it, the Creator God, is alone worthy of the titles that Domitian claimed. 'You are our Lord and our God, you are worthy of glory, honour and power.' The often perplexing symbolic language of the Book of Revelation is always at the service of this fundamental truth. There is only one who is worthy of the worship of our lives and hearts and that is the Creator God who, according to the reading, 'made all the universe' and by whose will 'everything was made and exists'. In the following chapter of this Book of Revelation, the risen Lord is honoured and worshipped on an equal footing with God: 'To the one seated on the throne and to the Lamb be blessing and honour and glory and might for ever and ever!' (Revelation 5:13). It is in and through his Son, the risen Lord, that God exercises his rule on earth. The author of this book was reassuring his persecuted churches that in a world where the emperor and various gods were demanding to be honoured and worshipped, the God of Jesus Christ was alone worthy of their total allegiance and worship. Such worship finds expression in liturgy but embraces all of our lives. Paul calls on the church in Rome, at the heart of Roman Empire, to 'present your bodies as a living sacrifice, holy and acceptable to God, which is your spiritual worship. Do not be conformed to this world, but be transformed by the renewing of your minds' (Romans 12:1–2). Today's gospel reading suggests that one of the ways we give expression to this spiritual worship, the worship of our lives, is by imaginatively using the gifts God has given us in the service of others. The time before the arrival of the glorious Son of Man is an opportunity for faithful and courageous service of the Lord and all created reality.

21 November, Thursday, Presentation of the Blessed Virgin Mary
Matthew 12:46–50

The feast of Mary's presentation in the Temple in Jerusalem as a child celebrates an important truth about Mary: From the beginning of her life, she was dedicated to God, given over to God's purposes. Because of her dedication to God from an early age, she was called by God to become a greater temple than the magnificent Temple in Jerusalem. If the Temple in Jerusalem was the house of God, the place where God was believed to be present in a special way, Mary became the house of the Lord in an even greater way, because she carried the Lord in her womb until she gave birth to him. God came to dwell in her, through Jesus, because she was open to God's presence from the earliest years of her life. She is the prime example of the group that Jesus refers to in today's gospel reading as those 'who do the will of my Father in heaven'. Today's feast celebrates the fact that from her childhood Mary did the will of God, and was therefore ready to become the temple of God's Son at the time of God's choosing. We too are called to do the will of the Father in heaven so that we too can become temples of the Lord, people who carry the Lord's presence to others, as Mary did. Writing to the church in Corinth, Paul says to each member, 'Do you not know that your body is a temple of the Holy Spirit within you?' (1 Corinthians 6:19). We ask Mary to pray for us now so that we may always do the will of the Father and so become temples of God as she was.

22 November, Friday, Thirty-third Week in Ordinary Time
Luke 19:45–48

In today's gospel reading Jesus shows his displeasure at what is happening in the Temple in Jerusalem. Instead of serving its original purpose as a house of prayer for everyone, it had come to serve the interests of a few. Every human institution needs ongoing reform and renewal, and that includes religious institutions, like the Church. The Lord is always prompting us to reform and renew our institutions so that they serve God's purposes more fully, rather than our own purposes. No human institution, no matter how revered, is perfect; it will always be in need of renewal, because it will always be shaped by people who are tainted by sin. What is important is to acknowledge this in an ongoing way and to be open to the Lord's call to repentance and renewal. This was not the case with those responsible for the Jewish Temple in Jerusalem. After Jesus' actions in the Temple, the gospel reading says that the chief priests and the scribes tried to do away with Jesus. To resist ongoing renewal is to resist the Lord. Our journey towards God, both as individuals and as communities, will always involve repentance, a willingness to keep on turning more fully towards what God wants for our lives, which is revealed to us through Jesus' life, death and resurrection.

23 November, Saturday, Thirty-third Week in Ordinary Time
Luke 20:27–40

The Sadducees who approach Jesus in today's gospel reading did not believe in any kind of resurrection from the dead. This view distinguished the Sadducees from other groups within Judaism at the time, such as the Pharisees. In the gospel reading, they present a situation to Jesus that seeks to make belief in any kind of afterlife appear ridiculous. However, the situation they present to Jesus presupposes that life beyond death will simply be an extension of this earthly life. In his reply, Jesus makes clear that life in what he calls 'the other world' is qualitatively different from what he refers to as life in 'this world'. In what does this qualitative difference consist? According to Jesus, it consists in the fact that in this world everybody dies, whereas in the other world 'they can no longer die'. Whereas those Jesus calls 'the children of this world' all have to succumb to the experience of death, 'the children of the resurrection' can no longer die. They live with a life that is eternal. Such a life is the life of God, because God is eternal. Jesus is saying that beyond the life of this world, we come to share in God's own life in a way that is not possible for us to do in this earthly life. To that extent, our relationship with God and with his Son, Jesus, is significantly deepened in the next life. Saint Paul expresses this deepening relationship with God beyond this life very succinctly and powerfully when he says in one of his letters, 'Now we see in a mirror, dimly, but then we will see face to face. Now I know only in part; then I will know fully, even as I have been fully known' (1 Corinthians 13:12). Not only will our communion with God be raised to another level, so also will our communion with all we have known and loved in this life.

25 November, Monday, Thirty-fourth Week in Ordinary Time
Luke 21:1–4
The term 'the widow's mite' has made its way into our daily speech. It is inspired by today's gospel reading. It is generally used to refer to someone who makes a small contribution that is generously given and that is all the person can afford. Jesus noticed the widow's very small contribution to the Temple treasury, two small coins. Yet he saw in that small contribution a tremendous generosity of heart, because in giving a little, she was giving her all. Others were giving far more money to the Temple treasury but, having given their contribution, they had plenty more to spare. When the widow gave her little contribution, she had nothing left. Generosity can be hard for us to measure. Someone who is making a small contribution to something, not just financial, can be displaying enormous generosity, because in giving that little they are giving their all. It is only the Lord who can judge how generous someone is, because only he can see into the heart of

others. In the gospel reading, the widow would probably have been invisible to most people; her tiny contribution to the Temple would have gone unnoticed. However, the Lord noticed the selfless generosity that her small contribution expressed and he brought her to the attention of others. There can come a time in all our lives when we feel we have very little to give. Our energy may be low; the state of our physical or mental health may be holding us back. Today's gospel reading reminds us that the little we give in those moments of weakness can reveal a greater generosity of heart and spirit than the great deal we might give when we are in moments of strength.

26 November, Tuesday, Thirty-fourth Week in Ordinary Time
Luke 21:5–11

As the curtain comes down on the liturgical year, the liturgical readings tend to highlight the reality of endings, of things coming to an end. In the gospel reading, Jesus announces the ending of the Temple in Jerusalem. This was a magnificent building; it had taken eighty years to complete. It dominated the city of Jerusalem. It must have seemed as if it would last for ever. It was considered by Jews to be the dwelling place of God. Yet, forty years after Jesus was crucified, it was destroyed by the Roman army. It was a tremendous loss for the Jewish people. We all have to deal with endings and losses of one kind or another. Sometimes such experiences of ending and loss can be traumatic for us, as traumatic as the destruction of the Temple and everything that went with it was for the people of Israel. When we experience some traumatic loss or ending, we can even wonder whether our own life is at an end, whether we ourselves are now lost. In such situations we need an anchor, something that doesn't change. That anchor is the Lord. The Book of Revelation, from which we are reading these days, speaks of the Lord as the one who was, who is and who is to come. In the midst of all our losses we know that the Lord endures and that his relationship with us never comes to an end. The Lord can be relied upon when all else fails, and he is always at work bringing new life out of our experiences of loss.

27 November, Wednesday, Thirty-fourth Week in Ordinary Time
Luke 21:12–19

In the gospel reading, Jesus is very clear about the difficulties his followers will experience in trying to be faithful to him. Many of them will end up in prison; others will be betrayed by family members. Yet Jesus goes on to assure them that he will be with them to support and strengthen them in those difficult moments when they may be tempted to turn from him. He will help them to endure, to stay faithful to him to the end. Most of us do not experience the difficulties Jesus mentions in our efforts to be faithful to him. Our faith in the Lord is unlikely to put us in prison or alienate us from our families. Yet we all struggle in various ways to be faithful to our baptismal calling, to the Lord's daily call. We are aware of times when our faith is put to the test, when we are tempted to take a path other than the one the Lord is calling us to take. At such times, the gospel reading assures us that we are not on our own. The Lord is with us, helping us to endure in faith, keeping us faithful to him. The Lord who calls us to take a certain path, goes with us down that path, helping us to travel it well when our faith is put to the test. Saint Paul expresses this truth very simply in his first letter to the Thessalonians: 'The one who calls you is faithful, and he will do this' (1 Thessalonians 5:24).

28 November, Thursday, Thirty-fourth Week in Ordinary Time
Luke 21:20–28

Many of the responses we say or sing at Mass are drawn from the Scriptures, such as 'Holy, Holy, Holy Lord ...', which comes from the prophet Isaiah. When the priest says, just before distributing Holy Communion, 'Behold the Lamb of God, behold him who takes away the sins of the world', it is drawn from the words of John the Baptist in the Gospel of John as he points out Jesus to his disciples. When the priest goes on to say, 'Blessed are those called to the supper of the Lamb', it is drawn from today's first reading from the Book of Revelation, 'Happy are those who are invited to the wedding feast of the Lamb'. The writer there was referring to the great feast in the kingdom of heaven, when the risen Lord, the Lamb of God, would gather people of every race and language who were open to his invitation. When the priest speaks of the 'supper of the Lamb', he is referring to the Eucharist at which we are gathered. The table of the Lord, the altar, from which we are fed by the Bread of Life, looks ahead to that final banquet of eternal life to which we are all called. This is the hope that our faith gives us. We never lose that hope even when a great darkness comes over our world, our cities, our lives. Jesus refers to such great darkness in today's gospel reading, but he goes on to say that he will come into this darkness with great power and glory, and we should therefore always stand erect, with our heads held high, full of hope. The Lord is always present at the heart of any darkness in which we find ourselves, and he is always at work to bring us to our final destiny, the banquet of eternal life.

29 November, Friday, Thirty-fourth Week in Ordinary Time
Luke 21:29–33

We have become used to rapid change in the course of our lifetime, especially for those who are now into their later years. So much has passed away, and so much that is new has come along to replace it. In today's gospel reading, Jesus speaks of heaven and earth passing away. The expression 'heaven and earth' suggests all reality as we know it. Yet this passing away of heaven and earth gives way to what

Jesus calls the kingdom of God, and to what the first reading calls a 'new heaven and a new earth', 'the holy city, the new Jerusalem'. God is always bringing something new out of what passes away. God is always the Creator. God is always at work creating a world that is an image of the kingdom of God. Jesus reveals God to be not only ever ancient but also ever new. The God who brought new life out of the death of Jesus is the Creator God who is always at work among us, in and through the risen Lord, bringing forth something new and wonderful from what is passing away. The risen Lord calls each of us to share in some way in this creative, life-giving work of God. By our values, our attitudes and our actions, we are called to create little openings for the coming of God's kingdom into our world. In this way we will be sharing in the continuous creative work of God the Father and his Son.

30 November, Saint Andrew, Apostle
Matthew 4:18–22

I chose Andrew as my Confirmation name. I am not sure why, but I knew he was one of the first people that Jesus called to follow him and that he was the brother of Simon Peter. The brothers were fishermen who made a good living by catching fish on the Sea of Galilee and selling the fish on to locals. It always struck me as interesting that Jesus called two sets of brothers when he began to form a group around himself: Peter and Andrew, and James and John. Peter and Andrew must have been a support to one another as they left one way of life that was familiar to them and started a whole new way of life that was very unfamiliar to them. From now on it is people they would be catching for Jesus rather than fish. Jesus needed people like Peter and Andrew, James and John, and many others, women and men, to bring his compassionate, healing presence to others. The Lord wants to work through us all to make him present to others.

None of us goes to the Lord alone. We need others to bring us to the Lord. We might reflect today on those who brought us to the Lord. In my case, I think of my parents, some teachers I had at school, the local priests in the parish, friends I made who were people of faith. We all came to the Lord through others, and the Lord wants to bring others to himself through each one of us. According to the Gospel of John, it was Andrew who met Jesus first, and it was Andrew who brought his brother Peter to Jesus. We can all be an Andrew to someone. We ask Saint Andrew today to grant us something of his willingness to bring others to the Lord, by sharing our faith in whatever way we can. We might also thank the Lord for all the 'Andrews' in our life who have brought us to him.